PRACTICUM MANUAL

for

COUNSELING and PSYCHOTHERAPY

Third Edition

Kenneth M. Dimick

Frank H. Krause

Accelerated Development Inc.
P. O. Box 667
Muncie, IN 47305

Library of Congress Catalog Card Number: 75-7444

ISBN 0-915202-05-0

© Copyright 1975 by Kenneth M. Dimick and Frank H. Krause

All rights reserved. No part of this publication may be reproduced or transmitted in any form or by any means, electronic or mechanical, including photocopy, recording, or any information storage and retrieval system, without permission in writing from the publisher.

Cover design by Kandy S. Scheick

For additional copies order from

Accelerated Development Inc.
P. O Box 667
Muncie, IN 47305

Cost: $7.95 plus 50¢ postage and handling in U.S. and Canada
In other countries, postage depends upon prevailing rates
Price is subject to change without notice.

PREFACE

In this edition of <u>The Practicum Manual for Counseling and Psychotherapy</u> the information has been re-evaluated, up-dated, and carefully scrutinized from the material presented in the first and second editions of our <u>Practicum Manual</u>. The original <u>Student Manual for Counseling Practicum</u> was prepared for use by our counseling practicum students at Ball State University because we could find no other suitable publication. Before developing the initial manual we wrote to over two hundred fifty counselor educators and asked for input from them about what they offered in their counseling practicums. From the material many were kind enough to send us and from our own experiences, we compiled the first edition of the <u>Student Manual for Counseling Practicum</u>. Apparently many other professors who teach and/or supervise counseling practicums felt a need for a counseling practicum text as we did because the first edition was adopted by many and necessitated a revised second edition.

We have analyzed the feedback given to us by practicum students and their supervisors to compile and write this third edition. <u>Practicum Manual for Counseling and Psychotherapy</u> presents not only a workbook for student counselors enrolled in practicum for counseling and psychotherapy, but also an orientation for the practicum supervisor and practicum counselor to innovative instructional approaches, mechanics of initiating a practicum, counseling techniques, basic foundations, ethics, evaluation procedures and the general conditions of counseling. Persons training to work as school and/or community members of the helping professions will find in the book a variety of approaches, suggestions and forms that will help them to become more effective counselors or psychotherapists.

April 1975

Kenneth M. Dimick
Frank H. Krause

ACKNOWLEDGEMENTS

The book was written and compiled because we felt in our own teaching of counseling practicum the need for such a manual. We express thanks to everyone who assisted us in the publication of this book. A number of individuals made significant contributions. Dr. Patsy A. Donn, Chairperson of our Department of Counseling Psychology and Guidance Services, has given us encouragement and continued support for several years. Dr. Joseph W. Hollis, Director of Doctoral Program in Counseling and Guidance at Ball State University, provided us with a model of commitment, persistence and understanding. We express our appreciation to the many professionals who contributed material for our consideration and to the following members of our Department who are committed to upgrading counseling practicums: Karen Baumann, Jerry Cartwright, Edward Daly, Jane Duckworth, Morton Dunham, Robert Hayes, Donald Hendrickson, Roger Hutchinson, Peter Mitchell, Kenneth Nunnelly, Christie Randolph, Mary Vestermark and Jay Zimmerman.

April 1975

Kenneth M. Dimick
Frank H. Krause

CONTENTS

	Form Number	Page
PREFACE		iii
ACKNOWLEDGMENTS		iv

I. INSTRUCTIONAL APPROACHES 1

    Practicum: A Growth Experience 1
    A Collage of Instructional Approaches to Teaching Practicum 2
    Innovations in Counseling Practicum: A Progress Report 4
    Developing Competency Statements for Counselor Education by Thomas C. Froehle . . 6
    The Practicum Experience Record by Thomas J. Caulfield 14
        Letter to the Practicum Site Supervisor 14
        Suggested Guidelines for Carrying out the Monitoring of Weekly
            Specific Behavioral Objectives 15
        Specific Behavioral Objectives 16
        Evaluation Form: Activities Listed by Weeks . . . . 1 copy Form 1 . 17
    Practicum Supervisors 21
    Criteria for Evaluating a Prospective Practicum Location 23

II. INITIATING PRACTICUM 25

    Suggested Course Requirements 27
    Role and Function 29
    Forms to Facilitate Communication Between Practicum Supervisors
        and Practicum Counselor 31
    Personal Data Sheet . . . . 1 copy Form 2 . 33
    Agreement Made by Practicum Counselor . . . . 1 copy Form 3 . 34
    Agreement Between Practicum Supervisor and Practicum Counselor . . 1 copy Form 4 . 35
    Practicum Counselor's Placement and Schedule . . . . 1 copy Form 5 . 36
    Summary of Time Utilization to Meet Course Requirements . . . 1 copy Form 6 . 37
    Example of a Weekly Schedule 38
    Weekly Schedule . . . . 14 copies Form 7 . 39

III. COUNSELING TECHNIQUES AND PROCESSES 53

    Counseling Techniques 53
    Techniques Used in Counseling and Psychotherapy by Joseph W. Hollis 58
    Suggestions for Counseling Practicum by John P. McGowan 63
    Interview Notes 65
    Initial Intake Form . . . . 10 copies Form 8 . 67
    Interview Notes Form . . . . 25 copies Form 9 . 87
    Case Study Guidelines 137
    A Note Regarding Case Reports by Ronald A. Ruble 138
    Example of Letter Sent to Referring Source Following Counseling
        by Ronald A. Ruble 140

II. ETHICS IN COUNSELING AND PSYCHOTHERAPY 143

    Ethical Standards of Psychologists, American Psychological Association . . . 144
    Ethical Standards, American Personnel and Guidance Association 152

V.	CLIENTS AND THE PRACTICUM COUNSELOR'S RESPONSIBILITIES	159
	Selection of Clients	159
	Responsibility to Clients	160
	Instruments for Determining Expectations and Effectiveness in Counseling by Joseph W. Hollis	162
	Example of a Clarifying Letter to Parents by Dennis Rumfelt	163
	Example of a Counselee Release Form	164
	Example of a Parent Release Form	164
	Example of a Form for the Release of Confidential Information	165
	Making Referrals by Patsy A. Donn	166
	Referral Form . . . . 4 copies Form 10	169
	Termination Report . . . . 10 copies Form 11	177
	Building Folder for Each Client by Joseph W. Hollis	197
	Check Sheet for Client Folder by Joseph W. Hollis . . . . . . 10 copies Form 12	199
VI.	TESTS, TEST INTERPRETATIONS AND THE COUNSELOR	219
	Test Selection and Interpretation	219
	Test Selection Guide by John A. Axelson	222
	Test Use and Interpretation by John P. McGowan	223
	Tests and Testing by Jane and Edwin Duckworth	224
VII.	INFORMATION PROCESSING	233
	Information Processes in Counseling and Psychotherapy by Joseph W. Hollis	235
	Protection of the Rights and Privacy of Parents and Students	238
	Major Amendments to the Family Educational Rights and Privacy Act of 1974	242
	Proposed Rules	243
VIII.	EVALUATION OF PRACTICUM STUDENT AND SUPERVISOR	247
	Possible Alternatives for Evaluating Counseling Practicum Students	248
	Cooperating Practicum Site Supervisor's Evaluation of Student Counselor by Thomas J. Caulfield . . . . 1 copy Form 13	251
	Counselee Rating Sheet by William E. Hopke . . . . 4 copies Form 14	255
	Self-Rating by the Student Counselor . . . . 4 copies Form 15	263
	Supervisor's Evaluation and Report Regarding Student Counselor . 2 copies Form 16	271
	Counseling Practicum Tapes: Weekly Evaluation Record . . . . 2 copies Form 17	275
	Counseling Practicum Interview Rating Form by Gordon Poling . . 5 copies Form 18	279
	Supervisor Evaluation of Practicum Counselor by Harold Hackney . 2 copies Form 19	289
	Student Counselor Evaluation of Supervisor by Harold Hackney . . 1 copy Form 20	297
BIBLIOGRAPHY		301
	The Counselor as a Person	301
	The Counseling Process	302
	Philosophical and Theoretical Base of Counseling	305
	Occupational and Educational Information	308
INDEX		310
ABOUT THE AUTHORS		313

CHAPTER I
INSTRUCTIONAL APPROACHES

This Manual provides structure and guidelines for the practicum counselor and his or her practicum supervisor(s). An approach to teaching counseling practicum that has been effective for the authors with their students is presented along with suggested records and related forms. The approach involves the student in the traditional role playing and taping, but expands counseling and psychotherapy practicum to multiexperiences also. Another key concept is that the student counselors enrolled in counseling practicum have active supervision in both the experiential setting and the university setting. Perhaps another major shift in emphasis from traditional counseling practicum is the dynamic involvement of the student counselor in each phase of the process including evaluation.

Counseling is an art. Although many attempts have been made to quantify, qualify and in other ways mold counseling into a science or pseudo-science, we feel it must be viewed as an art form. As with any art form, evaluation and re-evaluation of the process are difficult, complicated and may be even impossible tasks. Yet, evaluation and innovation remain a necessary part of counseling practicum.

PRACTICUM: A GROWTH EXPERIENCE

Practicum in counseling and psychotherapy, just like the student counselor, can continue to change and develop. Our emphasis is that practicum need not be as it currently exists, regardless of the setting. In order for practicum to be open to evolution and growth, it requires the creative effort of each practicum counselor and supervisor to view practicum, as well as the practicum experience, as having growth potential.

The hope then is that inherent in our presentation of innovations in counseling practicum the view will not be as goals to be attained, but rather means toward goals as yet undeveloped. Very appropriately, then, practicum can be viewed in terms of what it can be as opposed to what it is.

No "right" or "best" way for counseling practicum exists. Each situation, supervisor, and group of practicum students differ. The process in developing innovations in counseling is one of understanding the setting, identifying needs and, most importantly, answering the question of "how can change take place?" in terms of the setting and current needs rather than in terms of tradition.

Since no one way is best, an awareness of different approaches may enable the student and the practicum supervisor to gain better insight into what can be achieved in their situation and into the limitations of each approach. Increased awareness of different approaches not only provides greater freedom to grow through choice and implementation among alternatives but also enables more objective evaluation of whatever approach is used.

Our belief is that practicum in counseling regardless of the methodologies utilized is to be structured or maybe some would prefer to say unstructured so as to provide the practicum counselor the freedom to grow. Thus the desired practicum course is where

--freedom to grow exists rather than to be boxed-in with grades

--forms and paperwork facilitate action rather than to be just required detailed work

--professional consultation and supervision are provided so that the practicum student can try ideas and various techniques rather than supervisors who serve only as evaluators to check number of times a technique, form, or activity is or is not utilized.

A COLLAGE OF INSTRUCTIONAL APPROACHES TO TEACHING PRACTICUM

Within this practicum Manual are materials applicable to different instructional approaches. The major instructional approaches which seem to be used prominently in practicum courses are as follows:

1. Competency Based--this approach requires the identification of observable and measurable outcomes which are to be achieved before completing practicum. The outcomes are developed prior to the beginning of practicum. Thus a practicum student may "test" out of doing certain activities because he or she already has the competencies. The emphasis within practicum, when competency based instructional program is used, is to direct activities toward enabling each student to meet the predetermined goals--competencies.

2. Interpersonal Process Model--the emphases are upon the relationships, techniques, outcomes during the counseling process. Audio and video tapes are used extensively and often typescripts. IPR (Interpersonal Process Recall) technique of practicum supervision may be used. The interpersonal process model as an instructional approach places emphasis upon the counselor-client relationship rather than upon the allied activities such as committee work, administrative details, consultation, and other activities besides the counseling process that may be performed by the practicum counselor.

3. Simulation Model--the practicum student is provided opportunities to practice under simulation the activities which would be done in a real situation. Role-playing, in-basket activities, gaming, micro-counseling, and similar activities are used extensively.

4. Supervised Field Experience Model--the emphases are upon providing actual experiences in real settings with supervised-consultative relationship provided by an experienced counselor employed within the setting. The university supervisor may provide additional supervised and consultative activities. The practicum student is provided with experiences in keeping with his or her capabilities and to the extent of skills. The activities then are to be differentiated in terms of competencies needed and degree of difficulty. An intake interview will enable identification of clients who have needs with which potentially the practicum counselor can work or can work with consultation.

5. Contractual Model--the emphases are upon determining what the practicum student needs and then the practicum supervisor and practicum student make a contract for activities which will faciliate the desired outcomes. The determination of needs may be in consent and with advice of the university supervisor and in some instances the other class members. Once needs are determined and contract established the instructional approach is one of practicum counselor self direction. The supervisor becomes a facilitator of the desired outcomes.

6. MBO Model--Management By Objectives is an outgrowth of the behavioral movement. Specific objectives are stated for the course. Each objective includes what is to be learned, when it is to be learned, and how the determination will be made as to the achievement of the objective. The practicum supervisor and practicum counselor know what is expected, when it is expected, and how the achievement will be determined.

Often the instructional approach is a combination of two or more approaches. The innovations in practicum are bringing about new instructional approaches. Practicum students and supervisors are contributing to the changes.

Our basic approach however is one of encouraging practicum in each and every setting to be better today than it was yesterday, to establish goals tomorrow that were unthought of today, and to profit from yesterday's failures. Practicum, like the client or counselor, can change, it can grow, it can become, but only if change, growth and becoming are identified goals to be obtained.

Several written works contributing to the emphasis as set forth in this Manual are reproduced in this section. Our journal article originally appearing in <u>Counselor Education and Supervision</u> encourages the practicum supervisor to search for new and different methods of teaching practicum which facilitate maximum student counselor involvement. In "Developing Competency Statements for Counselor Education," by Thomas C. Froehle the more common approaches used in identifying, organizing, and classifying the competencies which need to be developed by student counselors are described. Another innovation which may be used in the practicum is "The Practicum Experience Record," which is a packet of material developed by Thomas Caulfield. The packet includes directions, behavioral objectives, and competencies for a practicum counselor.

INNOVATIONS IN COUNSELING PRACTICUM:
A PROGRESS REPORT

Kenneth M. Dimick and Frank H. Krause*

Our counseling practicum course has been restructured to incorporate what we feel are some unique ideas. Although this methodology has only been in practice for a few months, we are excited about the results and the possibilities for the future. Our goal is to provide students with a continuous practicum or practicum-related experience throughout their training. At the same time we want to assure our counselors in training that they have the opportunity to develop at their own speed. We also want to provide a working atmosphere that is optimally conducive to counselor growth, keeping in mind our professional responsibility to graduate only those students who have demonstrated their counseling competency.

In order that the reader may understand how our program is currently functioning, a brief description of the structure and composition of our counselor education department will be provided. Typically, we have 25 to 30 beginning practicum students per quarter, 15 to 20 enrolled in advanced practicum and 40 students enrolled in our prepracticum or techniques class. Approximately half of these students attend graduate school on a full-time basis, while the other half are enrolled part-time. In the past our practicum and advanced practicums have been divided into sections limited to 10 students with a faculty member and doctoral fellow supervising each section.

Innovations

Structure of the laboratory. All students enrolled in the practicum and advanced practicum are combined into one group. A classroom is assigned for use only as a practicum laboratory. Doctoral fellows and faculty members are each assigned to practicum instruction and each is individually responsible for a four-hour block of time in the laboratory room during each week.

Each student is required to spend a minimum of four hours a week in the laboratory. We suggest that students come to the laboratory experience at different times during each week in order that they might have contact with as many supervisors as possible. Activities engaged in during these four-hour blocks are: group tape-critiquing, encounter, discussion, and allied pursuits. Students are also encouraged to spend their free time in the laboratory. At present we are finding each student voluntarily coming to the laboratory experience approximately four extra hours a week. We do invite designated students, particularly those students experiencing specific difficulties, to spend more than the required four hours a week in the laboratory.

The laboratory experience is also open to students when a supervised group is not in progress. These are informal sessions where students may listen to tapes or participate in other activities not requiring formal supervision.

Supervision of prepracticum by practicum students. Tutorial supervision of beginning students by advanced students is not a totally new concept in counselor education (Meek & Parker 1966). We have attempted to incorporate this tutorial process in a manner that is advantageous to both beginning and advanced students.

Each prepracticum student from the counseling techniques class is required to spend a minimum of one hour per week in individual supervision or consultation with a beginning practicum student. During the periods when beginning practicum and advanced practicum are approximately equal in size, each beginning practicum student is required to spend a similar hour with an advanced practicum student. If these two classes are not approximately equal in size, supervision classes or doctoral student seminar classes are used to balance the sections, giving each practicum student the opportunity to work with a student in a higher level of training.

The nature of the experience provided during this hour is left to the discretion of the two students involved. Suggested activities include roleplaying, tape-critiquing, listening to

---

*Reprinted by permission from COUNSELOR EDUCATION AND SUPERVISION, XIII, No. 2 (December, 1973), pp. 144-146. Copyright 1973 American Personnel and Guidance Association.

tapes, viewing films or videotapes, and discussing common problems. (Recently one of our advanced practicum students told us that the best critique he had received came from a prepracticum student during one of these sessions.)

<u>Grading</u>. Assigning of grades to practicum students has been a millstone around counselor educators' necks (Dimick & Krause 1971). Our basic assumptions regarding the grading of practicum students were (a) that the practicum instructor could be a more effective agent of change if he was not responsible for assigning grades; (b) that the goal in practicum instruction would seem to be the development of competent counselors. We further concluded that this level of counseling competency can be demonstrated by some students in the first weeks of practicum, while others require several quarters or semesters to achieve these criteria.

It is our position that when a beginning practicum student can demonstrate an A level of competency in counseling skills, he should be moved from practicum to advanced practicum regardless of the number of weeks that it has taken him to achieve this competency. In order that the practicum instructor can assume more of a working-teaching role we developed a "board of evaluators." This board is composed of counselor educators in the department who are not directly involved with practicum instruction. Any time a student feels that he is counseling effectively he may request to appear before the board. (Practicum supervisors may encourage students to make this request.)

If the board certifies the student's competency (activities that take place during the evaluation session include audio- and videotapes of counseling sessions, roleplay, observation of counseling with a live client, and discussion. Similar to a doctoral or master's oral exam but involving only counseling ability and skills), then that student's grade is A. When the decision of the board is not favorable, comments are made to the student about his perceived weaknesses. It then becomes the responsibility of the practicum supervisors to help the student overcome these difficulties so that he may then be reevaluated by the board.

<u>Basic class requirements</u>. In addition to the four hours in the laboratory and one hour with a prepracticum student, the counselor in training is also required to see a minimum of four clients per week. Each week an hour is also to be spent in supervision with a member of the practicum supervisory team. We encourage the students to seek out various members of the team in order that they might experience a number of different supervisors and their models of supervision.

Conclusion

The most exciting part of this experience has been the discovery that practicum does not have to be taught in a traditional manner. Our message to counselor educators is not to suggest the adoption of this particular system, but to encourage all to look for new and different ways for more effectively teaching practicum.

References

Dimick, K. M., & Krause, F. H. Possible alternatives for evaluating counseling students. ILLINOIS GUIDANCE AND PERSONNEL QUARTERLY, 1971, 40, 15-17.

Meek, L. R., & Parker, A. W. Introductory counseling course: Use of practicum students. COUNSELOR EDUCATION AND SUPERVISION, 1966, 5, 154-158.

DEVELOPING COMPETENCY STATEMENTS FOR COUNSELOR EDUCATION

Thomas C. Froehle*

In this paper are described the more common approaches used in identifying, organizing, and classifying the competencies which counselor education programs seek to develop in counselors-in-training. While we do point out some possible sources of merit, we make no claim to a systematic consideration of merit or to a responsible evaluation of the approaches to the various tasks. For such discussion, the reader is referred to a related paper authored by Jackson (1974). The present paper does not attempt to describe or evaluate various delivery systems for making competency-based learning available to counselors-in-training. For a preliminary consideration of these distinguishing characteristics, you are referred to a paper titled, "Features of Competency-Based Counselor Education (Froehle, 1974)."

Some Definitions

Because no agreement exists on a definition of competency-based learning and/or competency-based education, the first necessity is to share with you key definitions specific to this paper. As a starter, competence is defined as "an organism's capacity to interact effectively with its environment." In the counselor-client environment considerable agreement exists that this capacity is functionally related to the knowledge and to the behavioral and judgment skills brought to that relationship (the order listed however should not suggest relative importance). For our purpose, then, a competency may be defined as "knowledge, skill, or judgment which the student will demonstrate at a predetermined proficiency level before initial and/or continuing certification (Cook, Newhauser, and Richey, 1972)."

Elsewhere in the literature, a competency has been operationally defined as a general statement covering a complex performance (Houston, 1972; Cottrell, 1970; Dodl, 1973). Attention should be directed to the description "general statement." Increasingly, competency statements are behavioral in nature but with no stated criteria. Detailed criteria are more typically included in the terminal performance objectives which give operational meaning to the competency statement. That is to say, terminal performance objectives make up a competency and achievement is used as evidence of competence.

---

*Dr. Thomas C. Froehle is Associate Professor, Department of Counseling and Guidance, Indiana University. Original material prepared for this publication based upon paper presented at North Central Association for Counselor Education and Supervision Convention, Chicago, November 4, 1974.

This brings us to the definition of competency-based counselor education (CBCE) which we define in terms of its programmatic features. Simply stated, a competency-based counselor education program is one in which the competencies to be acquired by a prospective counselor and the criteria to be applied in assessing those competencies are made explicit prior to instruction and training. Once specified, the competencies identify what a prospective counselor will know, what he or she will be like, what he or she will be able to do, and how the prospective counselor should be able to function in the real world of counseling (Froehle, 1974). In such a program both the training program and the counselor-in-training are evaluated in terms of the trainee's ability to demonstrate mastery of the prespecified competencies (Okey and Brown, 1973). CBCE programs differ principally from the more traditional programs in that CBCE programs focus more upon the competencies required for successful performance than upon the procedures used to develop those competencies.

Some Assumptions

Competency-based counselor education (CBCE) is predicated on the assumption that some knowledge and a range of behavioral and judgment skills exist which, upon possession by the practitioner, increase the likelihood of counselor effectiveness. In effect, CBCE assumes that prospective counselors who possess such skills will be successful in more client relationships than prospective counselors who do not have the skills--success being defined in terms of increments in client welfare.

Another assumption fundamental to CBCE is that this knowledge and these behavioral and judgment skills can be identified and promoted through the systematic arrangement of opportunities for learning and practice. Said another way, it assumes that the competencies are not that illusive that their acquisition, use and effect preclude systematic description, measurement and investigation.

Identifying Counselor Competencies

The identification and explication of competency statements is generally recognized as properly the first and most fundamental task to CBCE.[1] Okey and Brown (1973) describe four procedures for identifying competencies for teachers. They are as follows:

---

[1] This appears to be one of three efforts given special emphasis in CBCE. The two efforts which follow are: to develop procedures for _assessing_ individuals and awarding credentials for mastery of these _competencies_; and to design and develop educational experiences directly related to the attainment of these competencies. (HEW, 1973).

1. By <u>polling</u> interested parties: teachers, principals, supervisors, or teacher educators can be asked what skills they think teachers ought to learn.

2. By <u>poaching</u> from prepared lists: various institutions . . . and individuals . . . have listed teaching skills that can serve as sources for objectives.

3. By <u>observing</u> how experienced teachers act: observations can be made of master teachers at work in an effort to identify the teaching skills they use.

4. By <u>analyzing</u> the teaching act: Stolurow (1965) and others have suggested that teaching skills can be identified by analyzing the psychological requirements for learning to take place.

The methods described by Okey and Brown may be differentiated from each other on the basis of the type of activity in which the "identifier" engages.

In reality, according to the authors, most identification efforts use a combination of the four methods with an emphasis upon one or two methods. The authors prefer the "analyzing" method. Some interesting speculations emerge as one poses the questions: What is it that ultimately governs the selection of the method of choice? Could it be that the choice of method most accurately reflects the chooser's attribution of legitimacy to the source of and to the manner whereby the competency was identified? Under method one, for example, a teacher, a counselor, a principal, a counselor educator or whatever is presumed to be an expert source of opinion. In contrast, method three relies on expert, but non-participant observers, possibly because more value is placed upon observed performance than upon self-reported performance. But these and other speculations go much beyond the scope of this paper.

One of the better known descriptions of approaches to competency identification has been presented by Houston et al. (1972). They identify six approaches to competency generation: 1) program translation, 2) task analysis, 3) needs assessment, 4) cluster approach, 5) theoretical position, and 6) child-centered.

With the program translation approach you simply reformulate current courses into competency-based terms (e.g., rewrite learning objectives).

Under the task analysis approach, competent counselors in various work settings are observed in the act of counseling. Counselors may be asked to maintain a daily log or running diary, and to then reconstruct their daily activities in order to identify major competencies which they feel are necessary and/or contribute to their performance of these activities.

Using the needs assessment approach, the needs of society or the needs of a particular school, community, or population subculture are assessed. Based on these data, training objectives are derived deductively.

With the cluster approach several curriculum areas are identified which serve as the building blocks for counselor training. Competency clusters are then divided into competencies, and then into competency components, and then into behavioral objectives.

Under a theory directed approach a theoretical position is assumed and through a deductive approach competencies for the "effective counselor" are generated.

The last apporach described by Houston et al., the child-centered approach, involves analyzing children and the school and curriculum goals for the children. This information is then used to determine what children should be like and to identify the competencies needed to bring children to this ideal.

Close inspection reveals that the approaches described by Houston et al. are not discrete nor are they categorized in any systematic fashion. In practice, elements of each approach creep into any sustained effort to identify and explicate competency statements. In the next section of this paper we attempt a different ordering of the approaches and some slight modification in their respective definitions. And finally, we point to some possible programmatic advantages and disadvantages of each approach. These are summarized in Figure 1.

As with most everything else, each approach has its advantages and disadvantages. Expediency is the principal advantage of the program transformation approach (program translation for Houston, et al.). The task is accomplished easier by using this approach. However, this approach precludes total program reconstitution.

The major advantage of the competency cluster approach is the fact that it eliminates the mind-boggling problem of always dealing with the total process; on the other hand, it is not as limiting as the program transformation approach. The major disadvantages of this approach center around two problematic assumptions: 1) the assumption that the clusters selected are, in fact, adequate building blocks for an entire curriculum, and 2) the assumption that the deductively derived behavioral objectives are equally important for the prospective counselor. This approach also precludes, to some extent, total program reconstitution.

The principal advantages of the theoretical approach are the fact that 1) it permits a training institution to accurately describe where it's headed, and 2) it ensures continuity over time in a training program. Disadvantages include the fact that training procedures are governed not by client outcome but by beliefs associated with a process. It is "means oriented" rather than "outcome oriented."

APPROACHES	ADVANTAGES	DISADVANTAGES
PROGRAM TRANSFORMATION APPROACH	Expediency Ease of accomplishment Doesn't take as much time Not as threatening to counselor educators	Precludes total program reconstitution
COMPETENCY CLUSTER APPROACH	Not as mind-boggling as dealing with the total process - "counseling"; yet not as limiting as the Program Transformation Approach	Two problematic assumptions: 1) the assumption that the clusters selected are in fact adequate building blocks for an entire curriculum and 2) the assumption that the deductively derived behavioral objectives are equally important for the prospective counselor Precludes somewhat total program reconstitution
THEORETICAL APPROACH	Ensures continuity over time in a training program. Permits accurate definition	Training procedures are governed not by client outcome but by beliefs associated with a process
TASK ANALYSIS APPROACH	Permits precise description of professional performance and precise statements of training objectives	Excessive reliance upon current practice as the guide for training in the midst of uncertainty about the appropriateness of current practices
SYSTEM NEEDS ASSESSMENT APPROACH	Likely to win support of the system since it tends to perpetuate the status quo	High risk of oppressing individuals in the interest of system welfare
INDIVIDUAL NEEDS ASSESSMENT APPROACH	Potentially the most responsive to the needs of prospective clients	High risk that assessment data may dictate training in non-counseling kinds of performance. This may create problems for counseling as a "profession"

Figure 1. Advantages and Disadvantages of the Six Approaches

The task analysis approach permits detailed description and definition of counselor function and thereby makes possible very precise statements of training objectives, etc. Its major disadvantage is its excessive reliance upon the current practice of "Joe Counselor" as the guide for training in the midst of uncertainty about the appropriateness of current practices.

The product of the system needs assessment approach (simple needs assessment for Houston, et al.) is most likely to win support of the system, since it tends to perpetuate the status quo. The major disadvantage is its high risk of oppressing individuals in the interest of system welfare. Almost insignificant by comparison is the problem of the lag between getting a total fix on societal needs and the placement of counselors programmed to meet these needs.

The individual client needs assessment approach (child-centered approach for Houston, et al.) is potentially the most responsive to the needs of prospective clients; this is its greatest advantage. The principal disadvantage of this approach is the fact that assessment of individual client needs may dictate training in non-counseling kinds of performance. This may create problems for the "profession" of counseling. Secondly, no guarantee is provided that the training will be relevant because of the considerable time lag between assessment and completion of training.

Organizing and Classifying Competencies

Earlier we suggested a three-way classification for counselor competence: knowledge, behavioral skill, and judgment skill.[2] The inclusion of these three components reflects the growing belief that instruction and training must be directed not only to the accumulation of knowledge but also to its application and to the systematic investigation of the consequences of that application. Brief definitions of each competency type and a summary of the focus for evaluation of each competency type are presented in Figure 2.

COMPETENCY	FOCUS FOR EVALUATION
Knowledge Competencies	It's what the counselor knows and/or the amount of information or data which he possesses that counts.
Behavioral Skill Competencies	It's how the counselor performs that counts. It's what the counselor does with what he knows that counts.
Judgment Competencies	It's client welfare that counts. It's what the client knows, how he feels, or what he can do as a result of the counselor's efforts that counts.

Figure 2. Assessment Focus for Counselor Competencies

Knowledge competencies specify the knowledge, intellectual abilities, and information or data which the counselor is expected to demonstrate or somehow show evidence of having acquired. Knowledge competencies focus on what the counselor knows about counseling, not how well he or

---

[2]This classification system has been described in more detail in a chapter titled "Goal Analysis and Assessment: Helping Strategies," in D. J. Kurpius (Ed.), Modalities for Influencing Change in Education (University Associates, 1975).

she can perform the acts that go into that counseling, nor how successful he or she is in effecting desired client change through the use of these counseling procedures.

Behavioral skill competencies focus on the counselor's ability to draw upon information, data, knowledge and understanding in order to demonstrate or use a wide variety of prescribed counselor behaviors under specified conditions, either real or simulated conditions (e.g., "to use open-ended leads in a ten-minute microcounseling situation"; "to interpret accurately to a parent in a parent conference a student's score profile on an academic achievement test"; "to reward clients according to pre-specified contingencies"). In all three situations, it's the "live performance" in which we are interested. The actual questions are as follows: "Can the counselor use open-end leads to the satisfaction of some pre-specified criteria?" "Was the verbal interpretation of the test score profile an accurate one?" "Can the person administer and withhold rewards according to some pre-specified contingency (e.g., ten minutes of Monday night football on TV for every ten minutes of practice on the saxaphone)?" In none of the examples are we questioning the effect of the counselor's performance upon someone else. This is not the focus for behavioral skill competencies. Rather, behavioral skill competencies require assessment on the basis of the live performance of the counselor independent of any consideration of the effect of that performance upon someone (e.g., a client, a student).

Judgment competencies focus on the ability of a counselor to bring about change in others. Assessment therefore focuses not upon what the counselor knows or can do, but upon the results of knowing and doing, results which are demonstrated through change in someone else. Just as the acquisition of knowledge does not insure competence in the associated behavioral skills, neither does proficiency in the skill guarantee that the counselor trainee will decide correctly when to use which skills to meet the objectives of counseling and the needs of clients. Judicious decisions are critical to the success of a counselor, decisions about the most appropriate method of achieving the counseling goal, when the particular method should be used and what should precede and what should follow it (Paul, 1967). Such decisions confront the professional counselor every day and an effective counselor training program must help the prospective counselor become an effective decision maker.

In this short paper we have described briefly the more frequently used approaches to the development of statements of counselor competency. Our experience at Indiana University has convinced us that there is no easy way - no short cut to this all important function. Nor can one move on and bypass this stage even briefly because it is the foundation which ultimately governs the phases which follow, namely: 1) developing procedures for assessing individuals and awarding credentials for mastery of these competencies, and 2) designing and developing educational experiences directly related to the attainment of these competencies (HEW, 1973). To deviate from this sequence is to violate one of the most basic cannons of competency based learning. Only by steadfast adherence to the three part sequence suggested in this paper can we hope to promote learning which focuses upon desired outcomes rather than upon the procedures employed to promote those outcomes. This notion is fixed to the very core of competency based counselor education and the ultimate worth of this paper will be gauged by its success in promoting that notion.

References

Cook, F. S., Newhauser, C., & Richey, R. A working model of a competency-based teacher education system. Unpublished document, Wayne State University, 1973.

Cottrell, C. J. Model for curricula for vocational and technical teacher education: Report No. II, General Objectives, Set I, Columbus, Ohio. The Center for Vocational and Technical Education, 1970.

Department of Health, Education and Welfare. Fund for the improvement of post-secondary education: Program information and application procedures. Washington, D. C. HEW, 1973.

Dodl, N. The Florida catalog of teacher competencies. Tallahassee: Florida Department of Education, 1973.

Froehle, T. Features of competency-based counselor education. Paper disseminated through the Midwest Center for the Development of Pupil Personnel Services. Annual meeting of the American Personnel and Guidance Association. New Orleans, March, 1974.

Houston, W. R., et al. Developing instructional modules. (Work Text, Director's Guide), University of Houston, 1971.

Jackson, B. Individualization, humanization, and social change: Concepts to be considered in the generation of competencies. Paper presented at the annual meeting of the North Central Association for Counselor Education and Supervisors. Chicago, November, 1974.

Okey, J. R., & Brown, J. L. Competencies for performance-based teacher training. National Center for the Development of Training Materials in Teacher Education, Indiana University, Bloomington, Indiana.

Paul, G. L. Strategy of outcome research in psychotherapy. Journal of Consulting Psychology, 1967, 31, 109-118.

THE PRACTICUM EXPERIENCE RECORD*

Included in the packet of material for the Practicum Site Supervisor and the Practicum Student are (1) Letter to the Practicum Site Supervisor, (2) Suggested Guidelines for Carrying Out the Monitoring of Weekly Specific Behavioral Objectives, (3) Specific Behavioral Objectives, and (4) Evaluation Form: Activities Listed by Weeks.

The weekly evaluations by the Practicum Site Supervisor are to be shared with the Practicum Student and the University Practicum Supervisor. The purposes are to identify specially the behavioral objectives; increase communication among the Practicum Site Supervisor, Practicum Student, and University Practicum Supervisor; and provide the periodic evaluation of the extent to which the objectives are achieved.

Dear Practicum Site Supervisor:

The following list of events is designed to permit a wide range of experiences for student counselors enrolled in the practicum at Canisius College. These specific behavioral experiences have been selected in light of recommendation made by the New York State Bureau of Guidance, the New York State Personnel and Guidance Association, the Western New York School Counselors Association, and the Counselor Education Staff at Canisius.

If the schedule of events is followed closely, the student counselor will have an opportunity to demonstrate his competencies in a somewhat orderly manner of gradual complexity by the end of the semester. However, in no way is it mandatory that each week's activities must be ahdered to in a rigid manner. It is realized that individual differences exist in individuals and institutions which may well preclude strict adherence to each week's activities. These activities are presented as a minimal frame of reference and as a general guideline.

Your interest and cooperation in helping to prepare professional counselors is most appreciated and is a testament to your own commitment to the profession.

Sincerely,

The Canisius College
Counselor Education Staff

*Printed by permission from Dr. Thomas J. Caulfield, Chairman, Counselor Education, Canisius College.

SUGGESTED GUIDELINES FOR CARRYING OUT THE MONITORING
OF WEEKLY SPECIFIC BEHAVIORAL OBJECTIVES*

A wide range of methods may be employed for monitoring or observing the events listed. The methods employed are limited only by the cooperating counselor's ingenuity and environmental limitations. The methods suggested are included merely as guidelines to the cooperating counselor.

1. Individual Counseling Sessions, Group Counseling, Case Conferences, Parent Conferences, and Test Administration--These may be monitored in a variety of ways. Video taping, dual counseling, magnetic taping, use of observation rooms and interpersonal process recall are reasonable methods to use.

2. Making referrals and referral follow-up--It would seem appropriate for the cooperating counselor to discuss and "work through" the referral process as practiced in the school district. This process will vary in individual districts.

3. Conducting In-Service Sessions--The student counselor should have the opportunity to conduct an in-service session with teachers or guidance counselors. The area presented should be decided mutually by the cooperating counselor and the student counselor.

4. Orientation of New Students--The student counselor should have the opportunity to acquaint new students to the unique features of the school. Also he should have the opportunity to work through the scheduling process with new arrivals. The possibility of unique pupil needs should be considered at this time.

5. Guidance Department Meetings--The student counselor should have the opportunity of attending guidance department meetings. The learning and observation potential of such an experience is evident.

6. Counselors Evaluations of Student Counselor--This activity is suggested to provide the student counselor with an opportunity to gain insight into counselors' perceptions of counseling. It is suggested that the coordinating counselor _randomly_ select the evaluating counselees from among the population assigned to the student counselor.

7. Group Guidance Sessions--The student counselor should have the opportunity to conduct a group guidance session with a class/group of pupils. The area to be covered should be cooperatively agreed upon by the student counselor and the cooperating counselor. These areas can range from presenting occupational/educational information to personal/social concerns.

---

*Printed by permission from Dr. Thomas J. Caulfield, Chairman, Counselor Education, Canisius College.

SPECIFIC BEHAVIORAL OBJECTIVES*

Listing of Events to be Monitored or Observed during Practicum.

The following activities are strongly suggested for minimal fulfillment of practicum requirements. Strict adherence to the activities as listed is not mandatory. The list is provided as a guideline only and as a referent for providing the student counselor with an opportunity to display his or her competencies.

EVENTS	QUOTA PER SEMESTER
Individual Counseling Sessions	70 sessions ideal; 15 sessions minimum monitored for semester
Personal/Social Nature	3 sessions
Occupational/Educational	3 sessions
Test Interpretations	3 sessions
Group Counseling Sessions	3 sessions for semester
Number of Tests Administered	3 minimum for semester
Group Guidance Sessions	2 minimum
Case Conferences	3 sessions minimum for semester
In-Service Sessions	1 minimum
Parent Conferences	2 minimum for semester
Number of Referrals	3 contacts/1 referral minimum
Follow-up of Referral	2 minimum
Orientation of New Students	2 minimum
Student Evaluations of Counselor	3 minimum
Guidance Department Meeting	2 minimum
Meetings with Practicum Site Supervisor	15 minimum

*Printed by permission from Dr. Thomas J. Caulfield, Chairman, Counselor Education, Canisius College.

EVALUATION FORM
ACTIVITIES LISTED BY WEEKS

Practicum Site Supervisor_____   Student Counselor_____

FIRST WEEK   Date of
                              Activity   Completion

1. Student counselor introduction to practicum site supervisor . . . . _____
2. Practicum site supervisor introduces student counselor to school
   administrators and guidance staff. . . . . _____
3. Student counselor introduced to school faculty . . . . _____
4. Student counselor oriented to sources of information available in guidance
   offices (D.O.T., Occ/Ed literature, file system, cumulative records,
   standardized tests used in school district, etc.) . . . .   _____
5. Student counselor attends guidance department meeting . . . .   _____
6. Student counselor is oriented to school building . . . . _____
7. Practicum site supervisor discusses formal and informal organizational
   structure of school . . . .   _____
8. Student counselor is assigned work space compatible with carrying out
   counseling functions . . . .   _____
9. Student counselor is assigned a population of students with whom to work
   conjointly with practicing site supervisor . . . .   _____

COMMENTS:

                              Date_____ Signature_____

Directions: Circle the number which best   0. Not observed
            describes the performance of   1. Unsatisfactory
            the activity during the week.   2. Adequate
                                                            3. Does well
                                                            4. Outstanding

SECOND WEEK   Activity   Performance

1. Student counselor conducts group guidance session
   with at least 1 class of students 4 3 2 1 0
2. Student counselor administers one standardized test 4 3 2 1 0
3. Student counselor orients one new student to the school
   and schedules this student for classes 4 3 2 1 0
4. Practicum site supervisor discusses referral sources
   with student counselor 4 3 2 1 0
5. Student counselor begins counseling with at least one
   student 4 3 2 1 0
6. Student counselor attends guidance department meeting 4 3 2 1 0

COMMENTS:

                              Date_____ Signature_____

                                                            Form #1, p.1 of 4 pp.

Practicum Site Supervisor _____ Student Counselor _____

Directions: Circle the number which best
describes the performance of
the activity during the week.

                        0. Not observed
                        1. Unsatisfactory
                        2. Adequate
                        3. Does well
                        4. Outstanding

THIRD WEEK

1. Student counselor conducts group guidance session
   with at least 1 class of students 4 3 2 1 0
2. Student counselor administers one standardized test 4 3 2 1 0
3. Student counselor holds one test interpretation session 4 3 2 1 0
4. Student counselor orients one new student to the school
   and schedules this student for classes 4 3 2 1 0
5. Student counselor meets with practicum site supervisor 4 3 2 1 0
6. Individual counseling by student counselor 4 3 2 1 0

COMMENTS:

                    Date _____ Signature _____

FOURTH WEEK

1. Student counselor conducts an in-service session with teachers 4 3 2 1 0
2. Student counselor administers one standardized test 4 3 2 1 0
3. Student counselor holds one test interpretation session 4 3 2 1 0
4. Student counselor makes contact with one referral agency
   for orientation 4 3 2 1 0
5. Student counselor meets with practicum site supervisor 4 3 2 1 0
6. Individual counseling by student counselor 4 3 2 1 0

COMMENTS:

                    Date _____ Signature _____

FIFTH WEEK

1. Student counselor makes contact with one referral agency
   for orientation 4 3 2 1 0
2. Student counselor holds one test interpretation session 4 3 2 1 0
3. Student counselor conducts one case conference 4 3 2 1 0
4. Student counselor conducts one counseling session of
   personal/social nature 4 3 2 1 0
5. Student counselor conducts one counseling session of
   occupational/educational nature 4 3 2 1 0
6. Student counselor meets with practicum site supervisor 4 3 2 1 0

COMMENTS:

                    Date _____ Signature _____

Form #1, p.2 of 4 pp.

Practicum Site Supervisor_____ Student Counselor_____

Directions: Circle the number which best describes the performance of the activity during the week.

0. Not observed
1. Unsatisfactory
2. Adequate
3. Does well
4. Outstanding

SIXTH WEEK

1. Student counselor makes one contact with one referral agency for orientation 4 3 2 1 0
2. Student counselor conducts one counseling session of personal/social nature 4 3 2 1 0
3. Student counselor conducts one counseling session of occupational/educational nature 4 3 2 1 0
4. Student counselor conducts one case conference 4 3 2 1 0
5. Random student evaluation of counselor arranged by cooperating counselor 4 3 2 1 0
6. Student counselor meets with practicum site supervisor 4 3 2 1 0

COMMENTS:

Date_____ Signature_____

SEVENTH WEEK

1. Student counselor conducts one counseling session of personal/social nature 4 3 2 1 0
2. Student counselor conducts one counseling session of occupational/educational nature 4 3 2 1 0
3. Student counselor conducts one case conference 4 3 2 1 0
4. Student counselor arranges for referral of student to community agency 4 3 2 1 0
5. Open 4 3 2 1 0
6. Student counselor meets with practicum site supervisor 4 3 2 1 0

COMMENTS:

Date_____ Signature_____

EIGHTH WEEK

1. Student counselor conducts a minimum of two individual counseling sessions 4 3 2 1 0
2. Student counselor conducts one group counseling session ... 4 3 2 1 0
3. Student counselor conducts one parent conference 4 3 2 1 0
4. Student counselor meets with cooperating counselor 4 3 2 1 0
5. Practicum site supervisor conducts interim evaluation of student counselor 4 3 2 1 0

COMMENTS:

Date_____ Signature_____

Form #1, p.3 of 4 pp.

Practicum Site Supervisor_____   Student Counselor_____

Directions: Circle the number which best   0. Not observed
              describes the performance of   1. Unsatisfactory
              the activity during the week.   2. Adequate
                                                      3. Does well
                                                      4. Outstanding

NINTH WEEK

1. Student counselor conducts a minimum of two
   individual counseling sessions 4 3 2 1 0
2. Student counselor conducts a follow-up on referral
   made during the seventh week 4 3 2 1 0
3. Student counselor conducts one group counseling session 4 3 2 1 0
4. Student counselor conducts one parent conference 4 3 2 1 0
5. Random client evaluation of practicum counselor arranged
   by practicum site supervisor 4 3 2 1 0
6. Student counselor meets with practicum site supervisor 4 3 2 1 0

COMMENTS:

                                       Date_____ Signature_____

TENTH WEEK

1. Student counselor conducts a minimum of two
   individual counseling sessions 4 3 2 1 0
2. Student counselor conducts one group counseling session 4 3 2 1 0
3. Random client evaluation of practicum counselor arranged
   by practicum site supervisor 4 3 2 1 0
4. Student counselor meets with practicum site supervisor 4 3 2 1 0

COMMENTS:

                                       Date_____ Signature_____

ELEVENTH-FOURTEENTH WEEKS

Specific activities are left unscheduled purposely for these weeks to permit personal growth of the student counselor and to allow also for completion of minimum requirements. During this period the student counselor and the practicum site supervisor should meet weekly for growth and evaluative purposes. The student counselor should conduct a minimum of 3 counseling sessions each week. This period of time also permits opportunity for growth experiences not included in the minimum requirements but which are deemed appropriate mutually by the student and the practicum site supervisor.

EIGHTH WEEK AND FIFTEENTH WEEK

During these two weeks the student counselor and the practicum site supervisor should meet for evaluation.

                                                           Form #1, p. 4 of 4 pp.

PRACTICUM SUPERVISORS

Throughout this manual we make reference to the practicum supervisor. What is meant by this term? Does it communicate a different image to each individual utilizing this manual? To clarify, we see practicum as being supervised not only by a university professor but also by a professional counselor within the location where counseling practicum is being done. Thus each practicum counselor may have two or more supervisors. A student counselor may have a university practicum supervisor who is responsible for class work, a supervisor who serves as director of the counseling practicum laboratory at the university, and a supervisor in the setting where the student counselor is serving his or her counseling practicum.

Many practicum professors have moved from the traditional instructional approach (where the practicum professor is responsible for only his or her practicum counselors) to a teaching approach where a practicum counselor has two or more practicum supervisors. Many of us involved in training counselors/psychotherapists have evolved from the practicum supervisor being solely responsible for the critiquing of the student counselor to a sharing of the responsibility for a practicum counselor's growth with other professionals within and away from the training site.

Innovations not only have taken place with the number of practicum supervisors, but also with the variety of practicum settings available to a student counselor. By using more than one practicum supervisor and/or practicum setting, a student counselor may have the occasion for a number of growth experiences not usually available in a traditional approach. A student counselor may want the experience of working in a junior high school counseling office under the supervision of a qualified professional public school counselor, but the same practicum student also may want to experience counseling in the county jail under the supervision of the State Department of Correction psychologist. Therefore, if the university practicum supervisor uses the resources of the community, quite feasibly the student counselor will have more worthwhile counseling experiences. The traditional use of audio tapes and typescripts are beneficial. In addition, a practicum student's field experiences might be in a setting that has other valuable facilities and equipment available. A comprehensive mental health center might have observation rooms available for the practicum counselor. A diagnostic center for the State Department of Corrections might have video-tape equipment available for student counselor use.

Utilization of community resources and qualified personnel certainly is an instructional approach which we feel will enhance the student counselor's practicum experience. By involving practicum supervisors in approved practicum sites, the student counselor more than likely will have additional time to interact with practicum supervisors and will have two or more supervisors --university supervisor and one or more practicum site supervisors. The practicum supervisors might spend time at least in three areas: (1) supervision of the counseling and other practicum activities, (2) staffing cases with the practicum counselor, and (3) helping a practicum counselor with his or her own personal and professional growth.

In short, as an approach to teaching counseling practicum we have found the practicum counselor does benefit from having more than one practicum supervisor. Often the practicum counselor who has the opportunity to work with a number of high-functioning practicum supervisors has a far greater chance of becoming a high-level facilitator.

CRITERIA FOR EVALUATING A PROSPECTIVE PRACTICUM LOCATION

As we mentioned in the preceding section, numerous benefits are generated by a student counselor working in a variety of practicum locations. More than one practicum supervisor and his or her resources will often enhance the student counselor's training. However, as practicum supervisors responsible for the student counselors enrolled in our training program we do need to use some discretion in where to permit our student counselors to gain their experiences. This works two ways. As a valuable learning experience for the student counselor, it is also imperative that the student counselor make application to a practicum site. The practicum supervisor and/or appropriate university committee screen possible practicum sites. After a site has been approved the practicum site personnel have the responsibility to select only those practicum counselors who they feel will enhance their operation.

What are some criteria to look for when evaluating a school and/or other community agency as a potential practicum site? Personnel, professional associations of the school or agency, professional practices within the school or agency, administration of the proposed practicum location, and other pertinent information which would help the practicum supervisor evaluate the possible site seem like appropriate guidelines for us.

Let us examine these guidelines and ask some questions in order to spell out more specifically what to look for in a practicum location.

<u>Personnel</u> - What is the education and experience of the director and practicum supervisor? Is the director supportive of using and supervising practicum students? Is any financial support available to the student counselor (mileage, hourly pay, salary)? Is the practicum supervisor available for a minimum of two hours a week of individual supervision? What are the qualifications, professional affiliations, and other qualifications of staff members?

<u>Professional Association(s) of the School or Agency</u> - In what association(s) does the agency or school hold membership? Is the school or agency approved by other professional organizations? Does the school or agency have a working cooperation with other local agencies, colleges or universities and/or school systems?

<u>Professional Practices Within the School or Agency</u> - To what extent are ethics (i.e., APA, APGA, and NASW) followed? Which psychometric tests (i.e., ability, vocational, achievement, interest, and personality) are used and how? What resources such as the library are

available at the location? What opportunities do student counselors have to take an active developmental role as staff members rather than as outsiders? What are the intake procedures, treatment modalities, case loads, staffing procedures, and outreach programs, and are they in keeping with the objectives of practicum? How are counselee records kept (i.e., who keeps, where, security, etc.)?

<u>Administration of the School or Agency</u> - Who has control of the school or agency (i.e., corporation, governmental, board of directors, contributors)? How stable is the school or agency (i.e., source of support, length of service, tenure of director/staff, purposes or mandate of school or agency)?

<u>Other Pertinent Information</u> - What other information is needed by the local university requirements to help the practicum supervisor evaluate the school or agency? The following list of practicum settings illustrate the potential for a variety of sites where student counselors could have growth experiences. A university could start by evaluating a few sites and approving those which meet the criteria. The list could be expanded as settings meet the criteria and as students are available to be placed in the settings.

    Career or Vocational Area Schools
    Children's Homes
    Community Mental Health Centers
    Correctional Settings
    Counseling Departments located in public and/or private schools, K-12
    Counseling Centers located in Community or Junior Colleges
    Crisis Intervention Centers
    Drug and/or Alcohol Rehabilitation Centers
    Elementary Schools
    Family Planning Centers
    Geriatric Care Centers
    Hospitals for Mental Illnesses
    Mental Health Facilities
    Middle or Junior High Schools
    Pastoral Counseling Centers
    Physicians' Offices
    Psychiatric Centers
    Psychological Consultants to Business, Industry and/or Education
    Secondary or High Schools
    State Employment Agencies
    Suicide Prevention Centers
    Testing and Diagnostic Centers
    University Counseling Centers
    Vocational Placement Agencies
    Welfare Departments

CHAPTER II

INITIATING PRACTICUM

Practicum in counseling and/or psychotherapy is an opportunity for students to integrate the various cognitive and affective aspects of their counselor training program. Practicum consists of numerous actvities centered around actual counseling experiences with clients. The student counselor has a chance to gain experience, develop competencies, integrate past learning experiences, gain insight, and experience personal and professional growth under the tutelage of a supervisor. Counseling practicum is an "emerging" as opposed to "arriving" experience.

The practicum experience is tutorial in nature. The student counselor is given the opportunity to learn under the supervision of a qualified supervisor and in many instances under two or more supervisors.

The practicum counselor is in a process of growth and consequently he or she is _not_ expected to be, at the beginning of training, where he or she will be at the end of the practicum. At the beginning of the counseling practicum experience, greater emphasis is placed on openness to experience, willingness to examine the counseling interaction, recognition of issues, and meaningful involvement in one's own growth and development than on the demonstration of professional competence. Professional competence however is an essential and basic component that is required of the student counselor before making any counseling contacts or conducting interviews. As the practicum counselor progresses through the program, the emphasis does not shift but rather becomes broader to include the demonstration of a higher level of professional competence.

In addition to the opportunity of putting into practice the counseling abilities that the student counselor has acquired, practicum offers the unique opportunity for the integration of practical experience and theoretical knowledge. A strength of practicum is the development of counseling skills from real "on the job like" training as well as from textbooks and classroom experiences. The supervised practicum gives the practicum counselor the opportunities to transfer methodology and theories to applied situations.

Although requirement and format for various practicum classes will differ with instructors, the key to student counselor success in practicum appears to remain constant. The key is INVOLVEMENT with clients, supervisors and peers in meaningful professional experiences.

Responsibility placed upon the student counselor involved in counseling and psychotherapy practicum is paramount. In addition to the responsibility to clients and to one's self, the student counselor also represents the university where he or she is enrolled. The student counselor's actions, professionalism, and ability to function as an effective counselor or psychotherapist are scrutinized closely by a number of individuals, such as administrative and supervisory personnel, parents, other counselors, secretaries, and other employees in the school, agency or institutional setting.

Materials presented in this chapter have been selected as a result of careful screening. We feel that a student counselor can have a meaningful practicum experience by utilizing the information presented.

A practicum instructor might decide to have student counselors follow our recommendations completely, or he or she might decide to use a limited amount of the material. We believe that this chapter and the entire Manual supply those involved with practicum (both supervisor and supervisee) a number of resources, formats, and alternatives.

The Manual lends itself to being used in a workbook fashion. Included in this chapter are suggestions for starting the course, possible course requirements, and a variety of forms that we have found useful to assist both our practicum students and ourselves. If used, we feel both the student counselor and practicum supervisor can be assisted in viewing the accomplishments and progress of the practicum counselor.

SUGGESTED COURSE REQUIREMENTS

A practicum supervisor might want to have student counselors follow our suggested course requirements completely or to use some of these suggested requirements supplemented by one's personal requirements.

Class Meetings

Each practicum counselor is expected to spend a minimum of three and one-half hours a week in a group session. These students may use this time either in a didactic or an experiential activity. Student counselors might also use the class meeting time in the following ways:

1. As an opportunity to take part in role playing.

2. As an opportunity to listen and to discuss various recorded counseling sessions.

3. As an opportunity for listening and discussing counselor-in-training counseling tapes.

4. As an opportunity for discussing common problems, ideas, activities or concerns within the group.

5. As an opportunity for receiving feedback and an awareness as to how the counselor-in-training relates to his peers.

Counseling Sessions

Along with the weekly group meetings the practicum counselor is required to engage in a specified number of counseling interviews a week.

Individual Supervision Sessions

The counselor-in-training is expected to spend a minimum of one hour a week throughout the term with a practicum supervisor. These meetings are to discuss the development of the counselor trainee. Is the trainee facilitative in a counseling relationship? Is the student counselor perceptive? Is he or she able to demonstrate growth in counselees? Counselors-in-training generally find the individual supervision sessions to be one of their most meaningful experiences in practicum.

Tape Critiques

If at all possible, the practicum counselor is expected to tape all of his or her counseling sessions. Permission must be obtained from each counselee before any counseling session is taped. The tapes should be submitted weekly to the practicum supervisor in order that the counseling experiences may be shared and evaluated.

Each tape submitted for credit should be accompanied by a written or a typed critique. The critique should consist of the following information (see Forms #8 and #9):

1. Practicum counselor name, number of this tape, the number of hours of counseling time to date, and the date.

2. Client name, basic identifying data, e.g., 8th grade, shy girl, and the number of sessions to date with this client.

3. Brief summary of the content of the session. If this is a first session, include some background data and the reason for referral to you. Diagnostic material should be included in the summary.

4. Fairly detailed critique of what the counselor-in-training was trying to accomplish as a counselor and how well he or she feels the counseling was accomplished in terms of relationships, counselee growth, technique, etc.

5. Plans for further counseling with this client.

Client Folder

The practicum student might be held responsible for contributing information to a record file folder maintained by agency or school personnel in which the counseling sessions are held. Also, in many practicum courses the practicum counselor is asked to maintain a file folder on each client. In Chapter V of this Manual material is presented on how a practicum counselor can build a file folder for clients. Form #12 is a Check Sheet for Client Folder on to which can be recorded the activities and forms completed plus the dates.

Additional Requirements

Specific requirements may be identified by the practicum site supervisor, university supervisor, or professor. The following space is provided for listing additional requirements.

ROLE AND FUNCTION

In this day of emphasis regarding individual freedoms and especially in the profession of counseling which stresses such freedoms, it may seem inconsistent to discuss and demand some degree of adherence to a role. However, we feel that when the student counselor stops to realize that he or she is working in a practicum setting as a guest of that school, community agency, or other setting, then the student counselor will be able to view himself or herself in a position similar to those individuals that are contracted to the setting.

Not meaning to sound too parental but dress appropriately and in accordance with existing dress codes within the school, agency, or institution to which counselors-in-training are assigned. Behavior and dress reflect not only upon student counselors, but also upon the university and future student counselors who may wish to avail themselves of the particular practicum setting.

The best rule of thumb is common sense. The role of the practicum student is to obtain practice in counseling--not to change the system of the setting. The privileges that are extended to the student counselor certainly may be revoked by the school, agency, or institution at its discretion!

We suggest that those conflicts which might arise between the practicum student and the setting to which assigned offer a good opportunity for the student counselor to develop personal insight. The key to this situation would be look first at <u>oneself</u>, not at the system when a conflict arises and try to understand what it is about you that makes this situation a conflicting one.

NOTES

FORMS TO FACILITATE COMMUNICATON BETWEEN PRACTICUM SUPERVISORS AND PRACTICUM COUNSELOR

Practicum in counseling and/or psychotherapy necessitates cooperation among different people thus communication is essential. The professor, university supervisors, on-site supervisors, and practicum counselor must know one another by name, know the expectations of each other, be assured that ethical practices are understood and will be followed, and be informed as to the place, dates, hours, and activities to be performed by the practicum counselor as integral components of the practicum experiences. Included in this section of the Manual are forms which will faciliate the communication.

The Personal Data Sheet, Form #2, is designed to provide the practicum supervisors with basic information such as address, telephone numbers, work experiences, and the meanings of those experiences to student counselor. Also, the practicum counselor can communicate whether or not any arrangements have been made as to a location where the practicum activities are to be performed.

The practicum student is asked to study and be prepared to follow ethical procedures. The American Personnel and Guidance Association Ethical Standards and American Psychological Association Code of Ethics are reproduced in Chapter IV. The Agreement Made by the Practicum Counselor, Form #3, contains a statement regarding ethics. The Agreement also includes statements regarding keeping practicum supervisors informed regarding the practicum experiences; minimal level of counseling knowledge, skills, and attitudes; and preparation for and participation in supervisory sessions.

The practicum counseling sessions are to be with the consent of the faculty member. No practicum counselor is to begin counseling sessions until properly prepared and until adequate supervision is available. Form #4, Agreement Between Practicum Supervisor and Practicum Counselor, is a means of assuring that the professor has given approval for counseling sessions to begin at a designated location.

After the practicum student has met with the on-site supervisor, Form #5, Practicum Counselor's Placement and Schedule, can be completed. Once completed the form is to be submitted to the university practicum professor.

The practicum course is very time consuming and often requires a variety of activities. Form #6, Summary of Time Utilization To Meet Course Requirements, is a means of summarizing the activities and the times when each is to be performed. The primary function of the form is for the student; however, it may be submitted to the university professor and the supervisors for their review.

An Example of a Weekly Schedule, Form #7, is provided. This form is provided with multiple copies so that the practicum student can submit his or her Weekly Schedule. As to whether this schedule is to be submitted in terms of what was done or in terms of projected scheduled activities will be determined by the supervisor to whom the form is to be submitted. The practicum student will need to ask as to which procedure is to be followed.

PERSONAL DATA SHEET

DIRECTIONS: Practicum student is to submit this sheet to the Practicum Supervisor.

Practicum Student:

```
Please attach
a recent
photograph of
yourself.
```

Name _____

Address _____

_____

Telephone-Home _____
           Office _____

Date Submitted _____

Additional Information

What has been your professional and non-professional work experience?

What have these experiences meant to you?

Have you made any arrangements for obtaining practicum counselees? Yes____ No____

If yes, please supply the following:

    Place _____

    Name of Contact Person _____

    Arrangements you have made _____

    _____

    Other details if any _____

    _____

Form #2

AGREEMENT MADE BY THE PRACTICUM COUNSELOR

DIRECTIONS: Practicum student is to submit this sheet to the Practicum Supervisor.

(A) I hereby attest that I have read and understand the American Psychological Association and American Personnel and Guidance Association ethics (Chapter IV of this Manual) and will practice my counseling in accordance with these standards. I further understand that any breach of this code or any unethical behavior on my part will result in my receiving a failing grade and notification of such behavior will be placed in my permanent record.

(B) I understand that my responsibilities include keeping my practicum supervisor(s) informed regarding my practicum experiences.

(C) I understand that I will not be issued a passing grade until I have demonstrated a specified minimal level of counseling knowledges, skills, and attitudes.

(D) I further understand that my responsibilities include attending classes and supervisory sessions fully prepared as outlined by the course requirements. If such sessions are attended without my preparation, they will not be counted toward my minimal course requirements.

Practicum
Student
Signature_____

Date _____

Form #3

AGREEMENT BETWEEN PRACTICUM SUPERVISOR AND PRACTICUM COUNSELOR

DIRECTIONS: Practicum student is to have Practicum Supervisor sign this sheet before student makes arrangement to do practicum within school, community agency, or institution.

Date_____

Practicum Counselor Name_____ has permission to begin counseling interviews under my supervision.

Note:

The location(s) where the interviews may be held are as follows:

_____
_____
_____

Practicum Supervisor
Signature_____

Form #4

PRACTICUM COUNSELOR'S PLACEMENT AND SCHEDULE

DIRECTIONS: Practicum student submits this sheet to the university professor after the initial meeting with Supervisor in the practicum setting.

I am seeing clients at _____
under the supervision of _____. My tentative
schedule for my practicum in counseling is for the hours and dates as checked below:

	Monday	Tuesday	Wednesday	Thursday	Friday	Saturday
8- 9 a.m.	___	___	___	___	___	___
9-10	___	___	___	___	___	___
10-11	___	___	___	___	___	___
11-12	___	___	___	___	___	___
12- 1 p.m.	___	___	___	___	___	___
1- 2	___	___	___	___	___	___
2- 3	___	___	___	___	___	___
3- 4	___	___	___	___	___	___
4- 5	___	___	___	___	___	___
5- 6	___	___	___	___	___	___
7- 8	___	___	___	___	___	___
8- 9	___	___	___	___	___	___
9-10	___	___	___	___	___	___

Total Number of Hours _____

Comments:

Practicum Student Signature_____

Date_____

Form #5

SUMMARY OF TIME UTILIZATION TO MEET COURSE REQUIREMENTS

DIRECTIONS: Practicum student may use this form in two ways: (1) As a projected schedule of what is planned for the week and (2) As a completed form for submission to Practicum Supervisor after the requirements and schedule are met.

	Hours Per Week	Day	Time
1. Class Meetings	_____	_____	_____
2. Counseling Sessions	_____	_____	_____
3. Supervision	_____	_____	_____
4. Other Requirements	_____	_____	_____
Specify _____	_____	_____	_____
_____	_____	_____	_____
Total	_____		

Weekly Schedule of Practicum Experiences

	M	T	W	TH	F	SAT	SUN
8 a.m.	___	___	___	___	___	___	___
9	___	___	___	___	___	___	___
10	___	___	___	___	___	___	___
11	___	___	___	___	___	___	___
12 noon	___	___	___	___	___	___	___
1	___	___	___	___	___	___	___
2	___	___	___	___	___	___	___
3	___	___	___	___	___	___	___
4	___	___	___	___	___	___	___
5	___	___	___	___	___	___	___
Eve	___	___	___	___	___	___	___

Form #6

EXAMPLE OF A

WEEKLY SCHEDULE

DIRECTIONS: Practicum student may use this weekly schedule in two ways: (1) As a projected schedule of what is planned for the week to submit to Practicum Supervisor before week begins or (2) As a completed copy submitted to Practicum Supervisor after weekly interviews are over The practicum student will need to ask as to which procedure is to be followed.

Student Counselor: E. G. Rogers (Feb. 3 to Feb. 7)
Date Date

Practicum Supervisor: William Brown

Practicum Locations: CHS = Central High School   Total Hours: 8

PCC = Practicum Counseling Clinic   3

Day of Week	Location	Counselees	Time of Interview	Taped	Submitted Form (#8, 9, or 11)	Comments
Monday	CHS	Jane S.	9:00-10:00	Yes	11	Fifth Interview-Termination
	CHS	John N.	10:00-11:00	Yes	9	Second Interview-Continued
	CHS	Bill P.	11:15-11:30	No	None	Scholarship Information
Tues.	PCC	Sally M.	2:00- 3:00	No	8	First Interview-Continued
	PCC	Jack T.	3:15- 3:45	No	9	Second Interview-Continued
	PCC	Ann W.	4:00- 5:00	Yes	9 & 11	First Interview-No Return
Thurs.	CHS	Bill P.	9:00-10:00	Yes	9	Returned after scholarship information to discuss college plans-Continued
	CHS	Wilma J.	10:10-10:15	No	None	Information for term paper
	CHS	Jill Q.	10:30-11:00	Yes	9	Next year's schedule-No Return
	CHS	Steve D.	11:00-12:00	Yes	9 & 11	Third Interview-Closed
	CHS	Tim M.	12:15-12:50	No	8 & 11	First Interview-No Return

Example of Form #7

WEEKLY SCHEDULE

DIRECTIONS: Practicum student may use this weekly schedule in two ways: (1) As a projected schedule of what is planned for the week to submit to Practicum Supervisor before week begins or (2) As a completed copy submitted to Practicum Supervisor after weekly interviews are over. The practicum student will need to ask as to which procedure is to be followed.

Student Counselor: _____ (_____ to _____)
                                                      Date   Date
Practicum Supervisor: _____

Practicum Locations: _____ Total Hours: _____
                     _____   _____
                     _____   _____

Day of Week	Location	Counselees	Time of Interview	Taped	Submitted Form (#8, 9, or 11)	Comments
___	___	___	___	___	___	___
___	___	___	___	___	___	___
___	___	___	___	___	___	___
___	___	___	___	___	___	___
___	___	___	___	___	___	___
___	___	___	___	___	___	___
___	___	___	___	___	___	___
___	___	___	___	___	___	___
___	___	___	___	___	___	___
___	___	___	___	___	___	___
___	___	___	___	___	___	___
___	___	___	___	___	___	___
___	___	___	___	___	___	___
___	___	___	___	___	___	___
___	___	___	___	___	___	___
___	___	___	___	___	___	___

Form #7

WEEKLY SCHEDULE

DIRECTIONS: Practicum student may use this weekly schedule in two ways: (1) As a projected schedule of what is planned for the week to submit to Practicum Supervisor before week begins or (2) As a completed copy submitted to Practicum Supervisor after weekly interviews are over. The practicum student will need to ask as to which procedure is to be followed.

Student Counselor: _____ (_____ to _____)
                                              Date   Date
Practicum Supervisor: _____

Practicum Locations: _____ Total Hours: _____
                     _____
                     _____

Day of Week	Location	Counselees	Time of Interview	Taped	Submitted Form (#8, 9, or 11)	Comments

Form #7

WEEKLY SCHEDULE

DIRECTIONS: Practicum student may use this weekly schedule in two ways: (1) As a projected schedule of what is planned for the week to submit to Practicum Supervisor before week begins or (2) As a completed copy submitted to Practicum Supervisor after weekly interviews are over. The practicum student will need to ask as to which procedure is to be followed.

Student Counselor: _____   (_____ to _____)
                                                                 Date   Date
Practicum Supervisor: _____

Practicum Locations: _____   Total Hours: _____

Day of Week	Location	Counselees	Time of Interview	Taped	Submitted Form (#8, 9, or 11)	Comments

Form #7

WEEKLY SCHEDULE

DIRECTIONS: Practicum student may use this weekly schedule in two ways: (1) As a projected schedule of what is planned for the week to submit to Practicum Supervisor before week begins or (2) As a completed copy submitted to Practicum Supervisor after weekly interviews are over. The practicum student will need to ask as to which procedure is to be followed.

Student Counselor: _____ (_____ to _____)
                                              Date   Date
Practicum Supervisor: _____

Practicum Locations: _____ Total Hours: _____
                     _____   _____
                     _____   _____

Day of Week	Location	Counselees	Time of Interview	Taped	Submitted Form (#8, 9, or 11)	Comments
———	———	———	———	———	———	———
———	———	———	———	———	———	———
———	———	———	———	———	———	———
———	———	———	———	———	———	———
———	———	———	———	———	———	———
———	———	———	———	———	———	———
———	———	———	———	———	———	———
———	———	———	———	———	———	———
———	———	———	———	———	———	———
———	———	———	———	———	———	———
———	———	———	———	———	———	———
———	———	———	———	———	———	———
———	———	———	———	———	———	———
———	———	———	———	———	———	———
———	———	———	———	———	———	———
———	———	———	———	———	———	———

Form #7

WEEKLY SCHEDULE

DIRECTIONS: Practicum student may use this weekly schedule in two ways: (1) As a projected schedule of what is planned for the week to submit to Practicum Supervisor before week begins or (2) As a completed copy submitted to Practicum Supervisor after weekly interviews are over. The practicum student will need to ask as to which procedure is to be followed.

Student Counselor: _____ (_____ to _____)
                                                                                                       Date   Date

Practicum Supervisor: _____

Practicum Locations: _____   Total Hours: _____

Day of Week	Location	Counselees	Time of Interview	Taped	Submitted Form (#8, 9, or 11)	Comments
___	___	___	___	___	___	___
___	___	___	___	___	___	___
___	___	___	___	___	___	___
___	___	___	___	___	___	___
___	___	___	___	___	___	___
___	___	___	___	___	___	___
___	___	___	___	___	___	___
___	___	___	___	___	___	___
___	___	___	___	___	___	___
___	___	___	___	___	___	___
___	___	___	___	___	___	___
___	___	___	___	___	___	___
___	___	___	___	___	___	___
___	___	___	___	___	___	___
___	___	___	___	___	___	___
___	___	___	___	___	___	___
___	___	___	___	___	___	___

Form #7

WEEKLY SCHEDULE

DIRECTIONS: Practicum student may use this weekly schedule in two ways: (1) As a projected schedule of what is planned for the week to submit to Practicum Supervisor before week begins or (2) As a completed copy submitted to Practicum Supervisor after weekly interviews are over. The practicum student will need to ask as to which procedure is to be followed.

Student Counselor: _____ (_____ to _____)
                                                      Date   Date
Practicum Supervisor: _____

Practicum Locations: _____ Total Hours: _____
                     _____   _____
                     _____   _____

Day of Week	Location	Counselees	Time of Interview	Taped	Submitted Form (#8, 9, or 11)	Comments
___	___	___	___	___	___	___
___	___	___	___	___	___	___
___	___	___	___	___	___	___
___	___	___	___	___	___	___
___	___	___	___	___	___	___
___	___	___	___	___	___	___
___	___	___	___	___	___	___
___	___	___	___	___	___	___
___	___	___	___	___	___	___
___	___	___	___	___	___	___
___	___	___	___	___	___	___
___	___	___	___	___	___	___
___	___	___	___	___	___	___
___	___	___	___	___	___	___
___	___	___	___	___	___	___
___	___	___	___	___	___	___
___	___	___	___	___	___	___

Form #7

WEEKLY SCHEDULE

DIRECTIONS: Practicum student may use this weekly schedule in two ways: (1) As a projected schedule of what is planned for the week to submit to Practicum Supervisor before week begins or (2) As a completed copy submitted to Practicum Supervisor after weekly interviews are over. The practicum student will need to ask as to which procedure is to be followed.

Student Counselor: _____ (_____ to _____)
                                                      Date   Date
Practicum Supervisor: _____

Practicum Locations: _____   Total Hours: _____
                     _____   _____
                     _____   _____

Day of Week	Location	Counselees	Time of Interview	Taped	Submitted Form (#8, 9, or 11)	Comments

Form #7

WEEKLY SCHEDULE

DIRECTIONS: Practicum student may use this weekly schedule in two ways: (1) As a projected schedule of what is planned for the week to submit to Practicum Supervisor before week begins or (2) As a completed copy submitted to Practicum Supervisor after weekly interviews are over. The practicum student will need to ask as to which procedure is to be followed.

Student Counselor: _____ (_____ to _____)
                                                    Date   Date
Practicum Supervisor: _____

Practicum Locations: _____   Total Hours: _____
                     _____
                     _____

Day of Week	Location	Counselees	Time of Interview	Taped	Submitted Form (#8, 9, or 11)	Comments
___	___	___	___	___	___	___
___	___	___	___	___	___	___
___	___	___	___	___	___	___
___	___	___	___	___	___	___
___	___	___	___	___	___	___
___	___	___	___	___	___	___
___	___	___	___	___	___	___
___	___	___	___	___	___	___
___	___	___	___	___	___	___
___	___	___	___	___	___	___
___	___	___	___	___	___	___
___	___	___	___	___	___	___
___	___	___	___	___	___	___
___	___	___	___	___	___	___
___	___	___	___	___	___	___
___	___	___	___	___	___	___
___	___	___	___	___	___	___

Form #7

WEEKLY SCHEDULE

DIRECTIONS: Practicum student may use this weekly schedule in two ways: (1) As a projected schedule of what is planned for the week to submit to Practicum Supervisor before week begins or (2) As a completed copy submitted to Practicum Supervisor after weekly interviews are over. The practicum student will need to ask as to which procedure is to be followed.

Student Counselor: _____ (_____ to _____)
                                                                                            Date   Date

Practicum Supervisor: _____

Practicum Locations: _____   Total Hours: _____

Day of Week	Location	Counselees	Time of Interview	Taped	Submitted Form (#8, 9, or 11)	Comments
_____	_____	_____	_____	_____	_____	_____
_____	_____	_____	_____	_____	_____	_____
_____	_____	_____	_____	_____	_____	_____
_____	_____	_____	_____	_____	_____	_____
_____	_____	_____	_____	_____	_____	_____
_____	_____	_____	_____	_____	_____	_____
_____	_____	_____	_____	_____	_____	_____
_____	_____	_____	_____	_____	_____	_____
_____	_____	_____	_____	_____	_____	_____
_____	_____	_____	_____	_____	_____	_____
_____	_____	_____	_____	_____	_____	_____
_____	_____	_____	_____	_____	_____	_____
_____	_____	_____	_____	_____	_____	_____
_____	_____	_____	_____	_____	_____	_____
_____	_____	_____	_____	_____	_____	_____

Form #7

WEEKLY SCHEDULE

DIRECTIONS: Practicum student may use this weekly schedule in two ways: (1) As a projected schedule of what is planned for the week to submit to Practicum Supervisor before week begins or (2) As a completed copy submitted to Practicum Supervisor after weekly interviews are over. The practicum student will need to ask as to which procedure is to be followed.

Student Counselor: _____ (_____ to _____)
                                                                                                Date   Date

Practicum Supervisor: _____

Practicum Locations: _____ Total Hours: _____

Day of Week	Location	Counselees	Time of Interview	Taped	Submitted Form (#8, 9, or 11)	Comments

Form #7

WEEKLY SCHEDULE

DIRECTIONS: Practicum student may use this weekly schedule in two ways: (1) As a projected schedule of what is planned for the week to submit to Practicum Supervisor before week begins or (2) As a completed copy submitted to Practicum Supervisor after weekly interviews are over. The practicum student will need to ask as to which procedure is to be followed.

Student Counselor: _____ (_____ to _____)
                                                      Date   Date
Practicum Supervisor: _____

Practicum Locations: _____ Total Hours: _____

Day of Week	Location	Counselees	Time of Interview	Taped	Submitted Form (#8, 9, or 11)	Comments

Form #7

WEEKLY SCHEDULE

DIRECTIONS: Practicum student may use this weekly schedule in two ways: (1) As a projected schedule of what is planned for the week to submit to Practicum Supervisor before week begins or (2) As a completed copy submitted to Practicum Supervisor after weekly interviews are over. The practicum student will need to ask as to which procedure is to be followed.

Student Counselor: _____ (_____ to _____)
                                                                       Date   Date

Practicum Supervisor: _____

Practicum Locations: _____ Total Hours: _____

Day of Week	Location	Counselees	Time of Interview	Taped	Submitted Form (#8, 9, or 11)	Comments

Form #7

WEEKLY SCHEDULE

DIRECTIONS: Practicum student may use this weekly schedule in two ways: (1) As a projected schedule of what is planned for the week to submit to Practicum Supervisor before week begins or (2) As a completed copy submitted to Practicum Supervisor after weekly interviews are over. The practicum student will need to ask as to which procedure is to be followed.

Student Counselor: _____ (_____ to _____)
                                                      Date   Date
Practicum Supervisor: _____

Practicum Locations: _____   Total Hours: _____

Day of Week	Location	Counselees	Time of Interview	Taped	Submitted Form (#8, 9, or 11)	Comments
___	___	___	___	___	___	___
___	___	___	___	___	___	___
___	___	___	___	___	___	___
___	___	___	___	___	___	___
___	___	___	___	___	___	___
___	___	___	___	___	___	___
___	___	___	___	___	___	___
___	___	___	___	___	___	___
___	___	___	___	___	___	___
___	___	___	___	___	___	___
___	___	___	___	___	___	___
___	___	___	___	___	___	___
___	___	___	___	___	___	___
___	___	___	___	___	___	___
___	___	___	___	___	___	___

Form #7

WEEKLY SCHEDULE

DIRECTIONS: Practicum student may use this weekly schedule in two ways: (1) As a projected schedule of what is planned for the week to submit to Practicum Supervisor before week begins or (2) As a completed copy submitted to Practicum Supervisor after weekly interviews are over. The practicum student will need to ask as to which procedure is to be followed.

Student Counselor: _____ (_____ to _____)
                                               Date   Date
Practicum Supervisor: _____

Practicum Locations: _____   Total Hours: _____
                    _____   _____
                    _____   _____

Day of Week	Location	Counselees	Time of Interview	Taped	Submitted Form (#8, 9, or 11)	Comments
___	___	___	___	___	___	___
___	___	___	___	___	___	___
___	___	___	___	___	___	___
___	___	___	___	___	___	___
___	___	___	___	___	___	___
___	___	___	___	___	___	___
___	___	___	___	___	___	___
___	___	___	___	___	___	___
___	___	___	___	___	___	___
___	___	___	___	___	___	___
___	___	___	___	___	___	___
___	___	___	___	___	___	___
___	___	___	___	___	___	___
___	___	___	___	___	___	___
___	___	___	___	___	___	___

Form #7

CHAPTER III

COUNSELING TECHNIQUES AND PROCESSES

Currently in counseling and psychotherapy, many techniques and processes are being implemented. Role playing, interpreting, clarifying, confronting, and expressing feelings are but a few of the many therapeutic techniques. Included in this chapter are presentations which will enlighten the practicum counselor about techniques and other processes of counseling and psychotherapy.

At the start of this section are presented some personal views about student counselors and their development of counseling techniques. We summarize general overall approaches toward the total counseling session as to what the counselor does.

The chapter contains a list of techniques frequently used together with suggestions for considering your own techniques. You may want to expand your knowledge regarding techniques and your own philosophical bases for their use.

Also included in the chapter are suggestions for counseling practicum, information regarding interview notes, case study guidelines, and a note regarding case reports together with a sample letter. Forms also for the initial intake (Form #8) and the interview notes (Form #9) are provided.

COUNSELING TECHNIQUES

> Counselors-in-training are often told that categorizing or labeling as technique what occurs during the counseling session is a waste of a practitioner's time. Prospective counselors are encouraged to become more aware of one's own self and the relationship to one's clients. By doing this, an effective technique will be employed naturally. Yet, as our experience increases, we become more aware that with certain clients we do employ certain techniques or methods which lead to a more facilitative counseling session. (Krause and Hendrickson, 1972, p. 51)

The preceding brief statement alludes to the fact that approaches to techniques of counseling do differ among practitioners. The following paragraphs are directed toward emphasizing the need for techniques.

Just as a carpenter possibly could build a house without the use of tools, a counselor possibly could counsel without the use of techniques. The carpenter's house built without tools would most likely appear crude, have taken a long time to build, but probably would suffice as a place to live.

If the carpenter were given the use of one tool, the workmanship would most likely improve. The carpenter probably would learn to improvise and develop innovative ways of using this single tool in order to expedite the building process.

The good carpenter learns to use all tools in an efficient manner. He or she knows what the tools can do, how to use them, and what to substitute when tools are not available. Over a period of time certain tools become favorites and techniques are developed for using certain tools in ways no others have used them. As the individual becomes a master carpenter, the tools become part of the person, an extension of the carpenter's hands. He or she learns to build in the most efficient way possible and some tools are rejected as not being as useful as others. The carpenter learns to make the tools work so as to accomplish the desired goals.

The counselor's techniques can be seen as analogous to the carpenter's tools. The more the counselor learns about techniques and uses them, the closer they become to being an extension of the counselor. The master counselor learns to use techniques for accomplishing the desired goals more efficiently. (Dimick and Huff, 1971, p. 242)

Although much attention is given in counseling to the differences various counselors demonstrate, many commonalities in counseling do appear regardless of approach. You can adapt or adopt techniques from others to assist you in broadening your "tools" for helping clients.

A counseling atmosphere conducive to personal growth must be present for effective counseling to take place. Counseling has been referred to as "an invitation to health." Furthermore, it is an experience in health. The atmosphere, which is controlled to a large extent by the counselor, must represent health.

Counseling is a _process_ as opposed to specific problem solving. So often in class, we have heard counseling students pay lip service to such a belief and follow it with a statement such as "But what is the counselee's problem?" The counselee must be viewed as a person with problems as opposed to problems residing inside a person. Listening and knowing what is really being said and really felt are major keys to counseling.

Much discussion is given in contemporary counseling to directing dialogue to the "feeling level." Feelings and behaviors exist in unison not as separate entities. The counselor must be aware of both simultaneously not separately.

The old saying "Give a man a fish and he shall be fed for a day. Teach a man to fish and he shall be fed for a lifetime" has much application to counseling. Counselors cannot be in such a hurry to help that the client gets left out of the process.

Although practitioners vary as to the importance of here-and-now emphasis in counseling, every counselor needs to be aware continually of both his or her own feelings, as well as what the client appears to be feeling and thinking.

No rule exists that says all silence must be replaced with noise. Rather than learning to tolerate silence the counselor must learn to see silence as potentially productive.

An atmosphere built upon trust but differing from dependency must exist for effective counseling to take place. Such an atmosphere does not just happen but must be facilitated by the counselor.

Things are the way the client sees them. Although the client may change some perceptions during the counseling process, the important point to remember is that at any given minute the way the client sees things represents reality to the client at that time. Beliefs and feelings are not always logical. The counselor's presentation of logic does not always change the way things seem to the client.

In summary, the following list contains a number of general overall approaches, some may call them techniques, which are to be utilized by the counselor. A brief discussion of each is presented.

1. Create an _atmosphere_ which will enable the counselee to relax and feel free to discuss his or her concerns. The physical surroundings can assist in creating the atmosphere but far more important is the atmosphere created by the counselor and the interaction with the client.

2. Be willing to _listen_ (rather than probing) and provide the counselee an opportunity to present the situation as he or she sees it. Listening is an active, not passive, process. Learn and use the listening technique. It is important both as input and feedback for you.

3. Try to let the individual see that you are genuinely trying to <u>understand</u> his or her feelings. Understanding the cognitive domain is often easier than understanding either the affective or the psychomotor domains. The counselor must strive to understand all three domains.

4. Keep the focus on how the counselee <u>feels</u> about what has happened to him or her. Often the client only focuses on the cognitive but the counselor must help the client also focus on feelings.

5. <u>Respect</u> the counselee who trys to protect his or her feelings through verbal fumbling or misrepresenting his or her dilemma. What is being shared may be very personal, never revealed before, and may be hard to "face." Respect the counselee as he or she works through the feelings with you.

6. Make pertinent <u>reflective</u>, <u>clarifying</u>, <u>interpretative</u> or <u>confrontive</u> comments as you see fit. The counselor has many techniques from which to select for purposes of facilitating the client's feeling sharing, value clarification, exploration, or removal of ambivalence.

7. Draw out ideas as to what the counselee might be able to do by encouraging him or her to present <u>alternative courses of action</u> and <u>examining values involved</u>. Prior to the decision making process, the client will want to examine values held by self and possibly others as well as considering what alternatives are available and what the rewards and disadvantages are to each.

8. Help the counselee to appraise his or her plan of action on the grounds of <u>feelings</u> and <u>reality</u>. Counseling enables a client to consider more than just the mental processes, it also assists the client in integrating feelings into the process. Instead of separating or isolating these feelings, help the client get these into unison.

9. Allow the counselee to work out his or her own problem in his or her own way, regardless of what you think should be done. <u>Be patient</u>. The client's job is to grow--not merely to obtain information or be told what to do. Include the client in the process and <u>make growth</u>, rather than problem solving, <u>the goal</u>.

10. Try to understand the <u>role</u> the client is asking you to play--parent, sibling, pal-- and try to respect the counselee's need to project upon you. Transference is frequent by the client. Recognize it and know the techniques for handling it.

11. Keep the <u>counselee</u> rather than his or her problems <u>as the center of the counseling process</u>. Above all the counselor must keep in mind the welfare of the client. All techniques and theories utilized by the counselor are to be directed toward that end.

Be you!!! If you are effective, the you, not the counselor, is effective. A counselor's downfall often has been an effort to play the role of counselor instead of integrating counseling into his or her own being.

Finally, let it be re-emphasized that the art of counseling is an ongoing process. A practicum professor does expect you will make mistakes. The professor also expects you to learn to be a better artist today than you were yesterday. One learns from mistakes if one will allow self to do so. One regresses if he or she feels a need to hide or is afraid of mistakes.

TECHNIQUES USED IN COUNSELING AND PSYCHOTHERAPY

Joseph W. Hollis[*]

Major growth has occurred in the counseling and psychotherapy professions in recent years. Different philosophical positions have given rise to new theories which in turn have produced a search for additional approaches. The number of counselors, therapists, and clinicians has increased, while also expanding the scope of individuals with whom counseling services have been available.

Since no one counseling technique was appropriate for all clients or was flexible enough to use at the various depths required in counseling, additional counseling techniques became a necessity. Research and experimentation led to new techniques and to an identification of which techniques are most appropriate when using a specific theoretical base with a client in remedial, preventive, or developmental area. Thus, the counseling profession has developed to the stage where each counselor can select techniques according to his or her own philosophical base and according to the client's needs. When the counselor recognizes his or her own limitations in using a wide range of techniques, this would enable the counselor to refer certain clients, seek consultation when working with some clients, request co-counselor or co-therapist to work with specific clients, or limit one's practice to clients who can be assisted with the competencies held by the counselor.

The following list of counseling and psychotherapy techniques is not all inclusive but does represent techniques used by a broad spectrum of philosophical bases. The number of counseling techniques used by any one counselor varies. By a counselor reviewing his or her tape recordings from several sessions with different clients, ten to fifteen techniques may be identified which were used frequently with competency. An additional ten to fifteen may be identified which were used but used less frequently or in some cases with less professional competency.

The suggestions for using the techniques list are dependent upon your stage of professional development. Students in my courses use the list primarily in two ways: (1) to checkout and expand their knowledge about counseling techniques and (2) to introspect into their own counseling, philosophical bases, and treatment approaches.

---

[*] Dr. Joseph W. Hollis is Director of the Doctoral Program in Counseling and Guidance and Professor of Psychology-Counseling, Department of Counseling Psychology and Guidance Services, Ball State University. Original material prepared for this publication.

Directions for Use of Techniques List

First, look at the techniques listed in column one. Then technique by technique decide the extent to which you do or would be competent to use each. Indicate the extent of use or competency by circling the appropriate letter in column two. If you do not know the technique, then mark an "X" through the "N" for "none." Space is provided at the end of the techniques in column one to add other techniques.

Second, after completing the list and indicating your extent of use or competency, then go through the techniques list again and mark in the third column the theory or theories where each technique is appropriate. The third column, of course, can be marked only for the techniques with which you have knowledge.

The third task is to become more knowledgeable about the techniques which you do not know--the ones marked with X. As you gain knowledge relating to each technique, you can decide whether or not you will use it and with which kinds of clients and under what conditions.

The fourth task is to review columns two and three and determine whether or not the techniques in which you have the competencies are within one or two theories. If so, are the theories the ones which best reflect your self concept? Do the techniques marked reflect those most appropriate, as revealed in the literature, for the clients with whom you want to work?

(Read Preceding Two Pages Before Proceeding)

Technique	Extent of Use or Competency	Theories Where Technique is Most Appropriate
	N = None M = Minimal A = Average E = Extensive	Be = Behavior Modification (Wolpe) Cl = Client Center (Rogers) Co = Conjoint Family (Satir) Ex = Existential (May) Ge = Gestalt (Perls) Lo = Logo (Frankl) Ps = Psychoanalytic (Freud)
	Circle one to represent extent Mark X across the N if technique is unknown	RE = Rational Emotive Therapy (Ellis) TA = Transactional Analysis (Berne) TF = Trait Factor (Williamson) Circle one or more

```
acceptance . . . . . . . . . . . . . . . . N M A E . . . . . Be Cl Co Ex Ge Lo Ps RE TA TF
active imagination  . . . . . . . . . . .  N M A E . . . . . Be Cl Co Ex Ge Lo Ps RE TA TF
active listening  . . . . . . . . . . . .  N M A E . . . . . Be Cl Co Ex Ge Lo Ps RE TA TF
advice giving . . . . . . . . . . . . . .  N M A E . . . . . Be Cl Co Ex Ge Lo Ps RE TA TF
alter-ego . . . . . . . . . . . . . . . .  N M A E . . . . . Be Cl Co Ex Ge Lo Ps RE TA TF
analyzing symbols . . . . . . . . . . . .  N M A E . . . . . Be Cl Co Ex Ge Lo Ps RE TA TF
analysis  . . . . . . . . . . . . . . . .  N M A E . . . . . Be Cl Co Ex Ge Lo Ps RE TA TF
assertive training  . . . . . . . . . . .  N M A E . . . . . Be Cl Co Ex Ge Lo Ps RE TA TF
audiotape recorded models . . . . . . . .  N M A E . . . . . Be Cl Co Ex Ge Lo Ps RE TA TF
authoritarian approach  . . . . . . . . .  N M A E . . . . . Be Cl Co Ex Ge Lo Ps RE TA TF
aversion-aversive conditioning  . . . . .  N M A E . . . . . Be Cl Co Ex Ge Lo Ps RE TA TF
behavior modification . . . . . . . . . .  N M A E . . . . . Be Cl Co Ex Ge Lo Ps RE TA TF
bibliotherapy . . . . . . . . . . . . . .  N M A E . . . . . Be Cl Co Ex Ge Lo Ps RE TA TF
break-in, break-out . . . . . . . . . . .  N M A E . . . . . Be Cl Co Ex Ge Lo Ps RE TA TF
bumping in a circle . . . . . . . . . . .  N M A E . . . . . Be Cl Co Ex Ge Lo Ps RE TA TF
cajoling  . . . . . . . . . . . . . . . .  N M A E . . . . . Be Cl Co Ex Ge Lo Ps RE TA TF
case history  . . . . . . . . . . . . . .  N M A E . . . . . Be Cl Co Ex Ge Lo Ps RE TA TF
catharsis . . . . . . . . . . . . . . . .  N M A E . . . . . Be Cl Co Ex Ge Lo Ps RE TA TF
chemotherapy  . . . . . . . . . . . . . .  N M A E . . . . . Be Cl Co Ex Ge Lo Ps RE TA TF
clarifying feelings . . . . . . . . . . .  N M A E . . . . . Be Cl Co Ex Ge Lo Ps RE TA TF
commitment  . . . . . . . . . . . . . . .  N M A E . . . . . Be Cl Co Ex Ge Lo Ps RE TA TF
conditioning techniques . . . . . . . . .  N M A E . . . . . Be Cl Co Ex Ge Lo Ps RE TA TF
confession  . . . . . . . . . . . . . . .  N M A E . . . . . Be Cl Co Ex Ge Lo Ps RE TA TF
confrontation . . . . . . . . . . . . . .  N M A E . . . . . Be Cl Co Ex Ge Lo Ps RE TA TF
congruence  . . . . . . . . . . . . . . .  N M A E . . . . . Be Cl Co Ex Ge Lo Ps RE TA TF
contractual agreements  . . . . . . . . .  N M A E . . . . . Be Cl Co Ex Ge Lo Ps RE TA TF
co-therapist  . . . . . . . . . . . . . .  N M A E . . . . . Be Cl Co Ex Ge Lo Ps RE TA TF
counter propaganda  . . . . . . . . . . .  N M A E . . . . . Be Cl Co Ex Ge Lo Ps RE TA TF
counter transference  . . . . . . . . . .  N M A E . . . . . Be Cl Co Ex Ge Lo Ps RE TA TF
crying  . . . . . . . . . . . . . . . . .  N M A E . . . . . Be Cl Co Ex Ge Lo Ps RE TA TF
decision making . . . . . . . . . . . . .  N M A E . . . . . Be Cl Co Ex Ge Lo Ps RE TA TF
democratic  . . . . . . . . . . . . . . .  N M A E . . . . . Be Cl Co Ex Ge Lo Ps RE TA TF
desensitization . . . . . . . . . . . . .  N M A E . . . . . Be Cl Co Ex Ge Lo Ps RE TA TF
detailed inquiry  . . . . . . . . . . . .  N M A E . . . . . Be Cl Co Ex Ge Lo Ps RE TA TF
diagnosing  . . . . . . . . . . . . . . .  N M A E . . . . . Be Cl Co Ex Ge Lo Ps RE TA TF
doubling  . . . . . . . . . . . . . . . .  N M A E . . . . . Be Cl Co Ex Ge Lo Ps RE TA TF
dream interpretation  . . . . . . . . . .  N M A E . . . . . Be Cl Co Ex Ge Lo Ps RE TA TF
dreaming  . . . . . . . . . . . . . . . .  N M A E . . . . . Be Cl Co Ex Ge Lo Ps RE TA TF
drugs . . . . . . . . . . . . . . . . . .  N M A E . . . . . Be Cl Co Ex Ge Lo Ps RE TA TF
empathy . . . . . . . . . . . . . . . . .  N M A E . . . . . Be Cl Co Ex Ge Lo Ps RE TA TF
encouragement . . . . . . . . . . . . . .  N M A E . . . . . Be Cl Co Ex Ge Lo Ps RE TA TF
```

Term		Categories
environmental manipulation	N M A E	Be Cl Co Ex Ge Lo Ps RE TA TF
explaining	N M A E	Be Cl Co Ex Ge Lo Ps RE TA TF
fading	N M A E	Be Cl Co Ex Ge Lo Ps RE TA TF
family chronology	N M A E	Be Cl Co Ex Ge Lo Ps RE TA TF
family group counseling	N M A E	Be Cl Co Ex Ge Lo Ps RE TA TF
fantasizing	N M A E	Be Cl Co Ex Ge Lo Ps RE TA TF
feedback	N M A E	Be Cl Co Ex Ge Lo Ps RE TA TF
filmed models	N M A E	Be Cl Co Ex Ge Lo Ps RE TA TF
first memory	N M A E	Be Cl Co Ex Ge Lo Ps RE TA TF
free association	N M A E	Be Cl Co Ex Ge Lo Ps RE TA TF
frustration	N M A E	Be Cl Co Ex Ge Lo Ps RE TA TF
game theory techniques	N M A E	Be Cl Co Ex Ge Lo Ps RE TA TF
group centered	N M A E	Be Cl Co Ex Ge Lo Ps RE TA TF
group play	N M A E	Be Cl Co Ex Ge Lo Ps RE TA TF
homework	N M A E	Be Cl Co Ex Ge Lo Ps RE TA TF
hot seat	N M A E	Be Cl Co Ex Ge Lo Ps RE TA TF
identification of an animal, defend it	N M A E	Be Cl Co Ex Ge Lo Ps RE TA TF
identification of self as great personage	N M A E	Be Cl Co Ex Ge Lo Ps RE TA TF
inception inquiry	N M A E	Be Cl Co Ex Ge Lo Ps RE TA TF
informativity	N M A E	Be Cl Co Ex Ge Lo Ps RE TA TF
interpersonal process recall--IPR	N M A E	Be Cl Co Ex Ge Lo Ps RE TA TF
interpretation	N M A E	Be Cl Co Ex Ge Lo Ps RE TA TF
irrational behavior identification	N M A E	Be Cl Co Ex Ge Lo Ps RE TA TF
laissez faire groups	N M A E	Be Cl Co Ex Ge Lo Ps RE TA TF
life space	N M A E	Be Cl Co Ex Ge Lo Ps RE TA TF
live models	N M A E	Be Cl Co Ex Ge Lo Ps RE TA TF
magic mirror	N M A E	Be Cl Co Ex Ge Lo Ps RE TA TF
misinterpretation, deliberately	N M A E	Be Cl Co Ex Ge Lo Ps RE TA TF
modeling	N M A E	Be Cl Co Ex Ge Lo Ps RE TA TF
multiple counseling	N M A E	Be Cl Co Ex Ge Lo Ps RE TA TF
natural consequences	N M A E	Be Cl Co Ex Ge Lo Ps RE TA TF
negative practice	N M A E	Be Cl Co Ex Ge Lo Ps RE TA TF
negative reinforcement	N M A E	Be Cl Co Ex Ge Lo Ps RE TA TF
orientative	N M A E	Be Cl Co Ex Ge Lo Ps RE TA TF
paradoxical intention	N M A E	Be Cl Co Ex Ge Lo Ps RE TA TF
play therapy	N M A E	Be Cl Co Ex Ge Lo Ps RE TA TF
positive regard	N M A E	Be Cl Co Ex Ge Lo Ps RE TA TF
positive reinforcement	N M A E	Be Cl Co Ex Ge Lo Ps RE TA TF
predicting	N M A E	Be Cl Co Ex Ge Lo Ps RE TA TF
probing	N M A E	Be Cl Co Ex Ge Lo Ps RE TA TF
problem solving	N M A E	Be Cl Co Ex Ge Lo Ps RE TA TF
processing	N M A E	Be Cl Co Ex Ge Lo Ps RE TA TF
prognosing	N M A E	Be Cl Co Ex Ge Lo Ps RE TA TF
projection	N M A E	Be Cl Co Ex Ge Lo Ps RE TA TF
psychodrama	N M A E	Be Cl Co Ex Ge Lo Ps RE TA TF
punishment	N M A E	Be Cl Co Ex Ge Lo Ps RE TA TF
questioning	N M A E	Be Cl Co Ex Ge Lo Ps RE TA TF
rational	N M A E	Be Cl Co Ex Ge Lo Ps RE TA TF
reality testing	N M A E	Be Cl Co Ex Ge Lo Ps RE TA TF
reassurance	N M A E	Be Cl Co Ex Ge Lo Ps RE TA TF
recall	N M A E	Be Cl Co Ex Ge Lo Ps RE TA TF
reciprocity of affect	N M A E	Be Cl Co Ex Ge Lo Ps RE TA TF
reconscience	N M A E	Be Cl Co Ex Ge Lo Ps RE TA TF
re-education	N M A E	Be Cl Co Ex Ge Lo Ps RE TA TF
reflection	N M A E	Be Cl Co Ex Ge Lo Ps RE TA TF
regression	N M A E	Be Cl Co Ex Ge Lo Ps RE TA TF
reinforcement	N M A E	Be Cl Co Ex Ge Lo Ps RE TA TF
relaxation	N M A E	Be Cl Co Ex Ge Lo Ps RE TA TF
release therapy	N M A E	Be Cl Co Ex Ge Lo Ps RE TA TF
restatement of content	N M A E	Be Cl Co Ex Ge Lo Ps RE TA TF
reward	N M A E	Be Cl Co Ex Ge Lo Ps RE TA TF
rocking or cradling above head trust	N M A E	Be Cl Co Ex Ge Lo Ps RE TA TF

role playing	N M A E	Be Cl Co Ex Ge Lo Ps RE TA TF
role reversal	N M A E	Be Cl Co Ex Ge Lo Ps RE TA TF
self-modeling	N M A E	Be Cl Co Ex Ge Lo Ps RE TA TF
sensitivity exercises	N M A E	Be Cl Co Ex Ge Lo Ps RE TA TF
sensitivity training	N M A E	Be Cl Co Ex Ge Lo Ps RE TA TF
shaping	N M A E	Be Cl Co Ex Ge Lo Ps RE TA TF
silence	N M A E	Be Cl Co Ex Ge Lo Ps RE TA TF
simulation	N M A E	Be Cl Co Ex Ge Lo Ps RE TA TF
sociodrama	N M A E	Be Cl Co Ex Ge Lo Ps RE TA TF
sociometrics	N M A E	Be Cl Co Ex Ge Lo Ps RE TA TF
stimulation	N M A E	Be Cl Co Ex Ge Lo Ps RE TA TF
structuring	N M A E	Be Cl Co Ex Ge Lo Ps RE TA TF
SUD (Subjective Unit of Discomfort) . .	N M A E	Be Cl Co Ex Ge Lo Ps RE TA TF
summarization	N M A E	Be Cl Co Ex Ge Lo Ps RE TA TF
supporting	N M A E	Be Cl Co Ex Ge Lo Ps RE TA TF
systematic desensitization	N M A E	Be Cl Co Ex Ge Lo Ps RE TA TF
termination	N M A E	Be Cl Co Ex Ge Lo Ps RE TA TF
transference	N M A E	Be Cl Co Ex Ge Lo Ps RE TA TF
transparency	N M A E	Be Cl Co Ex Ge Lo Ps RE TA TF
trust walk	N M A E	Be Cl Co Ex Ge Lo Ps RE TA TF
urging	N M A E	Be Cl Co Ex Ge Lo Ps RE TA TF
value clarification	N M A E	Be Cl Co Ex Ge Lo Ps RE TA TF
value development	N M A E	Be Cl Co Ex Ge Lo Ps RE TA TF
verbal shock	N M A E	Be Cl Co Ex Ge Lo Ps RE TA TF
vicarious learning	N M A E	Be Cl Co Ex Ge Lo Ps RE TA TF
warmth	N M A E	Be Cl Co Ex Ge Lo Ps RE TA TF

ADD YOUR OWN

_____	. . . . . . N M A E	Be Cl Co Ex Ge Lo Ps RE TA TF
_____	. . . . . . N M A E	Be Cl Co Ex Ge Lo Ps RE TA TF
_____	. . . . . . N M A E	Be Cl Co Ex Ge Lo Ps RE TA TF

SUGGESTIONS FOR COUNSELING PRACTICUM

John P. McGowan*

I. <u>Initial Interview</u>

    A. Be yourself--Do not attempt to play a "role" or to change your natural style of verbal response to fit any particular counseling technique--rather, adopt a counseling technique to your own personality traits and familiar verbal delivery pattern.

       If you really want to help him, the client will know it, and this is one of the basic ideas or feelings that you need to communicate. If you are truly able to convey to the person with whom you are working the impression that you are sincerely interested in him and want to assist him, you can make many technical errors and still have a "good" relationship.

    B. Don't <u>tell</u> the client what counseling is, let him experience the relationship. Counseling represents a learning experience and he will learn from what you do as well as from what <u>you</u> say. In many cases when you attempt definite structuring, particularly later on in the interview, you are telling the client that things are not going the way you want them to and are actually instructing him on how he should act.

       "I can't hear what you are saying since your actions are speaking louder than your words."

    C. <u>Relax</u> and try to <u>go slow</u>, <u>go slow</u>, <u>go slow</u>!!! Give the client time to interact and to accept his share of the responsibility. Ninety-nine percent of beginning counselors move the interview too fast and as a result work far too hard themselves.

    D. Learn to <u>listen and observe</u>--try to forget about yourself and concentrate exclusively on the client--watch his behavior, it will tell you about his reactions to data that he is discussing as well as his reactions to what you are saying--learn to react to minimal behavioral cues.

    E. Learn to tolerate and feel at ease during reasonable periods of productive silence. Generally speaking, acceptance, reflective, and silences often result in further development of the problem at a more significant level and the development of understanding and insight on the part of the client. It also helps you to get a reasonable share of the responsibility placed over on the client and gives him time to think and integrate the things that are going on within the interview.

II. <u>Test Use and Interpretation</u>

    (For comments see Chapter VI.)

III. <u>General Suggestions</u>

    A. Do not try to "over-understand" the client particularly in fields related to psychological data. It is better to "know nothing" and to allow the client to develop his problem personally by verbalizing it to you. Remember that the insight you are working for should come on the part of the client, not the counselor--and, that no matter how well you understand the problem the thing you are working for is the client's understanding and acceptance of it.

    B. You are trained to <u>recognize and respond</u> to minimal cues; use and develop this skill. Feel free to play hunches and communicate them to clients, but in such a way that they can modify or change them in their reaction. If you are aware of the fact that something is happening within the counseling interview, even though you are picking it up

---

*Dr. John P. McGowan is Professor and Provost, University of Missouri. Printed by permission.

from the client's non-verbal behavior, feed this material back to the client in a non-threatening, permissive manner.

C. You are transmitting most of your own feelings and attitudes verbally and <u>non-verbally</u> in dealing with your clients. Get them out where the clients can deal with them and when it would help to clarify the relationship, go ahead and express them. However, do so objectively, without strong emotional feelings and identify them as your own.

Remember ". . . reality is, for the individual, the world as he perceives it"--avoid projecting your own attitudes, ideals, values, etc., onto the client, without identifying them as your own.

D. <u>Keep out</u> of the client's way when he is moving well by himself. Do not interrupt him <u>when he</u> is dealing with significant material or when he is involved in discussing highly emotional material. Most of the things that you would say are inappropriate anyway. Merely indicate that you are accepting and understanding the material.

E. Let the <u>needs</u> of the <u>client</u> determine your course of action. Try to adjust to the client <u>rather</u> than <u>having</u> the client adjust to you.

IV. <u>Know yourself</u>--know your <u>therapeutic ambition</u> and attempt to develop a relationship with <u>your clients</u> which is basically a healthy one. Set up as your final criteria for a counseling case "a personal feeling of a professional job well done."

INTERVIEW NOTES

During or following the counseling session, the practicum counselor will make notes of what occurred and possibly some comments regarding future plans. The extent and kind of notes made have been open to much discussion since records frequently are requested to be made available to the client or, if under 18 years of age, to the client's parents.

With the large number of clients seen and some often over an extended period of time, the interview notes are meaningful. The purposes and the recognition of who may some day see the notes will be guidelines to the contents.

In recording any information concerning the client, guidelines that have been developed to implement the 1974 Public Law 93-380 "Protection of the Rights and Privacy of Parents and Students" are to be followed. These guidelines may vary from one counseling setting to another; therefore, the student counselor is responsible for obtaining copies and following the local guidelines.

Function of Interview Notes

1. The record of the interview can reacquaint the counselor or psychotherapist with what had previously transpired in the contacts as well as with his or her original impressions of the therapeutic process.

2. Notes may serve as valuable aids in helping a different therapist (who may inherit the counselee) to understand the developmental nature of the previous contacts in addition to knowledge of the kind of treatment or methods attempted.

3. Of great importance is the value that interview notes have as a self-learning device. Notes can help us to check ourselves against the tendencies to be restricted, preoccupied or sterile in our contacts. The notes have decided utility in promoting a greater psychological understanding of behavior as displayed by a variety of individuals. Much of this can be accomplished by attempting to put into words our impressions and our feelings about the client that too often have been implicitly assumed.

4. Interview notes can be utilized in research and evaluation. They can aid in acquiring more ideas regarding the process itself and movement by the individual when certain techniques are used.

5. Notes serve to keep each one of us in contact with the work and methods of other professional workers in the same setting. The knowledge gained from what others are doing may serve to keep us more flexible and productive in our own counseling.

6. Notes may serve as a kind of protection for us since we can refer to these notes to clarify to ourselves and others what we actually did in the contacts.

Structure of Interview Notes

In view of the previous functions, notes might well reflect:

1. The status of the client (e.g., a recent divorcee thinking about the future, an inmate inquiring about welfare for spouse, a senior inquiring about a scholarship, a sophomore contemplating dropping out of school, etc.).

2. Presented problem as well as changes in perception of the problem area (e.g., is failing in marital relationship, can't get along with others, etc.).

3. Recapitulation of the counseling process (include client's cognitions, perceptions and attitudes--counselor's treatment of method--be as specific as possible).

4. Counselor's impression of the client (this may include progress and understanding exhibited by the client, suggestions for additional treatment of the case, probable course of counseling).

5. Plans for future counseling (a short statement as to what happens next in this case).

Forms of Recording Interview Notes

Two types of forms are provided in this Manual for recording interview notes. Form #8, Initial Intake Form, is used at the time of the initial intake and interview. The front side of the form is to be completed by the client. The information can be supplied by the client prior to seeing the counselor. The back side of the form is to be completed by the counselor. The information can be summarized under headings: Statement of Problem, Brief Dialogue of Interview, Treatment Suggestions, Prognosis, Recommendations, and Next Appointment.

Form #9, Interview Notes Form, provides a means of summarizing points generally significant from each counseling session. The headings include Statement of Problem, Brief Dialogue of Interview, Evaluation of Interview, Plans for Further Counseling, and Other Comments by Counselor. The form may be submitted with the audio or video tape to the practicum supervisor or the form may be placed in the client's folder. Space is provided for the supervisor's comments.

INITIAL INTAKE FORM

DIRECTIONS: (a) The front of this form is to be completed by the counselee before he or she is seen by the practicum counselor.
(b) The back of this form is to be completed by the practicum counselor after the initial interview is concluded.

Practicum Counselor_____ Interview Date_____

Client Name_____

Client Birth Date_____ Age_____ Sex M___ F___

Client Address_____ Telephone Number_____

Marital Status: Married_____ Single_____ Divorced_____ Widowed_____

Employment_____

Circle Last Educational
Grade Level Completed   1 2 3 4 5 6 7 8 9 10 11 12   College 1 2 3 4

If You Have Had Trade School or Special Program, Please Specify_____

_____

Referral Source: Self_____ Other (Please Specify)_____

Current Treatment (Medical and/or Psychological) (Kind and By Whom?)_____

_____

Are You Currently on Medication? Yes_____ No_____

Previous Treatment: Yes_____ No_____

If Yes, Please Give Location_____ Date_____

Are You in Good Health? Yes____ No____ If Not, Please Describe Your Condition_____

_____

Family Data	Names	Age	Living/Deceased
Parents	_____	___	_____
	_____	___	_____
Brothers & Sisters	_____	___	_____
	_____	___	_____
Children	_____	___	_____
	_____	___	_____
	_____	___	_____

Form #8 p.1 of 2 pp.

This side is to be completed by the counselor.

Statement of Problem

Brief Dialogue of Interview

Treatment Suggestions

Prognosis

Recommendations
    Referral to Another Source, Specify_____
    To Be Seen By ___Male or ___Female Counselor
    Type of Counseling
            Individual   _____
            Group   _____
            Multiple   _____
            Play Therapy   _____
            Other, Specify _____
    Testing, Specify_____
                    _____

Next Appointment Was Made for Date_____ Time_____
            Counselor Signature_____
                                                            Form #8 p.2 of 2 pp.

INITIAL INTAKE FORM

DIRECTIONS: (a) The front of this form is to be completed by the counselee before he or she is seen by the practicum counselor.
(b) The back of this form is to be completed by the practicum counselor after the initial interview is concluded.

Practicum Counselor_____ Interview Date_____

Client Name_____

Client Birth Date_____ Age_____ Sex M___ F___

Client Address_____ Telephone Number_____

Marital Status: Married_____ Single_____ Divorced_____ Widowed_____

Employment_____

Circle Last Educational
Grade Level Completed   1 2 3 4 5 6 7 8 9 10 11 12   College 1 2 3 4

If You Have Had Trade School or Special Program, Please Specify_____
_____

Referral Source: Self_____ Other (Please Specify)_____

Current Treatment (Medical and/or Psychological) (Kind and By Whom?)_____
_____

Are You Currently on Medication? Yes_____ No_____

Previous Treatment: Yes_____ No_____

If Yes, Please Give Location_____ Date_____

Are You in Good Health? Yes____ No____ If Not, Please Describe Your Condition_____
_____

Family Data	Names	Age	Living/Deceased
Parents	_____	____	_____
	_____	____	_____
Brothers & Sisters	_____	____	_____
	_____	____	_____
Children	_____	____	_____
	_____	____	_____
	_____	____	_____

Form #8 p.1 of 2 pp.

This side is to be completed by the counselor.

Statement of Problem

Brief Dialogue of Interview

Treatment Suggestions

Prognosis

Recommendations

    Referral to Another Source, Specify _____
    To Be Seen By   ___Male or   ___Female Counselor
    Type of Counseling
        Individual _____
        Group _____
        Multiple _____
        Play Therapy _____
        Other, Specify _____
    Testing, Specify _____

Next Appointment Was Made for Date _____ Time _____

    Counselor Signature _____

Form #8 p.2 of 2 pp.

INITIAL INTAKE FORM

DIRECTIONS: (a) The front of this form is to be completed by the counselee before he or she is seen by the practicum counselor.
(b) The back of this form is to be completed by the practicum counselor after the initial interview is concluded.

Practicum Counselor _____ Interview Date _____

Client Name _____

Client Birth Date _____ Age _____ Sex M ___ F ___

Client Address _____ Telephone Number _____

Marital Status: Married _____ Single _____ Divorced _____ Widowed _____

Employment _____

Circle Last Educational
Grade Level Completed   1 2 3 4 5 6 7 8 9 10 11 12   College 1 2 3 4

If You Have Had Trade School or Special Program, Please Specify _____

Referral Source: Self _____ Other (Please Specify) _____

Current Treatment (Medical and/or Psychological) (Kind and By Whom?) _____

Are You Currently on Medication? Yes _____ No _____

Previous Treatment: Yes _____ No _____

If Yes, Please Give Location _____ Date _____

Are You in Good Health? Yes _____ No _____ If Not, Please Describe Your Condition _____

Family Data	Names	Age	Living/Deceased
Parents	_____	___	_____
	_____	___	_____
Brothers & Sisters	_____	___	_____
	_____	___	_____
Children	_____	___	_____
	_____	___	_____
	_____	___	_____

Form #8 p.1 of 2 pp.

This side is to be completed by the counselor.

Statement of Problem

Brief Dialogue of Interview

Treatment Suggestions

Prognosis

Recommendations
        Referral to Another Source, Specify_____
        To Be Seen By ___Male or ___Female Counselor
        Type of Counseling
                Individual   _____
                Group   _____
                Multiple   _____
                Play Therapy   _____
                Other, Specify _____
        Testing, Specify_____
        _____

Next Appointment Was Made for Date_____ Time_____
            Counselor Signature_____

Form #8 p.2 of 2 pp.

INITIAL INTAKE FORM

DIRECTIONS: (a) The front of this form is to be completed by the counselee before he or she is seen by the practicum counselor.
(b) The back of this form is to be completed by the practicum counselor after the initial interview is concluded.

Practicum Counselor_____   Interview Date_____

Client Name_____

Client Birth Date_____ Age_____   Sex M___ F___
                                                    Telephone
Client Address_____   Number_____

Marital Status: Married_____ Single_____ Divorced_____ Widowed_____

Employment_____

Circle Last Educational
Grade Level Completed   1 2 3 4 5 6 7 8 9 10 11 12   College 1 2 3 4

If You Have Had Trade School or Special Program, Please Specify_____
_____

Referral Source: Self_____ Other (Please Specify)_____

Current Treatment (Medical and/or Psychological) (Kind and By Whom?)_____
_____

Are You Currently on Medication? Yes_____ No_____

Previous Treatment: Yes_____ No_____

If Yes, Please Give Location_____ Date_____

Are You in Good Health? Yes____ No____ If Not, Please Describe Your Condition_____
_____

Family Data	Names	Age	Living/Deceased
Parents	_____	___	___
	_____	___	___
Brothers & Sisters	_____	___	___
	_____	___	___
Children	_____	___	___
	_____	___	___
	_____	___	___

Form #8 p.1 of 2 pp.

This side is to be completed by the counselor.

Statement of Problem

Brief Dialogue of Interview

Treatment Suggestions

Prognosis

Recommendations

    Referral to Another Source, Specify _____
    To Be Seen By ___ Male or ___ Female Counselor _____
    Type of Counseling
        Individual _____
        Group _____
        Multiple _____
        Play Therapy _____
        Other, Specify_____
    Testing, Specify_____
    _____

Next Appointment Was Made for Date_____ Time_____

        Counselor Signature_____

Form #8 p.2 of 2 pp.

INITIAL INTAKE FORM

DIRECTIONS: (a) The front of this form is to be completed by the counselee before he or she is seen by the practicum counselor.
(b) The back of this form is to be completed by the practicum counselor after the initial interview is concluded.

Practicum Counselor_____   Interview Date_____

Client Name_____

Client Birth Date_____ Age_____   Sex M ___ F ___

Client Address_____   Telephone Number_____

Marital Status: Married_____ Single_____ Divorced_____ Widowed_____

Employment_____

Circle Last Educational
Grade Level Completed   1 2 3 4 5 6 7 8 9 10 11 12   College 1 2 3 4

If You Have Had Trade School or Special Program, Please Specify_____

_____

Referral Source: Self_____ Other (Please Specify)_____

Current Treatment (Medical and/or Psychological) (Kind and By Whom?)_____

_____

Are You Currently on Medication? Yes_____ No_____

Previous Treatment: Yes_____ No_____

If Yes, Please Give Location_____ Date_____

Are You in Good Health? Yes____ No____ If Not, Please Describe Your Condition_____

_____

Family Data	Names	Age	Living/Deceased
Parents	_____	___	_____
	_____	___	_____
Brothers & Sisters	_____	___	_____
	_____	___	_____
Children	_____	___	_____
	_____	___	_____
	_____	___	_____

Form #8 p.1 of 2 pp.

This side is to be completed by the counselor.

Statement of Problem

Brief Dialogue of Interview

Treatment Suggestions

Prognosis

Recommendations

    Referral to Another Source, Specify_____
    To Be Seen By   ___Male or   ___Female Counselor
    Type of Counseling
        Individual   _____
        Group   _____
        Multiple   _____
        Play Therapy   _____
        Other, Specify_____
    Testing, Specify_____
    _____

Next Appointment Was Made for Date_____   Time_____

    Counselor Signature_____

Form #8 p.2 of 2 pp.

INITIAL INTAKE FORM

DIRECTIONS: (a) The front of this form is to be completed by the counselee before he or she is seen by the practicum counselor.
(b) The back of this form is to be completed by the practicum counselor after the initial interview is concluded.

Practicum Counselor_____ Interview Date_____

Client Name_____

Client Birth Date_____ Age_____ Sex M___ F___

Client Address_____ Telephone Number_____

Marital Status: Married_____ Single_____ Divorced_____ Widowed_____

Employment_____

Circle Last Educational
Grade Level Completed   1 2 3 4 5 6 7 8 9 10 11 12   College 1 2 3 4

If You Have Had Trade School or Special Program, Please Specify_____

Referral Source: Self_____ Other (Please Specify)_____

Current Treatment (Medical and/or Psychological) (Kind and By Whom?)_____

Are You Currently on Medication? Yes_____ No_____

Previous Treatment: Yes_____ No_____

If Yes, Please Give Location_____ Date_____

Are You in Good Health? Yes_____ No_____ If Not, Please Describe Your Condition_____

Family Data	Names	Age	Living/Deceased
Parents	_____	___	_____
	_____	___	_____
Brothers & Sisters	_____	___	_____
	_____	___	_____
Children	_____	___	_____
	_____	___	_____
	_____	___	_____

Form #8 p.1 of 2 pp.

This side is to be completed by the counselor.

Statement of Problem

Brief Dialogue of Interview

Treatment Suggestions

Prognosis

Recommendations

    Referral to Another Source, Specify_____
    To Be Seen By ___Male or ___Female Counselor
    Type of Counseling
        Individual _____
        Group _____
        Multiple _____
        Play Therapy _____
        Other, Specify_____
    Testing, Specify_____

_____

Next Appointment Was Made for Date_____ Time_____

    Counselor Signature_____

Form #8 p.2 of 2 pp.

INITIAL INTAKE FORM

DIRECTIONS: (a) The front of this form is to be completed by the counselee before he or she is seen by the practicum counselor.
(b) The back of this form is to be completed by the practicum counselor after the initial interview is concluded.

Practicum Counselor _____ Interview Date _____

Client Name _____

Client Birth Date _____ Age _____ Sex M ___ F ___

Client Address _____ Telephone Number _____

Marital Status: Married _____ Single _____ Divorced _____ Widowed _____

Employment _____

Circle Last Educational
Grade Level Completed   1 2 3 4 5 6 7 8 9 10 11 12   College 1 2 3 4

If You Have Had Trade School or Special Program, Please Specify _____

Referral Source: Self _____ Other (Please Specify) _____

Current Treatment (Medical and/or Psychological) (Kind and By Whom?) _____

Are You Currently on Medication? Yes _____ No _____

Previous Treatment: Yes _____ No _____

If Yes, Please Give Location _____ Date _____

Are You in Good Health? Yes ____ No ____ If Not, Please Describe Your Condition _____

Family Data	Names	Age	Living/Deceased
Parents	_____	____	_____
	_____	____	_____
Brothers & Sisters	_____	____	_____
	_____	____	_____
Children	_____	____	_____
	_____	____	_____
	_____	____	_____

Form #8 p.1 of 2 pp.

This side is to be completed by the counselor.

Statement of Problem

Brief Dialogue of Interview

Treatment Suggestions

Prognosis

Recommendations

    Referral to Another Source, Specify_____
    To Be Seen By   ___Male or   ___Female Counselor
    Type of Counseling
        Individual   _____
        Group   _____
        Multiple   _____
        Play Therapy   _____
        Other, Specify_____
    Testing, Specify_____
    _____

Next Appointment Was Made for Date_____ Time_____

        Counselor Signature_____

Form #8 p.2 of 2 pp.

INITIAL INTAKE FORM

DIRECTIONS: (a) The front of this form is to be completed by the counselee before he or she is seen by the practicum counselor.
(b) The back of this form is to be completed by the practicum counselor after the initial interview is concluded.

Practicum Counselor_____ Interview Date_____

Client Name_____

Client Birth Date_____ Age_____ Sex M___ F___

Client Address_____ Telephone Number_____

Marital Status: Married_____ Single_____ Divorced_____ Widowed_____

Employment_____

Circle Last Educational
Grade Level Completed   1 2 3 4 5 6 7 8 9 10 11 12   College 1 2 3 4

If You Have Had Trade School or Special Program, Please Specify_____

_____

Referral Source: Self_____ Other (Please Specify)_____

Current Treatment (Medical and/or Psychological) (Kind and By Whom?)_____

_____

Are You Currently on Medication? Yes_____ No_____

Previous Treatment: Yes_____ No_____

If Yes, Please Give Location_____ Date_____

Are You in Good Health? Yes_____ No_____ If Not, Please Describe Your Condition_____

_____

Family Data	Names	Age	Living/Deceased
Parents	_____	___	_____
	_____	___	_____
Brothers & Sisters	_____	___	_____
	_____	___	_____
Children	_____	___	_____
	_____	___	_____
	_____	___	_____

Form #8 p.1 of 2 pp.

This side is to be completed by the counselor.

Statement of Problem

Brief Dialogue of Interview

Treatment Suggestions

Prognosis

Recommendations

    Referral to Another Source, Specify_____
    To Be Seen By   ___Male or   ___Female Counselor
    Type of Counseling
        Individual   _____
        Group   _____
        Multiple   _____
        Play Therapy   _____
        Other, Specify_____
    Testing, Specify_____

Next Appointment Was Made for Date_____ Time_____

        Counselor Signature_____

Form #8 p.2 of 2 pp.

INITIAL INTAKE FORM

DIRECTIONS: (a) The front of this form is to be completed by the counselee before he or she is seen by the practicum counselor.
(b) The back of this form is to be completed by the practicum counselor after the initial interview is concluded.

Practicum Counselor_____ Interview Date_____

Client Name_____

Client Birth Date_____ Age_____ Sex M___ F___

Client Address_____ Telephone Number_____

Marital Status: Married_____ Single_____ Divorced_____ Widowed_____

Employment_____

Circle Last Educational
Grade Level Completed   1 2 3 4 5 6 7 8 9 10 11 12   College 1 2 3 4

If You Have Had Trade School or Special Program, Please Specify_____

_____

Referral Source: Self_____ Other (Please Specify)_____

Current Treatment (Medical and/or Psychological) (Kind and By Whom?)_____

_____

Are You Currently on Medication? Yes_____ No_____

Previous Treatment: Yes_____ No_____

If Yes, Please Give Location_____ Date_____

Are You in Good Health? Yes____ No____ If Not, Please Describe Your Condition_____

_____

Family Data	Names	Age	Living/Deceased
Parents	_____	___	_____
	_____	___	_____
Brothers & Sisters	_____	___	_____
	_____	___	_____
Children	_____	___	_____
	_____	___	_____
	_____	___	_____

Form #8 p.1 of 2 pp.

This side is to be completed by the counselor.

Statement of Problem

Brief Dialogue of Interview

Treatment Suggestions

Prognosis

Recommendations
    Referral to Another Source, Specify_____
    To Be Seen By ___Male or ___Female Counselor
    Type of Counseling
        Individual _____
        Group _____
        Multiple _____
        Play Therapy _____
        Other, Specify_____
    Testing, Specify_____

Next Appointment Was Made for Date_____ Time_____
    Counselor Signature_____

Form #8 p.2 of 2 pp.

INITIAL INTAKE FORM

DIRECTIONS: (a) The front of this form is to be completed by the counselee before he or she is seen by the practicum counselor.
(b) The back of this form is to be completed by the practicum counselor after the initial interview is concluded.

Practicum Counselor_____ Interview Date_____

Client Name_____

Client Birth Date_____ Age_____ Sex M ___ F ___

Client Address_____ Telephone Number_____

Marital Status: Married_____ Single_____ Divorced_____ Widowed_____

Employment_____

Circle Last Educational
Grade Level Completed   1 2 3 4 5 6 7 8 9 10 11 12   College 1 2 3 4

If You Have Had Trade School or Special Program, Please Specify_____

Referral Source: Self_____ Other (Please Specify)_____

Current Treatment (Medical and/or Psychological) (Kind and By Whom?)_____

Are You Currently on Medication? Yes_____ No_____

Previous Treatment: Yes_____ No_____

If Yes, Please Give Location_____ Date_____

Are You in Good Health? Yes_____ No_____ If Not, Please Describe Your Condition_____

Family Data	Names	Age	Living/Deceased
Parents	_____	___	_____
	_____	___	_____
Brothers & Sisters	_____	___	_____
	_____	___	_____
Children	_____	___	_____
	_____	___	_____
	_____	___	_____

Form #8 p.1 of 2 pp.

This side is to be completed by the counselor.

Statement of Problem

Brief Dialogue of Interview

Treatment Suggestions

Prognosis

Recommendations

    Referral to Another Source, Specify_____
    To Be Seen By   ___Male or   ___Female Counselor
    Type of Counseling
        Individual   _____
        Group   _____
        Multiple   _____
        Play Therapy   _____
        Other, Specify_____
    Testing, Specify_____

Next Appointment Was Made for Date_____ Time_____

    Counselor Signature_____

Form #8 p.2 of 2 pp.

INTERVIEW NOTES FORM

DIRECTIONS: (a) One copy of this form is to be completed by the practicum counselor following each counseling session.
(b) When completed this might be submitted to the practicum supervisor.

Client Name _____

Practicum Counselor Name _____

Client Age _____ Client Sex _____ Date of Interview _____ Agency _____

Interview Number _____ with This Client.

Total Time (Approximately) Spent with Client to Date _____ Hours

Was Tape Recording Made? _____ Submitted for Supervisor's Review? _____

Statement of Problem

Brief Dialogue of Interview

Evaluation of Interview

Plans for Further Counseling

Form #9 p.1 of 2 pp.

Other Comments by Practicum Counselor

Supervisor's Comments

Practicum Supervisor Signature_____

Date_____

Form #9 p.2 of 2 pp.

INTERVIEW NOTES FORM

DIRECTIONS: (a) One copy of this form is to be completed by the practicum counselor following each counseling session.
(b) When completed this might be submitted to the practicum supervisor.

Client Name _____

Practicum Counselor Name _____

Client Age _____ Client Sex _____ Date of Interview _____ Agency _____

Interview Number _____ with This Client.

Total Time (Approximately) Spent with Client to Date _____ Hours

Was Tape Recording Made? _____ Submitted for Supervisor's Review? _____

Statement of Problem

Brief Dialogue of Interview

Evaluation of Interview

Plans for Further Counseling

Form #9 p.1 of 2 pp.

Other Comments by Practicum Counselor

Supervisor's Comments

Practicum Supervisor Signature_____

Date_____

Form #9 p.2 of 2 pp.

INTERVIEW NOTES FORM

DIRECTIONS: (a) One copy of this form is to be completed by the practicum counselor following each counseling session.
(b) When completed this might be submitted to the practicum supervisor.

Client Name _____

Practicum Counselor Name _____

Client Age _____   Client Sex _____   Date of Interview _____   Agency _____

Interview Number _____ with This Client.

Total Time (Approximately) Spent with Client to Date _____ Hours

Was Tape Recording Made? _____ Submitted for Supervisor's Review? _____

Statement of Problem

Brief Dialogue of Interview

Evaluation of Interview

Plans for Further Counseling

Form #9 p.1 of 2 pp.

Other Comments by Practicum Counselor

Supervisor's Comments

Practicum Supervisor Signature_____

Date_____

Form #9 p.2 of 2 pp.

INTERVIEW NOTES FORM

DIRECTIONS: (a) One copy of this form is to be completed by the practicum counselor following each counseling session.
(b) When completed this might be submitted to the practicum supervisor.

Client Name _____

Practicum Counselor Name _____

Client Age _____ Client Sex _____ Date of Interview _____ Agency _____

Interview Number ____ with This Client.

Total Time (Approximately) Spent with Client to Date _____ Hours

Was Tape Recording Made? _____ Submitted for Supervisor's Review? _____

Statement of Problem

Brief Dialogue of Interview

Evaluation of Interview

Plans for Further Counseling

Form #9 p.1 of 2 pp.

Other Comments by Practicum Counselor

Supervisor's Comments

Practicum Supervisor Signature_____

Date_____

Form #9 p.2 of 2 pp.

INTERVIEW NOTES FORM

DIRECTIONS: (a) One copy of this form is to be completed by the practicum counselor following each counseling session.
(b) When completed this might be submitted to the practicum supervisor.

Client Name _____

Practicum Counselor Name _____

Client Age _____ Client Sex _____ Date of Interview _____ Agency _____

Interview Number ____ with This Client.

Total Time (Approximately) Spent with Client to Date _____ Hours

Was Tape Recording Made? _____ Submitted for Supervisor's Review? _____

Statement of Problem

Brief Dialogue of Interview

Evaluation of Interview

Plans for Further Counseling

Form #9 p.1 of 2 pp.

Other Comments by Practicum Counselor

Supervisor's Comments

Practicum Supervisor Signature_____

Date_____

Form #9 p.2 of 2 pp.

INTERVIEW NOTES FORM

DIRECTIONS: (a) One copy of this form is to be completed by the practicum counselor following each counseling session.
(b) When completed this might be submitted to the practicum supervisor.

Client Name_____

Practicum Counselor Name_____

Client Age _____   Client Sex _____   Date of Interview _____   Agency_____

Interview Number _____ with This Client.

Total Time (Approximately) Spent with Client to Date _____ Hours

Was Tape Recording Made? _____ Submitted for Supervisor's Review? _____

Statement of Problem

Brief Dialogue of Interview

Evaluation of Interview

Plans for Further Counseling

Form #9 p.1 of 2 pp.

Other Comments by Practicum Counselor

Supervisor's Comments

Practicum Supervisor Signature_____

Date_____

Form #9 p.2 of 2 pp.

INTERVIEW NOTES FORM

DIRECTIONS: (a) One copy of this form is to be completed by the practicum counselor following each counseling session.
(b) When completed this might be submitted to the practicum supervisor.

Client Name_____

Practicum Counselor Name_____

Client Age _____   Client Sex _____   Date of Interview _____   Agency_____

Interview Number _____ with This Client.

Total Time (Approximately) Spent with Client to Date _____ Hours

Was Tape Recording Made? _____ Submitted for Supervisor's Review? _____

Statement of Problem

Brief Dialogue of Interview

Evaluation of Interview

Plans for Further Counseling

Form #9 p.1 of 2 pp.

Other Comments by Practicum Counselor

Supervisor's Comments

Practicum Supervisor Signature_____

Date_____

Form #9 p.2 of 2 pp.

INTERVIEW NOTES FORM

DIRECTIONS: (a) One copy of this form is to be completed by the practicum counselor following each counseling session.
(b) When completed this might be submitted to the practicum supervisor.

Client Name _____

Practicum Counselor Name _____

Client Age _____   Client Sex _____   Date of Interview _____   Agency _____

Interview Number ____ with This Client.

Total Time (Approximately) Spent with Client to Date _____ Hours

Was Tape Recording Made? _____ Submitted for Supervisor's Review? _____

Statement of Problem

Brief Dialogue of Interview

Evaluation of Interview

Plans for Further Counseling

Form #9 p.1 of 2 pp.

Other Comments by Practicum Counselor

Supervisor's Comments

Practicum Supervisor Signature_____

Date_____

Form #9 p.2 of 2 pp.

INTERVIEW NOTES FORM

DIRECTIONS: (a) One copy of this form is to be completed by the practicum counselor following each counseling session.
(b) When completed this might be submitted to the practicum supervisor.

Client Name _____

Practicum Counselor Name _____

Client Age _____   Client Sex _____   Date of Interview _____   Agency _____

Interview Number _____ with This Client.

Total Time (Approximately) Spent with Client to Date _____ Hours

Was Tape Recording Made? _____ Submitted for Supervisor's Review? _____

Statement of Problem

Brief Dialogue of Interview

Evaluation of Interview

Plans for Further Counseling

Form #9 p.1 of 2 pp.

Other Comments by Practicum Counselor

Supervisor's Comments

Practicum Supervisor Signature_____

Date_____

Form #9 p.2 of 2 pp.

INTERVIEW NOTES FORM

DIRECTIONS: (a) One copy of this form is to be completed by the practicum counselor following each counseling session.
(b) When completed this might be submitted to the practicum supervisor.

Client Name _____

Practicum Counselor Name _____

Client Age _____ Client Sex _____ Date of Interview _____ Agency _____

Interview Number _____ with This Client.

Total Time (Approximately) Spent with Client to Date _____ Hours

Was Tape Recording Made? _____ Submitted for Supervisor's Review? _____

Statement of Problem

Brief Dialogue of Interview

Evaluation of Interview

Plans for Further Counseling

Form #9 p.1 of 2 pp.

Other Comments by Practicum Counselor

Supervisor's Comments

Practicum Supervisor Signature_____

Date_____

Form #9 p.2 of 2 pp.

INTERVIEW NOTES FORM

DIRECTIONS: (a) One copy of this form is to be completed by the practicum counselor following each counseling session.
(b) When completed this might be submitted to the practicum supervisor.

Client Name _____

Practicum Counselor Name _____

Client Age _____   Client Sex _____   Date of Interview _____   Agency _____

Interview Number _____ with This Client.

Total Time (Approximately) Spent with Client to Date _____ Hours

Was Tape Recording Made? _____ Submitted for Supervisor's Review? _____

Statement of Problem

Brief Dialogue of Interview

Evaluation of Interview

Plans for Further Counseling

Form #9 p.1 of 2 pp.

Other Comments by Practicum Counselor

Supervisor's Comments

Practicum Supervisor Signature_____

Date_____

Form #9 p.2 of 2 pp.

INTERVIEW NOTES FORM

DIRECTIONS: (a) One copy of this form is to be completed by the practicum counselor following each counseling session.
(b) When completed this might be submitted to the practicum supervisor.

Client Name _____

Practicum Counselor Name _____

Client Age _____ Client Sex _____ Date of Interview _____ Agency _____

Interview Number _____ with This Client.

Total Time (Approximately) Spent with Client to Date _____ Hours

Was Tape Recording Made? _____ Submitted for Supervisor's Review? _____

Statement of Problem

Brief Dialogue of Interview

Evaluation of Interview

Plans for Further Counseling

Form #9 p.1 of 2 pp.

Other Comments by Practicum Counselor

Supervisor's Comments

Practicum Supervisor Signature_____

Date_____

Form #9 p.2 of 2 pp.

INTERVIEW NOTES FORM

DIRECTIONS: (a) One copy of this form is to be completed by the practicum counselor following each counseling session.
(b) When completed this might be submitted to the practicum supervisor.

Client Name _____

Practicum Counselor Name _____

Client Age _____ Client Sex _____ Date of Interview _____ Agency _____

Interview Number _____ with This Client.

Total Time (Approximately) Spent with Client to Date _____ Hours

Was Tape Recording Made? _____ Submitted for Supervisor's Review? _____

Statement of Problem

Brief Dialogue of Interview

Evaluation of Interview

Plans for Further Counseling

Form #9 p.1 of 2 pp.

Other Comments by Practicum Counselor

Supervisor's Comments

Practicum Supervisor Signature_____

Date_____

Form #9 p.2 of 2 pp.

INTERVIEW NOTES FORM

DIRECTIONS: (a) One copy of this form is to be completed by the practicum counselor following each counseling session.
(b) When completed this might be submitted to the practicum supervisor.

Client Name _____

Practicum Counselor Name _____

Client Age _____ Client Sex _____ Date of Interview _____ Agency _____

Interview Number ____ with This Client.

Total Time (Approximately) Spent with Client to Date _____ Hours

Was Tape Recording Made? _____ Submitted for Supervisor's Review? _____

Statement of Problem

Brief Dialogue of Interview

Evaluation of Interview

Plans for Further Counseling

Form #9 p.1 of 2 pp.

Other Comments by Practicum Counselor

Supervisor's Comments

Practicum Supervisor Signature_____

Date_____

Form #9 p.2 of 2 pp.

INTERVIEW NOTES FORM

DIRECTIONS: (a) One copy of this form is to be completed by the practicum counselor following each counseling session.
(b) When completed this might be submitted to the practicum supervisor.

Client Name _____

Practicum Counselor Name _____

Client Age _____ Client Sex _____ Date of Interview _____ Agency _____

Interview Number _____ with This Client.

Total Time (Approximately) Spent with Client to Date _____ Hours

Was Tape Recording Made? _____ Submitted for Supervisor's Review? _____

Statement of Problem

Brief Dialogue of Interview

Evaluation of Interview

Plans for Further Counseling

Form #9 p.1 of 2 pp.

Other Comments by Practicum Counselor

Supervisor's Comments

Practicum Supervisor Signature_____

Date_____

Form #9 p.2 of 2 pp.

INTERVIEW NOTES FORM

DIRECTIONS: (a) One copy of this form is to be completed by the practicum counselor following each counseling session.
(b) When completed this might be submitted to the practicum supervisor.

Client Name _____

Practicum Counselor Name _____

Client Age _____   Client Sex _____   Date of Interview _____   Agency _____

Interview Number _____ with This Client.

Total Time (Approximately) Spent with Client to Date _____ Hours

Was Tape Recording Made? _____ Submitted for Supervisor's Review? _____

Statement of Problem

Brief Dialogue of Interview

Evaluation of Interview

Plans for Further Counseling

Form #9 p.1 of 2 pp.

Other Comments by Practicum Counselor

Supervisor's Comments

Practicum Supervisor Signature_____

Date_____

Form #9 p.2 of 2 pp.

INTERVIEW NOTES FORM

DIRECTIONS: (a) One copy of this form is to be completed by the practicum counselor following each counseling session.
(b) When completed this might be submitted to the practicum supervisor.

Client Name _____

Practicum Counselor Name _____

Client Age _____ Client Sex _____ Date of Interview _____ Agency _____

Interview Number ____ with This Client.

Total Time (Approximately) Spent with Client to Date _____ Hours

Was Tape Recording Made? _____ Submitted for Supervisor's Review? _____

Statement of Problem

Brief Dialogue of Interview

Evaluation of Interview

Plans for Further Counseling

Form #9 p.1 of 2 pp.

Other Comments by Practicum Counselor

Supervisor's Comments

Practicum Supervisor Signature_____

Date_____

Form #9 p.2 of 2 pp.

INTERVIEW NOTES FORM

DIRECTIONS: (a) One copy of this form is to be completed by the practicum counselor following each counseling session.
(b) When completed this might be submitted to the practicum supervisor.

Client Name _____

Practicum Counselor Name _____

Client Age _____ Client Sex _____ Date of Interview _____ Agency _____

Interview Number _____ with This Client.

Total Time (Approximately) Spent with Client to Date _____ Hours

Was Tape Recording Made? _____ Submitted for Supervisor's Review? _____

Statement of Problem

Brief Dialogue of Interview

Evaluation of Interview

Plans for Further Counseling

Form #9 p.1 of 2 pp.

Other Comments by Practicum Counselor

Supervisor's Comments

Practicum Supervisor Signature_____

Date_____

Form #9 p.2 of 2 pp.

INTERVIEW NOTES FORM

DIRECTIONS: (a) One copy of this form is to be completed by the practicum counselor following each counseling session.
(b) When completed this might be submitted to the practicum supervisor.

Client Name _____

Practicum Counselor Name _____

Client Age _____   Client Sex _____   Date of Interview _____   Agency _____

Interview Number ____ with This Client.

Total Time (Approximately) Spent with Client to Date _____ Hours

Was Tape Recording Made? _____ Submitted for Supervisor's Review? _____

Statement of Problem

Brief Dialogue of Interview

Evaluation of Interview

Plans for Further Counseling

Form #9 p.1 of 2 pp.

Other Comments by Practicum Counselor

Supervisor's Comments

Practicum Supervisor Signature_____

Date_____

Form #9 p.2 of 2 pp.

INTERVIEW NOTES FORM

DIRECTIONS: (a) One copy of this form is to be completed by the practicum counselor following each counseling session.
(b) When completed this might be submitted to the practicum supervisor.

Client Name _____

Practicum Counselor Name _____

Client Age _____ Client Sex _____ Date of Interview _____ Agency _____

Interview Number _____ with This Client.

Total Time (Approximately) Spent with Client to Date _____ Hours

Was Tape Recording Made? _____ Submitted for Supervisor's Review? _____

Statement of Problem

Brief Dialogue of Interview

Evaluation of Interview

Plans for Further Counseling

Form #9 p.1 of 2 pp.

Other Comments by Practicum Counselor

Supervisor's Comments

Practicum Supervisor Signature_____

Date_____

Form #9 p.2 of 2 pp.

INTERVIEW NOTES FORM

DIRECTIONS: (a) One copy of this form is to be completed by the practicum counselor following each counseling session.
(b) When completed this might be submitted to the practicum supervisor.

Client Name _____

Practicum Counselor Name _____

Client Age _____   Client Sex _____   Date of Interview _____   Agency _____

Interview Number _____ with This Client.

Total Time (Approximately) Spent with Client to Date _____ Hours

Was Tape Recording Made? _____ Submitted for Supervisor's Review? _____

Statement of Problem

Brief Dialogue of Interview

Evaluation of Interview

Plans for Further Counseling

Form #9 p.1 of 2 pp.

Other Comments by Practicum Counselor

Supervisor's Comments

Practicum Supervisor Signature_____

Date_____

INTERVIEW NOTES FORM

DIRECTIONS: (a) One copy of this form is to be completed by the practicum counselor following each counseling session.
(b) When completed this might be submitted to the practicum supervisor.

Client Name _____

Practicum Counselor Name _____

Client Age _____   Client Sex _____   Date of Interview _____   Agency _____

Interview Number _____ with This Client.

Total Time (Approximately) Spent with Client to Date _____ Hours

Was Tape Recording Made? _____   Submitted for Supervisor's Review? _____

Statement of Problem

Brief Dialogue of Interview

Evaluation of Interview

Plans for Further Counseling

Form #9 p.1 of 2 pp.

Other Comments by Practicum Counselor

Supervisor's Comments

Practicum Supervisor Signature_____

Date_____

INTERVIEW NOTES FORM

DIRECTIONS: (a) One copy of this form is to be completed by the practicum counselor following each counseling session.
(b) When completed this might be submitted to the practicum supervisor.

Client Name _____

Practicum Counselor Name _____

Client Age _____   Client Sex _____   Date of Interview _____   Agency _____

Interview Number _____ with This Client.

Total Time (Approximately) Spent with Client to Date _____ Hours

Was Tape Recording Made? _____ Submitted for Supervisor's Review? _____

Statement of Problem

Brief Dialogue of Interview

Evaluation of Interview

Plans for Further Counseling

Form #9 p.1 of 2 pp.

Other Comments by Practicum Counselor

Supervisor's Comments

Practicum Supervisor Signature_____

Date_____

Form #9 p.2 of 2 pp.

INTERVIEW NOTES FORM

DIRECTIONS: (a) One copy of this form is to be completed by the practicum counselor following each counseling session.
(b) When completed this might be submitted to the practicum supervisor.

Client Name _____

Practicum Counselor Name _____

Client Age _____   Client Sex _____   Date of Interview _____   Agency _____

Interview Number _____ with This Client.

Total Time (Approximately) Spent with Client to Date _____ Hours

Was Tape Recording Made? _____ Submitted for Supervisor's Review? _____

Statement of Problem

Brief Dialogue of Interview

Evaluation of Interview

Plans for Further Counseling

Form #9 p.1 of 2 pp.

Other Comments by Practicum Counselor

Supervisor's Comments

Practicum Supervisor Signature_____

Date_____

Form #9 p.2 of 2 pp.

INTERVIEW NOTES FORM

DIRECTIONS: (a) One copy of this form is to be completed by the practicum counselor following each counseling session.
(b) When completed this might be submitted to the practicum supervisor.

Client Name _____

Practicum Counselor Name _____

Client Age _____   Client Sex _____   Date of Interview _____   Agency _____

Interview Number _____ with This Client.

Total Time (Approximately) Spent with Client to Date _____ Hours

Was Tape Recording Made? _____ Submitted for Supervisor's Review? _____

Statement of Problem

Brief Dialogue of Interview

Evaluation of Interview

Plans for Further Counseling

Form #9 p.1 of 2 pp.

Other Comments by Practicum Counselor

Supervisor's Comments

Practicum Supervisor Signature_____

Date_____

Form #9 p.2 of 2 pp.

CASE STUDY GUIDELINES

I. Purpose

   A. To provide experience in the writing of a case study.

   B. To increase self-knowledge awareness.

   C. To enable the practicum supervisors to better understand practicum counselors, so as to be able to offer better instruction and supervision

   D. To assess practicum students' skill in the interpretation and utilization of test results.

II. Suggested Headings

   These suggestions are offered to indicate areas of major importance and not meant to be the exact heading nor to be restrictive.

   A. Identification data.

   B. Statement of the problem--what questions are to be answered through the case study? This section serves as a guide to what is appropriate to include in the study and the amount of detail necessary.

   C. Home and family background.

   D. Development history.

   E. Work history.

   F. Educational history.

   G. Health history.

   H. Social emotional adjustment.

   I. Tests.

      1. The data. Indicate all tests taken and give all meaningful scores.
      2. Observations of behavior during testing.
      3. Interpretation--a major section. Account for test score discrepancies.

   J. Summary, conclusions and recommendations. All aspects of the case study should be integrated in terms of the questions to be answered and the goals to be realized. A case study should essentially always contain a prognosis and recommendations as to what the significant persons in the subject's life might do to help him or her realize meaningful, realistic goals.

III. Area of Emphasis and Length

   A. The section of the case study on tests will be detailed, will be carefully thought through, and will emphasize those things pertinent to the case. Interpret the results as if you were writing to a professional, but non-psychologically trained person, such as a teacher or school official. The language and detail of your interpretations should keep the recipient in mind.

   B. Length. No specific length is suggested. The case study should be long enough to treat each area adequately and resolve the questions of the study and yet not be unnecessarily lengthy and wordy. Typically, the case study will be between six and twelve double spaced typewritten pages.

A NOTE REGARDING CASE REPORTS

Ronald A. Ruble*

As you are engaged in the writing of different types of reports for your cases, it would seem that several questions might arise. The following is written to provide you with some guidelines. /In addition, be sure to follow the guidelines developed to implement federal legislation, Public Law 93-380, "Protection of the Rights and Privacy of Parents and Students." Copy of law is in this book./

1. Style of Reports. In general, reports written in the area of counseling are dispassionate and objective. As a means of assisting the counselor to carry through with this style, it is recommended that he use only third person in referring to his actions and those of the client, thus:

   (Poor)   I gave Joe the Kuder Preference Record, Form CH.
   (Better) Joe was administered the Kuder Preference Record, Form CH.

   It may be noted from the above, also, that the style is generally in a passive voice. This style is considered eminently acceptable for a report.

2. Organization of the Report. Most counselors and counselor educators feel that the reports which are most adequate are those which are highly organized. If you stop to think of the reasons why you are writing the report--i.e., the communication of information to others--you will see why this is so. Although it is not necessary to use formal organizational divisions such as headings, it may be that headings may assist you to organize your thoughts on paper. For example, in a report of a single interview (for inclusion in a case folder), you might find the following general outline sequence helpful:

   The Interview
   Client Behaviors
   Counselor Impressions
   Summary

3. The Length and Depth of Reports. One question which seems to arise time and time again in the Practicum is that of the length and depth of the report that is necessary. It must be admitted, however, that it is almost impossible to provide any specifications for you that would be meaningful.

   The only means we have of responding to this question is to indicate that, often, after clients have been seen in the Practicum, we receive inquiries from various sources for case summaries. This being the situation, it is necessary for us to go back to the case record and "reconstruct" the case from the information and reports which our practicum students have provided. If you wish therefore to do justice to the client, the report should be as long as necessary to convey pertinent information, and they should be as insightful as possible to allow others to return to the "raw data" at a later time and reconstruct significant aspects of the case.

A Note on Case Reports

4. Case Reports to the Client and/or His Family. Where the client has requested a report for himself or his family, the guiding consideration for the counselor in writing the report is communication. Such reports should mainly be positive in nature, they should emphasize the client's strengths and suggest positive behaviors which could lend to client "successes." If, during the interviews, information of a negative nature about familial relationships, sibling rivalry, etc. is developed, it would seem prudent to avoid direct mention of these factors unless they are obviously a matter of open concern to the family. A copy of any report made to the student and/or his family should be maintained in the case file.

---

*Dr. Ronald A. Ruble is Chairman and Professor, Division of Counselor Education, Saint Louis University. Printed by permission.

5. <u>Case Reports to the School</u>. In the case of a report to the school, often a copy of the case report may be sent to the client also. At other times, because of the information developed in the interviews or in testing, it may be desirable to develop a second report to the school in which some of the matters are reported in detail. If you have any questions about the advisability of communication of some information to the school, discuss it with one of your supervisors. Additionally, test data of a discrete type--scores, precise information--may be something both useful and desirable for the school. In such cases, information of this type should be included in a separate summary for the school. In any case, when a report goes to the school, a copy of that report should be maintained in the case file.

6. <u>The Case Summary</u>. In all cases, a summary of the interviews should be made and included in the student's folder. In this summary, the counselor should include all data which are thought to be relevant. In many cases, clients leaving the practicum have been motivated to seek further assistance from other agencies and the case summary can serve the counselor education staff as a model by which we may write a summary for a given agency.

7. <u>Reports to Parents, Clients, and Schools</u>. In the case of all reports which are sent to parents, clients, and/or schools, an indication of the approval of the supervisor must be included below and to the left of your signature as the counselor in the case. It is considered wise, on the next to the last meeting of the Practicum, to have draft copies of the reports ready for the supervisors' review. Corrections may be made before the last class meeting and the supervisor may then re-read the report and sign his approval before the report is sent out. The form for such approval on the report is as follows:

    APPROVED BY:

    (Counselor Educator Name)
    (Title)

It is important that, as you type the report, you leave sufficient room for the supervisor's signature (generally, in a typed report, you should leave four to five lines between "APPROVED BY:" and the Counselor Educator's name and title. The approval should appear below and to the left-hand margin from your own signature as counselor.

8. <u>Identification of Counselor on All Reports</u>. All reports, summaries of interviews, and any other papers appearing in the case file that have been placed there by and written by the counselor should have both the counselor's name and the date the report, summary, etc. was written. <u>No exceptions to this rule will be allowed</u>. Practicum students are requested to check case files carefully to be certain that this rule is observed before submitting reports.

9. <u>Materials Due in Each Case File</u>. For each case you carry during the practicum, a case file, maintained in a 9" x 12" folder should be developed. Information which should be in each would include the following:

    a. The Application Blank including the release form signed by both the client and a responsible adult--parent or guardian.
    b. Reports by the practicum counselor summarizing each interview.
    c. Copies of all test answer sheets.
    d. Copies of all test interpretative materials.
    e. Copies of all reports made to the client, family, school, etc.
    f. A case summary written by the practicum counselor.

10. <u>A Sample Report</u>. (Original on SLU letterhead, copy of white second sheet.)

EXAMPLE OF LETTER SENT TO REFERRING SOURCE FOLLOWING COUNSELING*

Following is presented a letter which a practicum counselor might want to use as an example when he or she is requested to give feedback about a counselee with whom he or she has worked.

SAINT LOUIS UNIVERSITY

April 25, 19__

Ms. Alice Greenly, Head Counselor
Nirvana High School
St. Louis, Missouri 63999

Dear Ms. Greenly:

Jean Jones was seen as a client in the Practicum Clinic seven times during the present semester (on February 24; March 6, 13, 20, 27; and April 9 and 16). She was referred to this service by you as her counselor at Nirvana High School primarily because you felt that she was having some difficulty in planning both her educational and occupational goals after high school. During four interviews, she and I as her counselor explored some of the factors which she seems to feel have a bearing on her decisions in this area, and in the last two interviews, she and I reviewed the results of the tests which were taken.

a. In her interviews with me, Jean seemed to feel that her interests in a number of possible educational and vocational alternatives make it difficult for her to narrow a choice down to just one educational or vocational area.

b. Jean seemed to have some question about her own intellectual abilities and the expectations of universities of students in this area. She seemed to feel that she might not be really capable of entering and graduating from a college level program in education, and, secondly, the choice of a teaching field--an area of concentration--seemed to be a difficult choice for her to make.

c. Additionally, Jean seemed concerned about the possible financial burdens that college might impose on her parents, and she and I explored the possibilities for financial assistance for a student with grades at the level of her own in high school (a B- average).

As a means of assisting Jean to explore her interests in a more systematic fashion, she and I discussed the possible advantages of her taking additional tests beyond those which she was administered (The Kuder Preference Record, Form CH, and the Differential Aptitude Tests), but it was decided that the information that these provided would be sufficient for her purposes.

On the Kuder Preference Record, Jean's high interests in scientific and mathematical areas seemed to suggest the possibility of a subject matter concentration in college in some scientific area. On the Differential Aptitude Tests, her Verbal Scale Score and the Numerical Score were both in the 90th percentile, suggesting that she should be able to compete effectively in college and be successful. Her aptitude scores in the areas of Abstract Reasoning (85th percentile) and Space Relations (79th percentile) appeared to support her interests with

---

*Printed by permission

Ms. Greenly
April 25, 19__
Page 2

definite aptitudes. These percentile scores indicate that Jean scored as high or higher than that percentage of the population on this test. She was compared with senior girls who have taken this test nationally and thus it would appear that her strengths are valid ones in these areas.

Jean did make some tentative decisions about her future. She decided to (a) write various colleges and universities for catalogs in order that she may find out more about the courses of study which are offered, (b) inquire about the possibilities of financial assistance from these institutions, and (c) investigate the possibility that her present school grades do not accurately reflect her real level of performance in high school.

Working with Jean has been a pleasure. Should she feel the need of further counseling assistance, it will be possible for her to return to the Practicum Clinic during any school semester. If she wishes further counseling, I would suggest that she telephone Dr. Ruble at 535-3300, Station 471 for an appointment.

Sincerely,

Pat Smith
Practicum Counselor

cc: Ms. Jean Jones

APPROVED BY:

Dr. Donald A. Ruble, Chairman and Professor
Division of Counselor Education

NOTES

CHAPTER IV

ETHICS IN COUNSELING AND PSYCHOTHERAPY

Ethical standards are published by both the American Psychological Association and the American Personnel and Guidance Association. Copies of both associations' ethical standards are included. Each counselor and psychotherapist while in practicum as well as after graduation is expected to conform to professional standards of conduct.

Both associations have committees which continually review the ethical stndards to make them comprehensive and timely. As conditions change, techniques improve, and professional advancements occur, the commonly accepted system of values is modified; however, the practicum student will need to follow carefully the principles of action accepted by the professional associations. The ethical standards can assist the counselor or psychotherapist in establishing moral and philosophical expectations of self during practicum and can help establish responsibilities to the client.

ETHICAL STANDARDS OF PSYCHOLOGISTS [1]

The psychologist believes in the dignity and worth of the individual human being. He is committed to increasing man's understanding of himself and others. While pursuing this endeavor, he protects the welfare of any person who may seek his service or of any subject, human or animal, that may be the object of his study. He does not use his professional position or relationships, nor does he knowingly permit his own services to be used by others, for purposes inconsistent with these values. While demanding for himself freedom of inquiry and communication, he accepts the responsibility this freedom confers: for competence where he claims it, for objectivity in the report of his findings, and for consideration of the best interests of his colleagues and of society.

Specific Principles

Principle 1. Responsibility. The psychologist,[2] committed to increasing man's understanding of man, places high value on objectivity and integrity, and maintains the highest standards in the services he offers.

a. As a scientist, the psychologist believes that society will be best served when he investigates where his judgment indicates investigation is needed; he plans his research in such a way as to minimize the possibility that his findings will be misleading; and he publishes full reports of his work, never discarding without explanation data which may modify the interpretation of results.

b. As a teacher, the psychologist recognizes his primary obligation to help others acquire knowledge and skill, and to maintain high standards of scholarship.

c. As a practitioner, the psychologist knows that he bears a heavy social responsibility because his work may touch intimately the lives of others.

Principle 2. Competence. The maintenance of high standards of professional competence is a responsibility shared by all psychologists, in the interest of the public and of the profession as a whole.

a. Psychologists discourage the practice of psychology by unqualified persons and assist the public in identifying psychologists competent to give dependable professional service. When a psychologist or a person identifying himself as a psychologist violates ethical standards, psychologists who know firsthand of such activities attempt to rectify the situation. When such a situation cannot be dealt with informally, it is called to the attention of the appropriate local, state, or national committee on professional ethics, standards, and practices.

b. Psychologists regarded as qualified for independent practice are those who (a) have been awarded a Diploma by the American Board of Examiners in Professional Psychology, or (b) have been licensed or certified by state examining boards, or (c) have been certified by voluntary boards established by state psychological associations. Psychologists who do not yet

---

[1] Copyrighted by the American Psychological Association, Inc., January 1963. Reprinted (and edited) from the *American Psychologist*, January 1963, and as amended by the APA Council of Representatives in September 1965 and December 1972.

[2] A student of psychology who assumes the role of psychologist shall be considered a psychologist for the purpose of this code of ethics.

meet the qualifications recognized for independent practice should gain experience under qualified supervision.

c. The psychologist recognizes the boundaries of his competence and the limitations of his techniques and does not offer services or use techniques that fail to meet professional standards established in particular fields. The psychologist who engages in practice assists his client in obtaining professional help for all important aspects of his problem that fall outside the boundaries of his own competence. This principle requires, for example, that provision be made for the diagnosis and treatment of relevant medical problems and for referral to or consultation with other specialists.

d. The psychologist in clinical work recognizes that his effectiveness depends in good part upon his ability to maintain sound interpersonal relations, that temporary or more enduring aberrations in his own personality may interfere with this ability or distort his appraisals of others. There he refrains from undertaking any activity in which his personal problems are likely to result in inferior professional services or harm to a client; or, if he is already engaged in such an activity when he becomes aware of his personal problems, he seeks competent professional assistance to determine whether he should continue or terminate his services to his client.

Principle 3. Moral and Legal Standards. The psychologist in the practice of his profession shows sensible regard for the social codes and moral expectations of the community in which he works, recognizing that violations of accepted moral and legal standards on his part may involve his clients, students, or colleagues in damaging personal conflicts, and impugn his own name and the reputation of his profession.

Principle 4. Misrepresentation. The psychologist avoids misrepresentation of his own professional qualifications, affiliations, and purposes, and those of the institutions and organizations with which he is associated.

a. A psychologist does not claim either directly or by implication professional qualifications that differ from his actual qualifications, nor does he misrepresent his affiliation with any institution, organization, or individual, nor lead others to assume he has affiliations that he does not have. The psychologist is responsible for correcting others who misrepresent his professional qualifications or affiliations.

b. The psychologist does not misrepresent an institution or organization with which he is affiliated by ascribing to it characteristics that it does not have.

c. A psychologist does not use his affiliation with the American Psychological Association or its Divisions for purposes that are not consonant with the stated purposes of the Association.

d. A psychologist does not associate himself with or permit his name to be used in connection with any services or products in such a way as to misrepresent them, the degree of his responsibility for them, or the nature of his affiliation.

Principle 5. Public Statements. Modesty, scientific caution, and due regard for the limits of present knowledge characterize all statements of psychologists who supply information to the public, either directly or indirectly.

a. Psychologists who interpret the science of psychology or the services of psychologists to clients or to the general public have an obligation to report fairly and accurately. Exaggeration, sensationalism, superficiality, and other kinds of misrepresentation are avoided.

b. When information about psychological procedures and techniques is given, care is taken to indicate that they should be used only by persons adequately trained in their use.

c. A psychologist who engages in radio or television activities does not participate in commercial announcements recommending purchase or use of a product.

Principle 6. Confidentiality. Safeguarding information about an individual that has been obtained by the psychologist in the course of his teaching, practice, or investigation is a primary obligation of the psychologist. Such information is not communicated to others unless certain important conditions are met.

    a. Information received in confidence is revealed only after most careful deliberation and when there is clear and imminent danger to an individual or to society, and then only to appropriate professional workers or public authorities.

    b. Information obtained in clinical or consulting relationships, or evaluative data concerning children, students, employees, and others are discussed only for professional purposes and only with persons clearly concerned with the case. Written and oral reports should present only data germane to the purposes of the evaluation, every effort should be made to avoid undue invasion of privacy.

    c. Clinical and other materials are used in classroom teaching and writing only when the identity of the persons involved is adequately disguised.

    d. The confidentiality of professional communications about individuals is maintained. Only when the originator and other persons involved give their express permission is a confidential professional communication shown to the individual concerned. The psychologist is responsible for informing the client of the limits of the confidentiality.

    e. Only after explicit permission has been granted is the identity of research subjects published. When data have been published without permission for identification, the psychologist assumes responsibility for adequately disguising their sources.

    f. The psychologist makes provisions for the maintenance of confidentiality in the preservation and ultimate disposition of confidential records.

Principle 7. Client Welfare. The psychologist respects the integrity and protects the welfare of the person or group with whom he is working.

    a. The psychologist in industry, education, and other situations in which conflicts of interest may arise among various parties, as between management and labor, or between the client and employer of the psychologist, defines for himself the nature and direction of his loyalties and responsibilities and keeps all parties concerned informed of these commitments.

    b. When there is a conflict among professional workers, the psychologist is concerned primarily with the welfare of any client involved and only secondarily with the interest of his own professional group.

    c. The psychologist attempts to terminate a clinical or consulting relationship when it is reasonably clear to the psychologist that the client is not benefiting from it.

    d. The psychologist who asks that an individual reveal personal information in the course of interviewing, testing, or evaluation, or who allows such information to be divulged to him, does so only after making certain that the responsible person is fully aware of the purposes of the interview, testing, or evaluation and of the ways in which the information may be used.

    e. In cases involving referral, the responsibility of the psychologist for the welfare of the client continues until this responsibility is assumed by the professional person to whom the client is referred or until the relationship with the psychologist making the referral has been terminated by mutual agreement. In situations where referral, consultation, or other changes in the conditions of the treatment are indicated and the client refuses referral, the psychologist carefully weighs the possible harm to the client, to himself, and to his profession that might ensue from continuing the relationship.

    f. The psychologist who requires the taking of psychological tests for didactic, classification, or research purposes protects the examinees by insuring that the tests and test results are used in a professional manner.

    g. When potentially disturbing subject matter is presented to students, it is discussed objectively, and efforts are made to handle constructively any difficulties that arise.

    h. Care must be taken to insure an appropriate setting for clinical work to protect both client and psychologist from actual or imputed harm and the profession from censure.

    i. In the use of accepted drugs for therapeutic purposes special care needs to be exercised by the psychologist to assure himself that the collaborating physician provides suitable safeguards for the client.

Principle 8. Client Relationship. The psychologist informs his prospective client of the important aspects of the potential relationship that might affect the client's decision to enter the relationship.

a. Aspects of the relationship likely to affect the client's decision include the recording of an interview, the use of interview material for training purposes, and observation of an interview by other persons.

b. When the client is not competent to evaluate the situation (as in the case of a child), the person responsible for the client is informed of the circumstances which may influence the relationship.

c. The psychologist does not normally enter into a professional relationship with members of his own family, intimate friends, close associates, or others whose welfare might be jeopardized by such a dual relationship.

Principle 9. Impersonal Services. Psychological services for the purpose of diagnosis, treatment, or personalized advice are provided only in the context of a professional relationship, and are not given by means of public lectures or demonstrations, newspaper or magazine articles, radio or television programs, mail, or similar media.

a. The preparation of personnel reports and recommendations based on test data secured solely by mail is unethical unless such appraisals are an integral part of a continuing client relationship with a company, as a result of which the consulting psychologist has intimate knowledge of the client's personnel situation and can be assured thereby that his written appraisals will be adequate to the purpose and will be properly interpreted by the client. These reports must not be embellished with such detailed analyses of the subject's personality traits as would be appropriate only after intensive interviews with the subject. The reports must not make specific recommendations as to employment or placement of the subject which go beyond the psychologist's knowledge of the job requirements of the company. The reports must not purport to eliminate the company's need to carry on such other regular employment or personnel practices as appraisal of the work history, checking of references, past performance in the company.

Principle 10. Announcement of Services. A psychologist adheres to professional rather than commercial standards in making known his availability for professional services.

a. A psychologist does not directly solicit clients for individual diagnosis or therapy.

b. Individual listings in telephone directories are limited to name, highest relevant degree, certification status, address, and telephone number. They may also include identification in a few words of the psychologist's major areas of practice; for example, child therapy, personnel selection, industrial psychology. Agency listings are equally modest.

c. Announcements of individual private practice are limited to a simple statement of the name, highest relevant degree, certification or diplomate status, address, telephone number, office hours, and a brief explanation of the types of services rendered. Announcements of agencies may list names of staff members with their qualifications. They conform in other particulars with the same standards as individual announcements, making certain that the true nature of the organization is apparent.

d. A psychologist or agency announcing nonclinical professional services may use brochures that are descriptive of services rendered but not evaluative. They may be sent to professional persons, schools, business firms, government agencies, and other similar organizations.

e. The use in a brochure of "testimonials from satisfied users" is unacceptable. The offer of a free trial of services is unacceptable if it operates to misrepresent in any way the nature or the efficacy of the services rendered by the psychologist. Claims that a psychologist has unique skills or unique devices not available to others in the profession are made only if the special efficacy of these unique skills or devices has been demonstrated by scientifically acceptable evidence.

f. The psychologist must not encourage (nor, within his power, even allow) a client to have exaggerated ideas as to the efficacy of services rendered. Claims made to clients about the efficacy of his services must no go beyond those which the psychologist would be willing to subject to professional scrutiny through publishing his results and his claims in a professional journal.

Principle 11. Interprofessional Relations. A psychologists acts with integrity in regard to colleagues in psychology and in other professions.

a. Each member of the Association cooperates with the duly constituted Committee on Scientific and Professional Ethics and Conduct in the performance of its duties by responding to inquiries with reasonable promptness and completeness. A member taking longer than 30 days to respond to such inquiries shall have the burden of demonstrating that he acted with "reasonable promptness."

b. A psychologist does not normally offer professional services to a person receiving psychological assistance from another professional worker except by agreement with the other worker or after the termination of the client's relationship with the other professional worker.

c. The welfare of clients and colleagues requires that psychologists in joint practice or corporate activities make an orderly and explicit arrangement regarding the conditions of their association and its possible termination. Psychologists who serve as employers of other psychologists have an obligation to make similar appropriate arrangements.

Principle 12. Remuneration. Financial arrangements in professional practice are in accord with professional standards that safeguard the best interest of the client and the profession.

a. In establishing rates for professional services, the psychologist considers carefully both the ability of the client to meet the financial burden and the charges made by other professional persons engaged in comparable work. He is willing to contribute a portion of his services to work for which he receives little or no financial return.

b. No commission or rebate or any other form of remuneration is given or received for referral of clients for professional services.

c. The psychologist in clinical or counseling practice does not use his relationships with clients to promote, for personal gain or the profit of an agency, commercial enterprises of any kind.

d. A psychologist does not accept a private fee or any other form of remuneration for professional work with a person who is entitled to his services through an institution or agency. The policies of a particular agency may make explicit provision for private work with its clients by members of its staff, and in such instances the client must be fully apprised of all policies affecting him.

Principle 13. Test Security. Psychological tests and other assessment devices, the value of which depends in part on the naivete of the subject, are not reproduced or described in popular publications in ways that might invalidate the techniques. Access to such devices is limited to persons with professional interests who will safeguard their use.

a. Sample items made up to resemble those of tests being discussed may be reproduced in popular articles and elsewhere, but scorable tests and actual test items are not reproduced except in professional publications.

b. The psychologist is responsible for the control of psychological tests and other devices and procedures used for instruction when their value might be damaged by revealing to the general public their specific contents or underlying principles.

Principle 14. Test Interpretation. Test scores, like test materials, are released only to persons who are qualified to interpret and use them properly.

a. Materials for reporting test scores to parents, or which are designed for self-appraisal purposes in schools, social agencies, or industry are closely supervised by qualified psychologists or counselors with provisions for referring and counseling individuals when needed.

b. Test results or other assessment data used for evaluation or classification are communicated to employers, relatives, or other appropriate persons in such a manner as to guard against misinterpretation or misuse. In the usual case, an interpretation of the test result rather than the score is communicated.

c. When test results are communicated directly to parents and students, they are accompanied by adequate interpretive aids or advice.

Principle 15. Test Publication. Psychological tests are offered for commercial publication only to publishers who present their tests in a professional way and distribute them only to qualified users.

a. A test manual, technical handbook, or other suitable report on the test is provided which describes the method of constructing and standardizing the test, and summarizes the validation research.

b. The populations for which the test has ben developed and the purposes for which it is recommended are stated in the manual. Limitations upon the test's dependability, and aspects of its validity on which research is lacking or incomplete, are clearly stated. In particular, the manual contains a warning regarding interpretations likely to be made which have not yet been substantiated by research.

c. The catalog and manual indicate the training or professional qualifications required for sound interpretation of the test.

d. The test manual and supporting documents take into account the principles enunicated in the *Standards for Educational and Psychological Tests and Manuals.*

e. Test advertisements are factual and descriptive rather than emotional and persuasive.

Principle 16. Research Precautions. The psychologist assumes obligations for the welfare of his research subjects, both animal and human.

The decision to undertake research should rest upon a considered judgment by the individual psychologist about how best to contribute to psychological science and to human welfare. The responsible psychologist weighs alternative directions in which personal energies and resources might be invested. Having made the decision to conduct research, psychologists must carry out their investigations with respect for the people who participate and with concern for their dignity and welfare. The Principles that follow make explicit the investigator's ethical responsibilities toward participants over the course of research, from the initial decision to pursue a study to the steps necessary to protect the confidentiality of research data. These Principles should be interpreted in terms of the contexts provided in the complete document [3] offered as a supplement to these Principles.

a. In planning a study the investigator has the personal responsibility to make a careful evaluation of its ethical acceptability, taking into account these Principles for research with human beings. To the extent that this appraisal, weighing scientific and humane values, suggests a deviation from any Principle, the investigator incurs an increasingly serious obligation to seek ethical advice and to observe more stringent safeguards to protect the rights of the human research participants.

b. Responsibility for the establishment and maintenance of acceptable ethical practice in research always remains with the individual investigator. The investigator is also responsible for the ethical treatment of research participants by collaborators, assistants, students, and employees, all of whom, however, incur parallel obligations.

c. Ethical practice requires the investigator to inform the participant of all features of the research that reasonably might be expected to influence willingness to participate, and to explain all other aspects of the research about which the participant inquires. Failure to make full disclosure gives added emphasis to the investigator's abiding responsibility to protect the welfare and dignity of the research participant.

---

[3] *Ethical Principles in the Conduct of Research with Human Participants*, available upon request from the American Psychological Association.

d. Openness and honesty are essential characteristics of the relationship between investigator and research participant. When the methodological requirements of a study necessitate concealment or deception, the investigator is required to ensure the participant's understanding of the reasons for this action and to restore the quality of the relationship with the investigator.

e. Ethical research practice requires the investigator to respect the individual's freedom to decline to participate in research or to discontinue participation at any time. The obligation to protect this freedom requires special vigilance when the investigator is in a position of power over the participant. The decision to limit this freedom gives added emphasis to the investigator's abiding responsibility to protect the participant's dignity and welfare.

f. Ethically acceptable research begins with the establishment of a clear and fair agreement between the investigator and the research participant that clarifies the responsibilities of each. The investigator has the obligation to honor all promises and commitments included in that agreement.

g. The ethical investigator protects participants from physical and mental discomfort, harm and danger. If the risk of such consequences exists, the investigator is required to inform the participant of that fact, secure consent before proceeding, and take all possible measures to minimize distress. A research procedure may not be used if it is likely to cause serious and lasting harm to participants.

h. After the data are collected, ethical practice requires the investigator to provide the participant with a full clarification of the nature of the study and to remove any misconceptions that may have arisen. Where scientific or humane values justify delaying or withholding information, the investigator acquires a special responsibility to assure that there are no damaging consequences for the participant.

i. Where research procedures may result in undesirable consequences for the participant, the investigator has the responsibility to detect and remove or correct these consequences, including, where relevant, long-term aftereffects.

j. Information obtained about the research participants during the course of an investigation is confidential. When the possibility exists that others may obtain access to such information, ethical research practice requires that this possibility, together with the plans for protecting confidentiality, be explained to the participants as a part of the procedure for obtaining informed consent.

k. A psychologist using animals in research adheres to the provisions of the Rules Regarding Animals, drawn up by the Committee on Precautions and Standards in Animal Experimentation and adopted by the American Psychological Association.

l. Investigations of human subjects using experimental drugs (for example: hallucinogenic, psychotomimetic, psychedelic, or similar substances) should be conducted only in such settings as clinics, hospitals, or research facilities maintaining appropriate safeguards for the subjects.

Principle 17. Publication Credit. Credit is assigned to those who have contributed to a publication, in proportion to their contribution, and only to these.

a. Major contributions of a professional character, made by several persons to a common project, are recognized by joint authorship. The experimenter or author who has made the principal contribution to a publication is identified as the first listed.

b. Minor contributions of a professional character, extensive clerical or similar nonprofessional assistance, and other minor contributions are acknowledged in footnotes or in an introductory statement.

c. Acknowledgment through specific citations is made for unpublished as well as published material that has directly influenced the research or writing.

d. A psychologist who compiles and edits for publication the contributions of others publishes the symposium or report under the title of the committee or symposium, with his own name appearing as chairman or editor among those of the other contributors or committee members.

Principle 18. Responsibility toward Organization. A psychologist respects the rights and reputation of the institute or organization with which he is associated.

a. Materials prepared by a psychologist as a part of his regular work under specific direction of his organization are the property of that organization. Such materials are released for use or publication by a psychologist in accordance with policies of authorization, assignment of credit, and related matters which have been established by his organization.

b. Other material resulting incidentally from activity supported by any agency, and for which the psychologist rightly assumes individual responsibility, is published with disclaimer for any responsibility on the part of the supporting agency.

Principle 19. Promotional Activities. The psychologist associated with the development or promotion of psychological devices, books, or other products offered for commercial sale is responsible for ensuring that such devices, books, or products are presented in a professional and factual way.

a. Claims regarding performance, benefits, or results are supported by scientifically acceptable evidence.

b. The psychologist does not use professional journals for the commercial exploitation of psychological products, and the psychologist-editor guards against such misuse.

c. The psychologist with a financial interest in the sale or use of a psychological product is sensitive to possible conflict of interest in his promotion of such products and avoids compromise of his professional responsibilities and objectives.

ETHICAL STANDARDS

American Personnel and Guidance Association*

Preamble

The American Personnel and Guidance Association is an educational, scientific, and professional organization whose members are dedicated to the enhancement of the worth, dignity, potential, and uniqueness of each individual and thus to the service of society.

The Association recognizes that the role definitions and work settings of its members include a wide variety of academic disciplines, levels of academic preparation, and agency services. This diversity reflects the breadth of the Association's interest and influence. It also poses challenging complexities in efforts to set standards for the performance of members, desired requisite preparation or practice, and supporting social, legal, and ethical controls.

The specification of ethical standards enables the Association to clarify to present and future members and to those served by members the nature of ethical responsibilities held in common by its members.

The existence of such standards serves to stimulate greater concern by members for their own professional functioning and for the conduct of fellow professionals such as counselors, guidance and student personnel workers, and others in the helping professions. As the ethical code of the Association, this document establishes principles which define the ethical behavior of Association members.

Section A: General

1. The member influences the development of the profession by continuous efforts to improve professional practices, teaching, services, and research. Professional growth is continuous throughout the member's career and is exemplified by the development of a philosophy that explains why and how a member functions in the helping relationship. Members are expected to gather data on their effectiveness and to be guided by the findings.

2. The member has a responsibility both to the individual who is served and to the institution within which the service is performed. The acceptance of employment in an institution implies that the member is in substantial agreement with the general policies and principles of the institution. Therefore the professional activities of the member are also in accord with the objectives of the institution. If, despite concerted efforts, the member cannot reach agreement with the employer as to acceptable standards of conduct that allow for changes in institutional policy conducive to the positive growth and development of counselees, then terminating the affiliation should be seriously considered.

3. Ethical behavior among professional associates, members and nonmembers, is expected at all times. When information is possessed which raises serious doubt as to the ethical behavior of professional colleagues, whether Association members or not, the member is obligated to take action to attempt to rectify such a condition. Such action shall utilize the institution's channels first and then utilize procedures established by the state, division, or Association.

The member can take action in a variety of ways: conferring with the individual in question, gathering further information as to the allegation, confer-

---

*Reprinted by permission. Taken from Guidepost, Vol. 17, July 4, 1974, pp. 4-5.

ring with local or national ethics committees, and so forth.

4. The member must not seek self-enhancement through expressing evaluations or comparisons that are damaging to others.

5. The member neither claims nor implies professional qualifications exceeding those possessed and is responsible for correcting any misrepresentations of these qualifications by others.

6. In establishing fees for professional services, members should take into consideration the fees charged by other professions delivering comparable services, as well as the ability of the counselee to pay. Members are willing to provide some services for which they receive little or no financial remuneration, or remuneration in food, lodging, and materials. When fees include charges for items other than professional services, that portion of the total which is for the professional services should be clearly indicated.

7. When members provide information to the public or to subordinates, peers, or supervisors, they have a clear responsibility to ensure that the content is accurate, unbiased, and consists of objective, factual data.

8. The member shall make a careful distinction between the offering of counseling services as opposed to public information services. Counseling may be offered only in the context of a reciprocal or face-to-face relationship. Information services may be offered through the media.

9. With regard to professional employment, members are expected to accept only positions that they are prepared to assume and then to comply with established practices of the particular type of employment setting in which they are employed in order to ensure the continuity of services.

Section B: Counselor-Counselee Relationship

This section refers to practices involving individual and/or group counseling relationships, and it is not intended to be applicable to practices involving administrative relationships.

To the extent that the counselee's choice of action is not imminently self- or other-destructive, the counselee must retain freedom of choice. When the counselee does not have full autonomy for reasons of age, mental incompetency, criminal incarceration, or similar legal restrictions, the member may have to work with others who exercise significant control and direction over the counselee. Under these circumstances the member must apprise counselees of restrictions that may limit their freedom of choice.

1. The member's *primary* obligation is to respect the integrity and promote the welfare of the counselee(s), whether the counselee(s) is (are) assisted individually or in a group relationship. In a group setting, the member-leader is also responsible for protecting individuals from physical and/or psychological trauma resulting from interaction within the group.

2. The counseling relationship and information resulting therefrom must be kept confidential, consistent with the obligations of the member as a professional person. In a group counseling setting the member is expected to set a norm of confidentiality regarding all group participants' disclosures.

3. If an individual is already in a counseling/therapy relationship with another professional person, the member does not begin a counseling relationship without first contacting and receiving the approval of that other professional. If the member discovers that the counselee is in another counseling/therapy relationship after the counseling relationship begins, the member is obligated to gain the consent of the other professional or terminate the relationship, unless the counselee elects to terminate the other relationship.

4. When the counselee's condition indicates that there is clear and imminent danger to the counselee or others, the member is expected to take direct personal action or to inform responsible authorities. Consultation with other professionals should be utilized where possible. Direct interventions, especially the assumption of responsibility for the counselee, should be taken only after careful deliberation. The counselee should be involved in the resumption of responsibility for his actions as quickly as possible.

5. Records of the counseling relationship including interview notes, test data, correspondence, tape recordings, and other documents are to be considered professional information for use in counseling, and they are not part of the public or official records of the institution or agency in which the counselor is employed. Revelation to others of counse-

ling material should occur only upon the express consent of the counselee.

6. Use of data derived from a counseling relationship for purposes of counselor training or research shall be confined to content that can be sufficiently disguised to ensure full protection of the identity of the counselee involved.

7. Counselees shall be informed of the conditions under which they may receive counseling assistance at or before the time when the counseling relationship is entered. This is particularly so when conditions exist of which the counselee would be unaware. In individual and group situations, particularly those oriented to self-understanding or growth, the member-leader is obligated to make clear the purposes, goals, techniques, rules of procedure, and limitations that may affect the continuance of the relationship.

8. The member has the responsibility to screen prospective group participants, especially when the emphasis is on self-understanding and growth through self-disclosure. The member should maintain an awareness of the group participants' compatibility throughout the life of the group.

9. The member reserves the right to consult with any other professionally competent person about a counselee. In choosing a consultant, the member avoids placing the consultant in a conflict of interest situation that would preclude the consultant's being a proper party to the member's efforts to help the counselee.

10. If the member is unable to be of professional assistance to the counselee, the member avoids initiating the counseling relationship or the member terminates it. In either event, the member is obligated to refer the counselee to an appropriate specialist. (It is incumbent upon the member to be knowledgable about referral resources so that a satisfactory referral can be initiated.) In the event the counselee declines the suggested referral, the member is not obligated to continue the relationship.

11. When the member learns from counseling relationships of conditions that are likely to harm others, the member should report *the condition* to the responsible authority. This should be done in such a manner as to conceal the identity of the counselee.

12. When the member has other relationships, particularly of an administrative, supervisory, and/or evaluative nature, with an individual seeking counseling services, the member should not serve as the counselor but should refer the individual to another professional. Only in instances where such an alternative is unavailable and where the individual's condition definitely warrants counseling intervention should the member enter into and/or maintain a counseling relationship.

13. All experimental methods of treatment must be clearly indicated to prospective recipients, and safety precautions are to be adhered to by the member.

14. When the member is engaged in short-term group treatment/training programs, e.g., marathons and other encounter-type or growth groups, the member ensures that there is professional assistance available during and following the group experience.

15. Should the member be engaged in a work setting that calls for any variation from the above statements, the member is obligated to consult with other professionals whenever possible to consider justifiable alternatives. The variations that may be necessary should be clearly communicated to other professionals and prospective counselees.

Section C: Measurement and Evaluation

The primary purpose of educational and psychological testing is to provide descriptive measures that are objective and interpretable in either comparative or absolute terms. The member must recognize the need to interpret the statements that follow as applying to the whole range of appraisal techniques including test and nontest data. Test results constitute only one of a variety of pertinent sources of information for personnel, guidance, and counseling decisions.

1. It is the member's responsibility to provide adequate orientation or information to the examinee(s) prior to and following the test administration so that the results of testing may be placed in proper perspective with other relevant factors. In so doing, the member must recognize the effects of socioeconomic, ethnic, and cultural factors on test scores. It is the member's professional responsibility to use additional unvalidated information cautiously in modifying interpretation of the test results.

2. In selecting tests for use in a given situation or with a particular counselee,

the member must consider carefully the specific validity, reliability, and appropriateness of the test(s). "General" validity, reliability, and the like may be questioned legally as well as ethically when tests are used for vocational and educational selection, placement, or counseling.

3. When making any statements to the public about tests and testing, the member is expected to give accurate information and to avoid false claims or misconceptions. Special efforts are often required to avoid unwarranted connotations of such terms as IQ and grade equivalent scores.

4. Different tests demand different levels of competence for administration, scoring, and interpretation. Members have a responsibility to recognize the limits of their competence and to perform only those functions for which they are prepared.

5. Tests should be administered under the same conditions that were established in their standardization. When tests are not administered under standard conditions or when unusual behavior or irregularities occur during the testing session, those conditions should be noted and the results designated as invalid or of questionable validity. Unsupervised or inadequately supervised test-taking, such as the use of tests through the mails, is considered unethical. On the other hand, the use of instruments that are so designed or standardized to be self-administered and self-scored, such as interest inventories, is to be encouraged.

6. The meaningfulness of test results used in personnel, guidance, and counseling functions generally depends on the examinee's unfamiliarity with the specific items on the test. Any prior coaching or dissemination of the test materials can invalidate test results. Therefore, test security is one of the professional obligations of the member. Conditions that produce most favorable test results should be made known to the examinee.

7. The purpose of testing and the explicit use of the results should be made known to the examinee prior to testing. The counselor has a responsibility to ensure that instrument limitations are not exceeded and that periodic review and/or retesting are made to prevent counselee stereotyping.

8. The examinee's welfare and explicit prior understanding should be the criteria for determining the recipients of the test results. The member is obligated to see that adequate interpretation accompanies any release of individual or group test data. The interpretation of test data should be related to the examinee's particular concerns.

9. The member is expected to be cautious when interpreting the results of research instruments possessing insufficient technical data. The specific purposes for the use of such instruments must be stated explicitly to examinees.

10. The member must proceed with extreme caution when attempting to evaluate and interpret the performance of minority group members or other persons who are not represented in the norm group on which the instrument was standardized.

11. The member is obligated to guard against the appropriation, reproduction, or modifications of published tests or parts thereof without the express permission and adequate recognition of the original author or publisher.

12. Regarding the preparation, publication, and distribution of tests, reference should be made to:

a. *Standards for Educational and Psychological Tests and Manuals,* revised edition, 1973, published by the American Psychological Association on behalf of itself, the American Educational Research Association, and the National Council on Measurement in Education.

b. "The Responsible Use of Tests: A Position Paper of AMEG, APGA, and NCME," published in *Measurement and Evaluation in Guidance* Vol. 5, No. 2, July 1972, pp. 385–388.

Section D: Research and Publication

1. Current American Psychological Association guidelines on research with human subjects shall be adhered to (*Ethical Principles in the Conduct of Research with Human Participants.* Washington, D.C.: American Psychological Association, Inc., 1973).

2. In planning any research activity dealing with human subjects, the member is expected to be aware of and responsive to all pertinent ethical principles and to ensure that the research problem, design, and execution are in full compliance with them.

3. Responsibility for ethical research practice lies with the principal researcher, while others involved in the research

activities share ethical obligation and full responsibility for their own actions.

4. In research with human subjects, researchers are responsible for their subjects' welfare throughout the experiment, and they must take all reasonable precautions to avoid causing injurious psychological, physical, or social effects on their subjects.

5. It is expected that all research subjects be informed of the purpose of the study except when withholding information or providing misinformation to them is essential to the investigation. In such research, the member is responsible for corrective action as soon as possible following the research.

6. Participation in research is expected to be voluntary. Involuntary participation is appropriate only when it can be demonstrated that participation will have no harmful effects on subjects.

7. When reporting research results, explicit mention must be made of all variables and conditions known to the investigator that might affect the outcome of the investigation or the interpretation of the data.

8. The member is responsible for conducting and reporting investigations in a manner that minimizes the possibility that results will be misleading.

9. The member has an obligation to make available sufficient original research data to qualified others who may wish to replicate the study.

10. When supplying data, aiding in the research of another person, reporting research results, or in making original data available, due care must be taken to disguise the identity of the subjects in the absence of specific authorization from such subjects to do otherwise.

11. When conducting and reporting research, the member is expected to be familiar with and to give recognition to previous work on the topic, as well as to observe all copyright laws and follow the principle of giving full credit to all to whom credit is due.

12. The member has the obligation to give due credit through joint authorship, acknowledgement, footnote statements, or other appropriate means to those who have contributed significantly to the research, in accordance with such contributions.

13. The member is expected to communicate to other members the results of any research judged to be of professional or scientific value. Results reflecting unfavorably on institutions, programs, services, or vested interests should not be withheld for such reasons.

14. If members agree to cooperate with another individual in research and/or publication, they incur an obligation to cooperate as promised in terms of punctuality of performance and with full regard to the completeness and accuracy of the information provided.

Section E: Consulting and Private Practice

Consulting refers to a voluntary relationship between a professional helper and help-needing social unit (industry, business, school, college, etc.) in which the consultant is attempting to give help to the client in the solution of some current or potential problem. When "client" is used in this section it refers to an individual, group, or organization served by the consultant. (This definition of "consulting" is adapted from "Dimensions of the Consultant's Job" by Ronald Lippitt, *Journal of Social Issues,* Vol. 15, No. 2, 1959.)

1. Members who act as consultants must have a high degree of self-awareness of their own values and needs in entering helping relationships that involve change in social units.

2. There should be understanding and agreement between consultant and client as to the task, the directions or goals, and the function of the consultant.

3. Members are expected to accept only those consulting roles for which they possess or have access to the necessary skills and resources for giving the kind of help that is needed.

4. The consulting relationship is defined as being one in which the client's adaptability and growth toward self-direction are encouraged and cultivated. For this reason, the consultant is obligated to maintain consistently the role of a consultant and to avoid becoming a decision maker for the client.

5. In announcing one's availability for professional services as a consultant, the member follows professional rather than commercial standards in describing services with accuracy, dignity, and caution.

6. For private practice in testing, counseling, or consulting, all ethical principles defined in this document are pertinent. In addition, any individual, agency, or institution offering educational, personal, or vocational counseling should meet the

standards of the International Association of Counseling Services, Inc.

7. The member is expected to refuse a private fee or other remuneration for consultation with persons who are entitled to these services through the member's employing institution or agency. The policies of a particular agency may make explicit provisions for private practice with agency counselees by members of its staff. In such instances, the counselees must be apprised of other options open to them should they seek private counseling services.

8. It is unethical to use one's institutional affiliation to recruit counselees for one's private practice.

Section F: Personnel Administration

It is recognized that most members are employed in public or quasi-public institutions. The functioning of a member within an institution must contribute to the goals of the institution and vice versa if either is to accomplish their respective goals or objectives. It is therefore essential that the member and the institution function in ways to: (a) make the institution's goals explicit and public; (b) make the member's contribution to institutional goals specific; and (c) foster mutual accountability for goal achievement.

To accomplish these objectives it is recognized that the member and the employer must share responsibilities in the formulation and implementation of personnel policies.

1. Members should define and describe the parameters and levels of their professional competency.

2. Members should establish interpersonal relations and working agreements with supervisors and subordinates regarding counseling or clinical relationships, confidentiality, distinction between public and private material, maintenance and dissemination of recorded information, work load, and accountability. Working agreements in each instance should be specified and made known to those concerned.

3. Members are responsible for alerting their employers to conditions that may be potentially disruptive or damaging.

4. Members are responsible for informing employers of conditions that may limit their effectiveness.

5. Members are expected to submit regularly to review and evaluation.

6. Members are responsible for in-service development of self and/or staff.

7. Members are responsible for informing their staff of goals and programs.

8. Members are responsible for providing personnel practices that guarantee and enhance the rights and welfare of each recipient of their service.

9. Members are expected to select competent persons and assign responsibilities compatible with their skills and experiences.

Section G: Preparation Standards

Members who are responsible for training others should be guided by the preparation standards of the Association and relevant division(s). The member who functions in the capacity of trainer assumes unique ethical responsibilities that frequently go beyond that of the member who does not function in a training capacity. These ethical responsibilities are outlined as follows:

1. Members are expected to orient trainees to program expectations, basic skills development, and employment prospects prior to admission to the program.

2. Members in charge of training are expected to establish programs that integrate academic study and supervised practice.

3. Members are expected to establish a program directed toward developing the trainees' skills, knowledge, and self-understanding, stated whenever possible in competency or performance terms.

4. Members are expected to identify the level of competency of their trainees. These levels of competency should accommodate the paraprofessional as well as the professional.

5. Members, through continual trainee evaluation and appraisal, are expected to be aware of the personal limitations of the trainee that might impede future performance. The trainer has the responsibility of not only assisting the trainee in securing remedial assistance, but also screening from the program those trainees who are unable to provide competent services.

6. Members are expected to provide a program that includes training in research commensurate with levels of role functioning. Paraprofessional and tech-

nician-level personnel should be trained as consumers of research. In addition, these personnel should learn how to evaluate their own and their program effectiveness. Advanced graduate training, especially at the doctoral level, should include preparation for original research by the member.

7. Members are expected to make trainees aware of the ethical responsibilities and standards of the profession.

8. Training programs are expected to encourage trainees to value the ideals of service to individuals and to society. In this regard, direct financial remuneration or lack thereof should not influence the quality of service rendered. Monetary considerations should not be allowed to overshadow professional and humanitarian needs.

9. Members responsible for training are expected to be skilled as teachers and practitioners.

10. Members are expected to present thoroughly varied theoretical positions so that trainees may make comparisons and have the opportunity to select a position.

11. Members are obligated to develop clear policies within their training institution regarding field placement and the roles of the trainee and the trainer in such placements.

12. Members are expected to ensure that forms of training focusing on self-understanding or growth are voluntary, or if required as part of the training program, are made known to prospective trainees prior to entering the program. When the training program offers a growth experience with an emphasis on self-disclosure or other relatively intimate or personal involvement, the member should have no administrative, supervisory, or evaluative authority regarding the participant.

13. Members are obligated to conduct a training program in keeping with the most current guidelines of the American Personnel and Guidance Association and its various divisions.

CHAPTER V

CLIENTS AND THE PRACTICUM COUNSELOR'S RESPONSIBILITIES

Perhaps emphasizing the client as the major focus of counseling is unnecessary, but the client can become "lost in the shuffle" if the practicum counselor becomes unduly concerned about counseling processes and techniques. The student counselor may "lose sight of the forest because of the trees." The practicum counselor at all times must hold the client and the client's well being above all else. When the student counselor makes decisions, plans strategies, or implements techniques, the client and the client's well being must be the important factors.

Not all practicum counselors can work well with all clients. The practicum counselor has a responsibility to know his or her own strengths and weaknesses, to be able to assess each client and then to determine whether or not the practicum counselor holds the potential for assisting the client. The client comes first and all else is secondary. The practicum counselor who cannot be sure that his or her client comes above all else must consider whether or not he or she deserves the right to enter into a counseling relationship. Counseling techniques utilized, referrals made to other professionals, and the determination of when and under what conditions the breaking of confidences is justified must all be identified in terms of what is best for the client!

SELECTION OF CLIENTS

Often student counselors will find themselves in a role that does not allow for the best possible client selection. A problem that exists for many student counselors is to meet the requirements of their counseling practicum course. A practicum counselor often will be so concerned about meeting the course requirement to make 40 or more tapes that any criteria for selecting clients are given low priority in importance. The concern is only to find a sufficient number of clients in order to satisfy the practicum requirements. Often the client or potential client is not perceived as being as important as the class requirements. If a student counselor is in a position of being able to select clients, selection is best done by truly knowing one's self. Counseling is not, at its best, a process of meeting counselor needs but rather client needs. The student counselor needs to be aware of his or her needs so as not to confuse them with clients' needs. What can I do and what can I do well? What am I not willing to do? What do I like to do that I do not do very well? What are the specific needs of this client? What other sources are available for this client if I don't feel qualified or willing to work with this person? What are the capabilities of my colleagues?

Selection of clients, like many questions in counseling, must be looked at not only from the point of view of what is best for the client, but also from consideration in terms of the setting and available resources. The counselor must be familiar with the strengths of available co-workers and compute this information in the final selection decision. Selection of clients, although a seemingly complicated process, is simplified by the answer to the question: "Is the selection of this client the best available thing that can happen to this client?"

Finally, selection does not mandate or even suggest that it is forever. It is the mature, competent practicum counselor who realizes after the counseling process has begun that his or her client would best be served by another professional person and makes the appropriate referral.

RESPONSIBILITY TO CLIENTS

The responsibility of counseling is the responsibility of the practicum counselor to the client. In this regard a number of specific responsibilities seem to exist:

1. Clients need to know what is expected of them--often the student counselor makes such statements as "You may do whatever you want in this hour." Rarely is that what the counselor means. The student counselor needs to make clear his or her expectations for the client as well as any limitations that are to be placed upon the counseling relationship. The practicum counselor is supposedly the expert in the counseling process. The client has the right to expect and the practicum counselor the responsibility to provide guidelines as to what the counseling process will be.

2. Professional behavior--the practicum counselor has the responsibility to his or her client to subscribe to and participate within the framework of a professional code of ethics.

3. Confidentiality--the student counselor has the responsibility of maintaining confidentiality regarding his or her clients and informing the client of any potential breach of this confidentiality.

4. To provide the best possible service--the most important of all practicum counselor responsibilities is to provide the best available service to his or her client.

Professional responsibility assumes an internal framework and an internal enforcement. The practicum counselor is responsible to remain appraised of new professional information, techniques and community resources available for referral. Professional responsibility needs to be maintained by self discipline and self responsibility and not dependent upon or subscription to responsible behaviors toward the client.

Included in this chapter is a variety of materials which can be of benefit to practicum supervisors and student counselors in their work with clients. An example of a clarifying letter to parents describing the role and functions of the school counselor is included in order that others who have to "sell" themselves to a school community might have a model from which to work.

The practicum counselor needs to be familiar with referral procedures. Included in this chapter is an article elaborating upon making referrals and also presented is a referral form. Termination reports and case folders also are described in order to help the practicum supervisor and student counselor work more efficiently with each client--the all important client.

INSTRUMENTS FOR DETERMINING EXPECTATIONS
AND EFFECTIVENESS IN COUNSELING

Joseph W. Hollis*

Effectiveness in counseling has been determined for years by examining the counseling techniques used and the counselor's behavior. Practicum programs in counseling use rating sheets which are completed by supervisors, peers, or panel of experts. The ratings have been made by observing and hearing the counseling processes either directly or by means of video tape, listening to audio tapes, or reading transcriptions of the counseling processes. The rating sheets primarily have focused attention on the counselor and what the counselor does. Only minimal attention has been focused on the client's expectations and whether or not the expectations have been fulfilled.

The first question is "What are the areas in which counseling has been effective?" The answers have come from experts and from research. The answers not only identify areas but also identify techniques and philosophical bases which are most successful with different areas. With the information available and, if applied, the counselor would be able to tell a client whether or not the expectations (outcomes) from counseling were within the scope of the counselor's competencies. To provide the client with that kind of information, the counselor needs: first, to be able to determine the client's expectations; second, to know the counselor's counseling competencies.

The Client Expectancy Inventory[1] (CEI) developed by Thro and Hollis was designed to measure the client's expectations at or near the beginning of counseling. The scoring keys permit determining expectations within the cognitive and affective domains separately or by four separate diagnostic scales including personal-social, vocational, information utilization, and internal reorganization.

Since many clients come to counseling by their own choice and since they attend with the expectations of certain outcomes, one measurement of counseling effectiveness would be the extent to which the client's expectations were fulfilled. The Inventory of Fulfillment of Client Expectancy[2] (IFCE) is designed to measure extent of satisfaction in the cognitive and affective domains separately or in the diagnostic scales.

The CEI and IFCE can be used independently or in conjunction with one another. The client's time needed to take the inventories is approximately twenty-five minutes each. Scoring time is five minutes or less and the results can be discussed with the client immediately.

---

*Dr. Joseph W. Hollis is Director of Doctoral Program in Counseling and Guidance and Professor of Psychology-Counseling, Ball State University. Original material prepared for this publication.

[1]Client Expectancy Inventory, Ernest G. Thro and Joseph W. Hollis, Accelerated Development Inc., P. O. Box 667, Muncie, IN 47305.

[2]Inventory of Fulfillment of Client Expectancy, Ernest G. Thro and Joseph W. Hollis, Accelerated Development Inc., P. O. Box 667, Muncie, IN 47305.

EXAMPLE OF A CLARIFYING LETTER TO PARENTS*

DIRECTIONS: The following letter is an example of a letter sent to parents by an elementary school counselor early in the school year. The letter is presented to illustrate what might be done rather than to be used as is.

If used, the letter is to be duplicated (mimeographed, offset, or printed) on letterhead stationery.

September, 19__

Dear Parents:

During the school year as in this past summer, _____ School will have the services of a full-time counselor just as junior and senior high schools have had these services in the past. In the future more and more elementary schools will be served by a counselor, but now _____ is the only school with the services of a full-time elementary school counselor. Parents and students are encouraged to make use of the counselor's services.

Many parents may wonder what the work of an elementary school counselor might be. The counselor's job is to work with teachers, social worker, principal, school nurse, and other school personnel to help the child better understand self and the world around him or her. The counselor is interested especially in working with parents as they encourage and guide their growing children. Of course, the counselor talks and works with individual pupils, too. The counselor is a person who has had experience as a teacher and also has received special training in helping children to understand themselves better. The counselor does not punish children but is concerned with helping those who may be in trouble. Contrary to some thinking, the principal work is not with "bad children" or "troublemakers," but the concern is with each and every child in school because each child, no matter who, sometimes needs help with school studies, in trying to decide what to do with his or her life, or in living a worthwhile and happy life. Every person, too, must make a great number of decisions about different things, and one of the principal jobs of the counselor is to help the child make decisions regarding present behavior and potential alternatives. The use of play materials such as clay, magic markers and many other materials becomes a natural part of many of the contacts with the children. Children communicate well in play and these play materials help them to communicate much that they are unable to say in words.

As you may see now, I am here to work with you in a special way. I realize how difficult it is to rear children and to help them as they grow and work in school. I do not feel that I know all the answers, but I am willing to help you find possible ways of working with your children. I am especially willing to help you understand better the things your children are doing in school.

I would enjoy meeting and working with each and every parent. It would be a pleasure to talk with you about the pleasant experiences and/or the concerns you have with your growing child. I am sure I will continue to enjoy working with you and your children.

Sincerely,

Dennis Rumfelt
Counselor

---

*This letter was prepared by Dennis Rumfelt, Elementary School Counselor, Goshen, Indiana. Printed by permission.

EXAMPLE OF A COUNSELEE RELEASE FORM
(To be used with counselees 18 years of age or older)

My signature below indicates that I understand that the counseling service is designed to help me help myself as I make vocational plans, educational plans, and various other adjustments. I further understand that the counseling service will be rendered by graduate students under competent supervision, that portions of sessions may be recorded and observed for educational purposes, and that all relationships with the counselors and supervisors will be kept confidential.

SIGNATURE_____

LOCAL ADDRESS_____

PHONE_____ DATE_____

NATURE OF PROBLEM_____

_____

_____

EXAMPLE OF A PARENT RELEASE FORM
(To be used with counselees under 18 years of age)

My son/daughter _____ has my permission to participate in counseling sessions to be conducted in conjunction with the counselor training program at _____ (Name of University). I understand that

1. The counselor will be a graduate student working under the direct supervision of a qualified university professor.

2. Results of the interview will be made available, upon request, to both the counselee and the parents. The information may include interests, problems, study habits, and other helpful information.

3. All, or part of, the sessions may be temporarily recorded on audio or video tape or viewed on closed-circuit TV, but, at no time, will the individual's identity be disclosed to anyone but the interviewing counselor and supervisor.

4. Precaution will be taken to avoid personal embarrassment to my son/daughter or to us, the parents.

Date_____   Signed (Parent)_____

Date_____   Signed (Parent)_____

Date_____   Signed (Counselor)_____

EXAMPLE OF A FORM FOR THE RELEASE OF CONFIDENTIAL INFORMATION

Schools, colleges, employment agencies, employers, or parents often request information concerning an individual's visits to the Practicum Counseling Center. However, any decision on release of information is entirely up to the individual if 18 years of age or to the parents if under 18 years of age. Please check what you want us to do:

_____ 1. Test results may be released

_____ 2. Counselor's notes may be released.

_____ 3. I do not want information released to anyone. (State exceptions.)

_____
_____
_____
_____

_____ 4. I would like test results sent to the following:

_____
_____
_____
_____

_____ 5. Video or audio tapes (if any were recorded) may be used for instructional purposes by the Practicum Supervisor.

Date_____   Counselee_____
                                    (Signed)

The parents must also sign   Parent_____
if counselee is under 18   (Signed)
years of age.
                                Parent_____
                                          (Signed)

165

MAKING REFERRALS

Patsy A. Donn*

<u>The Attitude</u>

Learning when and how to make referrals is almost as important for the student counselor as learning to counsel. No counselor or therapist can be all things to all clients in all situations, and each counselor needs to learn this limitation at the beginning of a counseling career.

The student counselor or therapist often has difficulty accepting certain realistic conditions or limitations that necessitate making client referrals. For example, the practicum counselor may lack the experience and background necessary to work with a severely disturbed client or the student counselor may be embroiled in a debilitating counter transference that necessitates a referral. The student counselor should make a referral when he or she feels a presenting problem would be served better by another counselor with more expertise and with a knowledge of techniques that seem indicated.

A client may be referred to another counselor, intra-professional referral. The counselor may be within the same practicum course, within the practicum site where the practicum counselor is holding the practicum counseling sessions, or in a different agency. In addition, the student counselor frequently will need to make inter-professional referrals for various reasons--to a physician for medical reasons or a psychometrist for diagnostic evaluation.

The practicum counselor, as well as the experienced one, might do well to accept the likelihood that he or she cannot save the whole of suffering humanity single-handedly. If the student counselor accepts this likelihood along with the knowledge that he or she cannot serve all clients equally well, nor help some clients at all, then he or she will be open to making appropriate referrals.

The most discouraging part of making referrals is the paucity of referral sources. The student counselor may be shocked by the lack of referral sources for clients who have no financial resources to pay for the service. This situation is particularly true in smaller communities. Most large communities have community agencies, such as child and adult mental health clinics, as well as mental health practitioners in private practice. As a rule, mental health

---

*Dr. Patsy A. Donn is Professor and Chairperson, Department of Counseling Psychology and Guidance Services, Ball State University. Original material prepared for this publication.

associations in larger communities coordinate and publish directories containing basic information about agencies in their area. Every counselor and clinician should obtain and use such directories in making referrals. In addition to using published directories and materials, the practicum counselor should attempt to learn about referral agencies and resources through professional colleagues and associations. In the process of getting to know colleagues, people in related professions and the community, the student counselor will develop his or her own "directory" of people and places for making referrals.

The Mechanics of Making Referrals

The mechanics of making referrals are the practicum counselor's responsibility. The procedure for obtaining persmission to refer will vary from one school or agency to another. The practicum counselor must follow the procedures of the setting and those of the college or university supervisor. In addition, the practicum counselor has the responsibility to do the following:

1. Determine when a referral is necessary and what purposes will be served.
2. Discuss the referral with the client, since any referral is a mutual decision.
3. Identify and validate the agency or person to whom the referral is being made.
4. Personally make the initial contact with the referral person or agency in the process of facilitating the referral.
5. Obtain a signed "Release of Information" form from the client.
6. Prepare a written report for the person or agency to whom the referral is made.

Referral to Physician

Many psychological problems are accompanied by physiological problems. The practicum counselor always is to be alert for somatic difficulties. If even the possibility exists that a physical condition may be causing or relating to the psychological problem, then a referral is to be made for a complete physical work-up.

The physician to whom the referral is made probably will request a report. ". . . the content of the report will depend on the purpose of the referral and the sophistication of the person to whom the referral is being made (Hollis and Donn, 1973, p. 181)." A suggested content outline is provided by Hollis and Donn (1973, p. 182) and includes the following:

>Name and Demographic Data on the Person
>
>Purpose(s) for Referral
>
>>"Why are you referring this person to me?"

Previous Treatment by Referring Person

"What have you done with the client while working with him or her?"

Biographical Data

Past Medical and/or Psychological Data

Client's Problem

"Detail narrative as to what the client's problem is and whether or not the client is or has been on medication for the problem."

Referral for Psychometric Work-Up

The practicum counselor's competencies for administering, scoring, interpreting, and utilizing tests probably will vary from test to test. Standardized group tests which are frequently taught in tests and measurement courses may be known while the projective and other diagnostic tests may be less well known. Each practicum counselor may have need for psychometric instruments with some clients and the evaluation tools which would be most helpful may be ones in which the practicum counselor does not have sufficient skills. In such cases, a referral for psychometric work-up would be advisable. The procedure will depend upon the school or agency in which the counseling is being done. Regardless of whether the referral is made to a peer practicum counselor, a psychometrist or psychologist within the school or agency setting, or another professional person outside of the setting, a referral form or letter is to be prepared. The contents and format will vary. Many counseling centers use a checklist of tests (Hollis and Donn, 1973, p. 186) on which the specific tests requested can be marked. The checklist may be accompanied by a referral letter.

Reference

Hollis, Joseph W., and Patsy A. Donn. Psychological Report Writing: Theory and Practice. Accelerated Development Inc., Muncie, Indiana, 1973.

REFERRAL FORM

DIRECTIONS: Complete the following information for the person to whom the referral is being made.

Date_____

To: _____
    Name of person to whom referral is made

    _____
    Address or Agency

    _____

(Complete Reverse Side)

Form #10 p.1 of 2 pp.

Name of person being referred _____

Address _____

_____

_____

Sex: _____ Age: _____ Birth Date: _____

Parents name if needed _____

_____

The reason for the referral is as follows: (Briefly describe the problem.)

A report is _____ or is not _____ needed from you.
If needed, please supply the following:

Referred by: Name _____

Title _____

Telephone Number _____ Address _____

_____

Form #10 p.2 of 2 pp.

REFERRAL FORM

DIRECTIONS: Complete the following information for the person to whom the referral is being made.

Date_____

To: _____
     Name of person to whom referral is made

     _____
     Address or Agency

     _____

     _____

(Complete Reverse Side)

Form #10 p.1 of 2 pp.

Name of person being referred _____

Address _____
_____
_____

Sex: _____   Age: _____   Birth Date: _____

Parents name if needed _____
_____

The reason for the referral is as follows: (Briefly describe the problem.)

A report is _____ or is not _____ needed from you.
If needed, please supply the following:

        Referred by: Name_____
              Title_____

Telephone Number_____ Address_____
                _____

Form #10 p.2 of 2 pp.

REFERRAL FORM

DIRECTIONS: Complete the following information for the person to whom the referral is being made.

Date _____

To: _____
      Name of person to whom referral is made

    _____
      Address or Agency

    _____

    _____

(Complete Reverse Side)

Form #10 p.1 of 2 pp.

Name of person being referred _____

Address _____

_____

_____

Sex: _____ Age: _____ Birth Date: _____

Parents name if needed_____

_____

The reason for the referral is as follows: (Briefly describe the problem.)

A report is _____ or is not _____ needed from you.
If needed, please supply the following:

                       Referred by: Name_____

                                    Title_____

        Telephone Number_____ Address_____

                                                 _____

REFERRAL FORM

DIRECTIONS: Complete the following information for the person to whom the referral is being made.

Date _____

To: _____
      Name of person to whom referral is made

   _____
      Address or Agency

   _____

   _____

(Complete Reverse Side)

Form #10 p.1 of 2 pp.

Name of person being referred _____

Address _____
_____
_____

Sex: _____   Age: _____   Birth Date: _____

Parents name if needed _____
_____

The reason for the referral is as follows: (Briefly describe the problem.)

A report is _____ or is not _____ needed from you.
If needed, please supply the following:

                        Referred by: Name_____
                                      Title_____
        Telephone Number_____ Address_____
                                      _____

Form #10 p.2 of 2 pp.

TERMINATION REPORT   CONFIDENTIAL

DIRECTIONS: The practicum counselor is to complete the following at the time of termination of
             counseling with each client. The report is to be filed in the folder maintained
             regarding the client.

I.   IDENTIFYING DATA

     Counselee Name_____ Age_____ Sex_____

     Address_____

     Agency or School Where Counselee Has Been Seen_____

     Additional background information deemed pertinent_____

     _____

     _____

II. NUMBER OF INTERVIEW

     Total number of times client was seen including intake_____

     Average length of each interview_____ Total time spent with this counselee_____

     Dates on which interviews were conducted:

     1. Intake_____   4. _____   7. _____   10. _____
     2. _____   5. _____   8. _____   11. _____
     3. _____   6. _____   9. _____   12. _____

III. PROBLEMS REVEALED IN COUNSELING

     Include the presenting problem or problems, subsequent concerns presented by the coun-
     selee, and the reason for termination; a brief sequence of the context of counseling;
     and a summary of tests used and their results if administered.

                                                                    Form #11 p.1 of 2 pp.

IV. SUMMARY

Synthesize a brief summary statement about the counselee and the contacts made by your school or agency. This paragraph should combine the most pertinent data as stated in the preceding material.

V. RECOMMENDATIONS

State recommendations as to the present and future status of the counselee. An example of a recommendation could be in terms of stating what experiences, if any, might be useful to the counselee in the future.

Signed_____ Date_____

Name Typed_____ Position_____

Address_____ _____

Form #11 p.2 of 2 pp.

TERMINATION REPORT   CONFIDENTIAL

DIRECTIONS: The practicum counselor is to complete the following at the time of termination of counseling with each client. The report is to be filed in the folder maintained regarding the client.

I. IDENTIFYING DATA

   Counselee Name_____ Age____ Sex_____

   Address_____

   Agency or School Where Counselee Has Been Seen_____

   Additional background information deemed pertinent_____
   _____
   _____

II. NUMBER OF INTERVIEW

   Total number of times client was seen including intake_____

   Average length of each interview_____ Total time spent with this counselee_____

   Dates on which interviews were conducted:

   1. Intake_____   4. _____   7. _____   10. _____
   2. _____   5. _____   8. _____   11. _____
   3. _____   6. _____   9. _____   12. _____

III. PROBLEMS REVEALED IN COUNSELING

   Include the presenting problem or problems, subsequent concerns presented by the counselee, and the reason for termination; a brief sequence of the context of counseling; and a summary of tests used and their results if administered.

Form #11 p.1 of 2 pp.

IV. SUMMARY

   Synthesize a brief summary statement about the counselee and the contacts made by your school or agency. This paragraph should combine the most pertinent data as stated in the preceding material.

V. RECOMMENDATIONS

   State recommendations as to the present and future status of the counselee. An example of a recommendation could be in terms of stating what experiences, if any, might be useful to the counselee in the future.

Signed_____   Date_____

Name Typed_____   Position_____

Address_____   _____

Form #11 p.2 of 2 pp.

TERMINATION REPORT   CONFIDENTIAL

DIRECTIONS: The practicum counselor is to complete the following at the time of termination of counseling with each client. The report is to be filed in the folder maintained regarding the client.

I. IDENTIFYING DATA

   Counselee Name_____ Age____ Sex_____

   Address_____

   Agency or School Where Counselee Has Been Seen_____

   Additional background information deemed pertinent_____
   _____
   _____

II. NUMBER OF INTERVIEW

   Total number of times client was seen including intake_____

   Average length of each interview_____ Total time spent with this counselee_____

   Dates on which interviews were conducted:

   1. Intake_____   4. _____   7. _____   10. _____
   2. _____   5. _____   8. _____   11. _____
   3. _____   6. _____   9. _____   12. _____

III. PROBLEMS REVEALED IN COUNSELING

   Include the presenting problem or problems, subsequent concerns presented by the counselee, and the reason for termination; a brief sequence of the context of counseling; and a summary of tests used and their results if administered.

Form #11 p.1 of 2 pp.

IV. SUMMARY

Synthesize a brief summary statement about the counselee and the contacts made by your school or agency. This paragraph should combine the most pertinent data as stated in the preceding material.

V. RECOMMENDATIONS

State recommendations as to the present and future status of the counselee. An example of a recommendation could be in terms of stating what experiences, if any, might be useful to the counselee in the future.

Signed_____   Date_____

Name Typed_____   Position_____

Address_____   _____

Form #11 p.2 of 2 pp.

TERMINATION REPORT   CONFIDENTIAL

DIRECTIONS: The practicum counselor is to complete the following at the time of termination of
              counseling with each client. The report is to be filed in the folder maintained
              regarding the client.

I. IDENTIFYING DATA

   Counselee Name_____ Age____ Sex_____

   Address_____

   Agency or School Where Counselee Has Been Seen_____

   Additional background information deemed pertinent_____

   _____

   _____

II. NUMBER OF INTERVIEW

   Total number of times client was seen including intake_____

   Average length of each interview_____   Total time spent with this counselee_____

   Dates on which interviews were conducted:

   1. Intake_____   4. _____   7. _____   10. _____
   2. _____   5. _____   8. _____   11. _____
   3. _____   6. _____   9. _____   12. _____

III. PROBLEMS REVEALED IN COUNSELING

   Include the presenting problem or problems, subsequent concerns presented by the counselee, and the reason for termination; a brief sequence of the context of counseling;
   and a summary of tests used and their results if administered.

Form #11 p.1 of 2 pp.

IV. SUMMARY

Synthesize a brief summary statement about the counselee and the contacts made by your school or agency. This paragraph should combine the most pertinent data as stated in the preceding material.

V. RECOMMENDATIONS

State recommendations as to the present and future status of the counselee. An example of a recommendation could be in terms of stating what experiences, if any, might be useful to the counselee in the future.

Signed_____   Date_____

Name Typed_____   Position_____

Address_____   _____

Form #11 p.2 of 2 pp.

TERMINATION REPORT   CONFIDENTIAL

DIRECTIONS: The practicum counselor is to complete the following at the time of termination of counseling with each client. The report is to be filed in the folder maintained regarding the client.

I. IDENTIFYING DATA

   Counselee Name_____ Age____ Sex_____

   Address_____

   Agency or School Where Counselee Has Been Seen_____

   Additional background information deemed pertinent_____
   _____
   _____

II. NUMBER OF INTERVIEW

   Total number of times client was seen including intake_____

   Average length of each interview_____ Total time spent with this counselee_____

   Dates on which interviews were conducted:

   1. Intake_____   4. _____   7. _____   10. _____
   2. _____   5. _____   8. _____   11. _____
   3. _____   6. _____   9. _____   12. _____

III. PROBLEMS REVEALED IN COUNSELING

   Include the presenting problem or problems, subsequent concerns presented by the counselee, and the reason for termination; a brief sequence of the context of counseling; and a summary of tests used and their results if administered.

Form #11 p.1 of 2 pp.

IV. SUMMARY

Synthesize a brief summary statement about the counselee and the contacts made by your school or agency. This paragraph should combine the most pertinent data as stated in the preceding material.

V. RECOMMENDATIONS

State recommendations as to the present and future status of the counselee. An example of a recommendation could be in terms of stating what experiences, if any, might be useful to the counselee in the future.

Signed_____   Date_____

Name Typed_____   Position_____

Address_____   _____

TERMINATION REPORT   CONFIDENTIAL

DIRECTIONS: The practicum counselor is to complete the following at the time of termination of counseling with each client. The report is to be filed in the folder maintained regarding the client.

I. IDENTIFYING DATA

   Counselee Name_____ Age____ Sex_____

   Address_____

   Agency or School Where Counselee Has Been Seen_____

   Additional background information deemed pertinent_____

   _____

   _____

II. NUMBER OF INTERVIEW

   Total number of times client was seen including intake_____

   Average length of each interview_____   Total time spent with this counselee_____

   Dates on which interviews were conducted:

   1. Intake_____   4. _____   7. _____   10. _____
   2. _____   5. _____   8. _____   11. _____
   3. _____   6. _____   9. _____   12. _____

III. PROBLEMS REVEALED IN COUNSELING

   Include the presenting problem or problems, subsequent concerns presented by the counselee, and the reason for termination; a brief sequence of the context of counseling; and a summary of tests used and their results if administered.

Form #11 p.1 of 2 pp.

IV. SUMMARY

   Synthesize a brief summary statement about the counselee and the contacts made by your school or agency. This paragraph should combine the most pertinent data as stated in the preceding material.

V. RECOMMENDATIONS

   State recommendations as to the present and future status of the counselee. An example of a recommendation could be in terms of stating what experiences, if any, might be useful to the counselee in the future.

Signed_____   Date_____

Name Typed_____   Position_____

Address_____   _____

Form #11 p.2 of 2 pp.

TERMINATION REPORT   CONFIDENTIAL

DIRECTIONS: The practicum counselor is to complete the following at the time of termination of counseling with each client. The report is to be filed in the folder maintained regarding the client.

I. IDENTIFYING DATA

   Counselee Name_____ Age____ Sex_____

   Address_____

   Agency or School Where Counselee Has Been Seen_____

   Additional background information deemed pertinent_____

   _____

   _____

II. NUMBER OF INTERVIEW

   Total number of times client was seen including intake_____

   Average length of each interview_____ Total time spent with this counselee_____

   Dates on which interviews were conducted:

   1. Intake_____   4. _____   7. _____   10. _____
   2. _____   5. _____   8. _____   11. _____
   3. _____   6. _____   9. _____   12. _____

III. PROBLEMS REVEALED IN COUNSELING

   Include the presenting problem or problems, subsequent concerns presented by the counselee, and the reason for termination; a brief sequence of the context of counseling; and a summary of tests used and their results if administered.

Form #11 p.1 of 2 pp.

IV. SUMMARY

   Synthesize a brief summary statement about the counselee and the contacts made by your school or agency. This paragraph should combine the most pertinent data as stated in the preceding material.

V. RECOMMENDATIONS

   State recommendations as to the present and future status of the counselee. An example of a recommendation could be in terms of stating what experiences, if any, might be useful to the counselee in the future.

Signed_____ Date_____

Name Typed_____ Position_____

Address_____ _____

Form #11 p.2 of 2 pp.

TERMINATION REPORT   CONFIDENTIAL

DIRECTIONS: The practicum counselor is to complete the following at the time of termination of counseling with each client. The report is to be filed in the folder maintained regarding the client.

I. IDENTIFYING DATA

   Counselee Name_____ Age____ Sex_____

   Address_____

   Agency or School Where Counselee Has Been Seen_____

   Additional background information deemed pertinent_____
   _____
   _____

II. NUMBER OF INTERVIEW

   Total number of times client was seen including intake_____

   Average length of each interview_____ Total time spent with this counselee_____

   Dates on which interviews were conducted:

   1. Intake_____   4. _____   7. _____   10. _____
   2. _____   5. _____   8. _____   11. _____
   3. _____   6. _____   9. _____   12. _____

III. PROBLEMS REVEALED IN COUNSELING

   Include the presenting problem or problems, subsequent concerns presented by the counselee, and the reason for termination; a brief sequence of the context of counseling; and a summary of tests used and their results if administered.

Form #11 p.1 of 2 pp.

IV. SUMMARY

Synthesize a brief summary statement about the counselee and the contacts made by your school or agency. This paragraph should combine the most pertinent data as stated in the preceding material.

V. RECOMMENDATIONS

State recommendations as to the present and future status of the counselee. An example of a recommendation could be in terms of stating what experiences, if any, might be useful to the counselee in the future.

Signed_____ Date_____

Name Typed_____ Position_____

Address_____ _____

Form #11 p.2 of 2 pp.

TERMINATION REPORT   CONFIDENTIAL

DIRECTIONS: The practicum counselor is to complete the following at the time of termination of counseling with each client. The report is to be filed in the folder maintained regarding the client.

I. IDENTIFYING DATA

   Counselee Name_____ Age____ Sex_____

   Address_____

   Agency or School Where Counselee Has Been Seen_____

   Additional background information deemed pertinent_____
   _____
   _____

II. NUMBER OF INTERVIEW

   Total number of times client was seen including intake_____

   Average length of each interview_____ Total time spent with this counselee_____

   Dates on which interviews were conducted:

   1. Intake_____   4. _____   7. _____   10. _____
   2. _____   5. _____   8. _____   11. _____
   3. _____   6. _____   9. _____   12. _____

III. PROBLEMS REVEALED IN COUNSELING

   Include the presenting problem or problems, subsequent concerns presented by the counselee, and the reason for termination; a brief sequence of the context of counseling; and a summary of tests used and their results if administered.

Form #11 p.1 of 2 pp.

IV. SUMMARY

Synthesize a brief summary statement about the counselee and the contacts made by your school or agency. This paragraph should combine the most pertinent data as stated in the preceding material.

V. RECOMMENDATIONS

State recommendations as to the present and future status of the counselee. An example of a recommendation could be in terms of stating what experiences, if any, might be useful to the counselee in the future.

Signed_____   Date_____

Name Typed_____   Position_____

Address_____   _____

Form #11 p.2 of 2 pp.

TERMINATION REPORT   CONFIDENTIAL

DIRECTIONS: The practicum counselor is to complete the following at the time of termination of counseling with each client. The report is to be filed in the folder maintained regarding the client.

I. IDENTIFYING DATA

   Counselee Name_____ Age____ Sex_____

   Address_____

   Agency or School Where Counselee Has Been Seen_____

   Additional background information deemed pertinent_____
   _____
   _____

II. NUMBER OF INTERVIEW

   Total number of times client was seen including intake_____

   Average length of each interview_____ Total time spent with this counselee_____

   Dates on which interviews were conducted:

   1. Intake_____   4. _____   7. _____   10. _____
   2. _____   5. _____   8. _____   11. _____
   3. _____   6. _____   9. _____   12. _____

III. PROBLEMS REVEALED IN COUNSELING

   Include the presenting problem or problems, subsequent concerns presented by the counselee, and the reason for termination; a brief sequence of the context of counseling; and a summary of tests used and their results if administered.

Form #11 p.1 of 2 pp.

IV. SUMMARY

Synthesize a brief summary statement about the counselee and the contacts made by your school or agency. This paragraph should combine the most pertinent data as stated in the preceding material.

V. RECOMMENDATIONS

State recommendations as to the present and future status of the counselee. An example of a recommendation could be in terms of stating what experiences, if any, might be useful to the counselee in the future.

Signed_____   Date_____

Name Typed_____   Position_____

Address_____   _____

Form #11 p.2 of 2 pp.

BUILDING FOLDER FOR EACH CLIENT

Joseph W. Hollis*

The practicum student probably will be responsible for contributing information to the file folder maintained by the agency or school in which the counseling sessions are held. The procedure will depend upon the policies of the agency or school. Each practicum student is to become well informed regarding kinds of information desired and kinds to be omitted, when and how information is to be added to the folder, and the security procedures to be followed.

Since the practicum course may have objectives in addition to those held by the agency or school in which counseling is done, a separate folder may be required for each client. The folder would be reviewed by the agency or school supervisor, the college or university supervisor, and the practicum counselor.

The purposes in practicum of a folder for each client may include any or all of the following:

1. To teach the practicum counselor how to build a folder for each client similar to what might be required on-the-job.

2. To provide a sequential collection of pertinent data applicable to the client, i.e., intake interview notes, release forms, correspondence with other agencies, referrals, test data and interpretations, counseling notes, and reports.

3. To enable the practicum counselor and supervisor(s) to review the progress made by the client and by the counselor.

4. To summarize the counseling activities which have been done by the counselor and the client, i.e., counseling techniques, homework, other persons involved such as the family members or other community agencies, and involvement in groups.

5. To encourage a dialogue with a record of the dialogue between the practicum counselor and the supervisor, i.e., critiques, suggestions, recommendations, and requests.

Form #12 entitled CHECK SHEET FOR CLIENT FOLDER is an illustration of a summary sheet for recording what is included in the file folder. One copy is placed in the front of each folder. As the practicum student completes an activity or form the date is recorded in the second column labeled "Completion Date."

---

*Dr. Joseph W. Hollis is Director of Doctoral Program in Counseling and Guidance and Professor of Psychology-Counseling, Ball State University. Original material written for this publication.

The date the form or report is submitted to the faculty for review is recorded in the third column entitled "Submitted (Date)." Thus, a record is kept of when an activity was performed in column two and when it was submitted in column three.

The date the material is reviewed by the faculty member and the faculty initials are recorded in columns four and five. The dates in columns two, three, and four (completion, submitted, and reviewed) can be very important data in reviewing the dialogue, timing of supervision, and appropriateness of feedback in terms of where a practicum counselor may be with a client. The faculty member may want to add comments during or following the review. Column six provides space for a word or phrase to be added or to place a check mark to indicate that comments have been written on the back (Form #12, p.2).

The first column entitled "Activity or Form" can provide a summary of the activities performed during the counseling sessions with a client. A review of several client folders could provide a means of determining the breadth of activities in which a practicum student was engaged during the counseling aspect of practicum.

CHECK SHEET FOR CLIENT FOLDER
Joseph W. Hollis*

One copy in each Case File

Counselor _____ Counselor No. ____

Client _____ M ___ F ___ Age ____ Client No. ____
Marital Status Single ____ Married ____ Separated ____ Divorced ____ Widowed ____
Number of Children Total ____ In home ____

Activity or Form	Completion Date	Submitted Date	Faculty Date	Reviewed Initials	Supervisor's Comments
Intake Form #8	___	___	___	___	(Check here. Record on back.)
Release Form Parents	___	___	___	___	
Client	___	___	___	___	
Tape(s) Session 1	___	___	___	___	___
2	___	___	___	___	___
3	___	___	___	___	___
4	___	___	___	___	___
5	___	___	___	___	___
6	___	___	___	___	___
Interview Notes Form #9 plus notes to supervisor Session 1	___	___	___	___	___
2	___	___	___	___	___
3	___	___	___	___	___
4	___	___	___	___	___
5	___	___	___	___	___
6	___	___	___	___	___
Copies of Test Answer Sheets	___	___	___	___	___
Copies of Test Interpretation	___	___	___	___	___
Inquiries (letters) to					
_____	___	___	___	___	___
_____	___	___	___	___	___
Reports to					
_____	___	___	___	___	___
_____	___	___	___	___	___
Other Activities or Forms					
_____	___	___	___	___	___
_____	___	___	___	___	___
Termination Form #11	___	___	___	___	___
Case Summary	___	___	___	___	___

*Dr. Joseph W. Hollis is Director of Doctoral Program in Counseling and Guidance and Professor of Psychology-Counseling, Ball State University. Printed by permission.

Form #12, p.1 of 2 pp.

Supervisor's Comments (Please date and sign each one):

Form #12, p.2 of 2 pp.

CHECK SHEET FOR CLIENT FOLDER
Joseph W. Hollis*

One copy in each Case File

Counselor _____ Counselor No. ____

Client _____ M ___ F ___ Age ____ Client No. ____
Marital Status Single ____ Married ____ Separated ____ Divorced ____ Widowed ____
Number of Children Total ____ In home ____

Activity or Form	Completion Date	Submitted Date	Faculty Reviewed Date	Initials	Supervisor's Comments
Intake Form #8	_____	_____	_____	_____	(Check here.
Release Form Parents	_____	_____	_____	_____	Record on
Client	_____	_____	_____	_____	back.)
Tape(s) Session 1 ..	_____	_____	_____	_____	_____
2 ..	_____	_____	_____	_____	_____
3 ..	_____	_____	_____	_____	_____
4 ..	_____	_____	_____	_____	_____
5 ..	_____	_____	_____	_____	_____
6 ..	_____	_____	_____	_____	_____
Interview Notes Session 1 ..	_____	_____	_____	_____	_____
Form #9 2 ..	_____	_____	_____	_____	_____
plus notes to 3 ..	_____	_____	_____	_____	_____
supervisor 4 ..	_____	_____	_____	_____	_____
5 ..	_____	_____	_____	_____	_____
6 ..	_____	_____	_____	_____	_____
Copies of Test Answer Sheets	_____	_____	_____	_____	_____
Copies of Test Interpretation	_____	_____	_____	_____	_____
Inquiries (letters) to					
_____	_____	_____	_____	_____	_____
_____	_____	_____	_____	_____	_____
Reports to					
_____	_____	_____	_____	_____	_____
_____	_____	_____	_____	_____	_____
Other Activities or Forms					
_____	_____	_____	_____	_____	_____
_____	_____	_____	_____	_____	_____
Termination Form #11	_____	_____	_____	_____	_____
Case Summary	_____	_____	_____	_____	_____

*Dr. Joseph W. Hollis is Director of Doctoral Program in Counseling and Guidance and Professor of Psychology-Counseling, Ball State University. Printed by permission.

Form #12, p.1 of 2 pp.

Supervisor's Comments (Please date and sign each one):

Form #12, p.2 of 2 pp.

CHECK SHEET FOR CLIENT FOLDER
Joseph W. Hollis*

One copy in each Case File

Counselor _____ Counselor No. ____

Client _____ M ___ F ___ Age ____ Client No. ____
Marital Status   Single ____ Married ____ Separated ____ Divorced ____ Widowed ____
Number of Children   Total _____   In home _____

Activity or Form	Completion Date	Submitted Date	Faculty Reviewed Date	Initials	Supervisor's Comments
Intake Form #8					(Check here. Record on back.)
Release Form Parents					
Client					
Tape(s) Session 1					
2					
3					
4					
5					
6					
Interview Notes Session 1					
Form #9 2					
plus notes to 3					
supervisor 4					
5					
6					
Copies of Test Answer Sheets					
Copies of Test Interpretation					
Inquiries (letters) to					
_____					
_____					
Reports to					
_____					
_____					
Other Activities or Forms					
_____					
Termination Form #11					
Case Summary					

---

*Dr. Joseph W. Hollis is Director of Doctoral Program in Counseling and Guidance and Professor of Psychology-Counseling, Ball State University. Printed by permission.

Form #12, p.1 of 2 pp.

Supervisor's Comments (Please date and sign each one):

CHECK SHEET FOR CLIENT FOLDER
Joseph W. Hollis*

One copy in each Case File

Counselor _____ Counselor No. ____

Client _____ M ___ F ___ Age ___ Client No. ____
Marital Status Single ___ Married ___ Separated ___ Divorced ___ Widowed ___
Number of Children Total ___ In home ___

Activity or Form	Completion Date	Submitted Date	Faculty Date	Reviewed Initials	Supervisor's Comments
Intake Form #8	_____	_____	_____	_____	(Check here. Record on back.)
Release Form Parents	_____	_____	_____	_____	
Client	_____	_____	_____	_____	
Tape(s) Session 1 ..	_____	_____	_____	_____	_____
2 ..	_____	_____	_____	_____	_____
3 ..	_____	_____	_____	_____	_____
4 ..	_____	_____	_____	_____	_____
5 ..	_____	_____	_____	_____	_____
6 ..	_____	_____	_____	_____	_____
Interview Notes Session 1 ..	_____	_____	_____	_____	_____
Form #9 2 ..	_____	_____	_____	_____	_____
plus notes to 3 ..	_____	_____	_____	_____	_____
supervisor 4 ..	_____	_____	_____	_____	_____
5 ..	_____	_____	_____	_____	_____
6 ..	_____	_____	_____	_____	_____
Copies of Test Answer Sheets	_____	_____	_____	_____	_____
Copies of Test Interpretation	_____	_____	_____	_____	_____
Inquiries (letters) to					
_____	_____	_____	_____	_____	_____
_____	_____	_____	_____	_____	_____
Reports to					
_____	_____	_____	_____	_____	_____
_____	_____	_____	_____	_____	_____
Other Activities or Forms					
_____	_____	_____	_____	_____	_____
_____	_____	_____	_____	_____	_____
Termination Form #11	_____	_____	_____	_____	_____
Case Summary	_____	_____	_____	_____	_____

*Dr. Joseph W. Hollis is Director of Doctoral Program in Counseling and Guidance and Professor of Psychology-Counseling, Ball State University. Printed by permission.

Form #12, p.1 of 2 pp.

Supervisor's Comments (Please date and sign each one):

Form #12, p.2 of 2 pp.

CHECK SHEET FOR CLIENT FOLDER
Joseph W. Hollis*

One copy in each Case File

Counselor _____ Counselor No. _____

Client _____ M___ F___ Age___ Client No. _____
Marital Status Single___ Married___ Separated___ Divorced___ Widowed___
Number of Children Total_____ In home_____

Activity or Form	Completion Date	Submitted Date	Faculty Date	Reviewed Initials	Supervisor's Comments
Intake Form #8	_____	_____	_____	_____	(Check here. Record on back.)
Release Form Parents	_____	_____	_____	_____	
Client	_____	_____	_____	_____	
Tape(s) Session 1 ..	_____	_____	_____	_____	_____
2 ..	_____	_____	_____	_____	_____
3 ..	_____	_____	_____	_____	_____
4 ..	_____	_____	_____	_____	_____
5 ..	_____	_____	_____	_____	_____
6 ..	_____	_____	_____	_____	_____
Interview Notes Session 1 ..	_____	_____	_____	_____	_____
Form #9 2 ..	_____	_____	_____	_____	_____
plus notes to 3 ..	_____	_____	_____	_____	_____
supervisor 4 ..	_____	_____	_____	_____	_____
5 ..	_____	_____	_____	_____	_____
6 ..	_____	_____	_____	_____	_____
Copies of Test Answer Sheets	_____	_____	_____	_____	_____
Copies of Test Interpretation	_____	_____	_____	_____	_____
Inquiries (letters) to					
_____	_____	_____	_____	_____	_____
_____	_____	_____	_____	_____	_____
Reports to					
_____	_____	_____	_____	_____	_____
_____	_____	_____	_____	_____	_____
Other Activities or Forms					
_____	_____	_____	_____	_____	_____
_____	_____	_____	_____	_____	_____
Termination Form #11	_____	_____	_____	_____	_____
Case Summary	_____	_____	_____	_____	_____

_____

*Dr. Joseph W. Hollis is Director of Doctoral Program in Counseling and Guidance and Professor of Psychology-Counseling, Ball State University. Printed by permission.

Form #12, p.1 of 2 pp.

Supervisor's Comments (Please date and sign each one):

Form #12, p.2 of 2 pp.

CHECK SHEET FOR CLIENT FOLDER
Joseph W. Hollis*

One copy in each Case File

Counselor _____ Counselor No. _____

Client _____ M___ F___ Age___ Client No.___
Marital Status Single___ Married___ Separated___ Divorced___ Widowed___
Number of Children Total_____ In home_____

Activity or Form	Completion Date	Submitted Date	Faculty Reviewed Date	Initials	Supervisor's Comments
Intake Form #8	____	____	____	____	(Check here.
Release Form Parents	____	____	____	____	Record on
Client	____	____	____	____	back.)
Tape(s) Session 1 ..	____	____	____	____	____
2 ..	____	____	____	____	____
3 ..	____	____	____	____	____
4 ..	____	____	____	____	____
5 ..	____	____	____	____	____
6 ..	____	____	____	____	____
Interview Notes Session 1 ..	____	____	____	____	____
Form #9 2 ..	____	____	____	____	____
plus notes to 3 ..	____	____	____	____	____
supervisor 4 ..	____	____	____	____	____
5 ..	____	____	____	____	____
6 ..	____	____	____	____	____
Copies of Test Answer Sheets	____	____	____	____	____
Copies of Test Interpretation	____	____	____	____	____

Inquiries (letters) to

_____ ..... ____ ____ ____ ____ ____

_____ ..... ____ ____ ____ ____ ____

Reports to

_____ ..... ____ ____ ____ ____ ____

_____ ..... ____ ____ ____ ____ ____

Other Activities or Forms

_____ ..... ____ ____ ____ ____ ____

_____ ..... ____ ____ ____ ____ ____

Termination Form #11 .... ____ ____ ____ ____ ____

Case Summary .... ____ ____ ____ ____ ____

---

*Dr. Joseph W. Hollis is Director of Doctoral Program in Counseling and Guidance and Professor of Psychology-Counseling, Ball State University. Printed by permission.

Form #12, p.1 of 2 pp.

Supervisor's Comments (Please date and sign each one):

Form #12, p.2 of 2 pp.

CHECK SHEET FOR CLIENT FOLDER
Joseph W. Hollis*

One copy in each Case File

Counselor _____ Counselor No. _____

Client _____ M ___ F ___ Age ___ Client No. ___
Marital Status Single ___ Married ___ Separated ___ Divorced ___ Widowed ___
Number of Children Total ___ In home ___

Activity or Form	Completion Date	Submitted Date	Faculty Date	Reviewed Initials	Supervisor's Comments
Intake Form #8					(Check here. Record on back.)
Release Form Parents					
Client					
Tape(s) Session 1					
2					
3					
4					
5					
6					
Interview Notes Session 1					
Form #9 2					
plus notes to 3					
supervisor 4					
5					
6					
Copies of Test Answer Sheets					
Copies of Test Interpretation					
Inquiries (letters) to					
_____					
_____					
Reports to					
_____					
_____					
Other Activities or Forms					
_____					
Termination Form #11					
Case Summary					

---

*Dr. Joseph W. Hollis is Director of Doctoral Program in Counseling and Guidance and Professor of Psychology-Counseling, Ball State University. Printed by permission.

Form #12, p.1 of 2 pp.

Supervisor's Comments (Please date and sign each one):

CHECK SHEET FOR CLIENT FOLDER
Joseph W. Hollis*

One copy in each Case File

Counselor _____ Counselor No. ____

Client _____ M ___ F ___ Age ___ Client No. ____
Marital Status Single ___ Married ___ Separated ___ Divorced ___ Widowed ___
Number of Children Total ___ In home ___

Activity or Form	Completion Date	Submitted Date	Faculty Reviewed Date	Initials	Supervisor's Comments
Intake Form #8	___	___	___	___	(Check here.
Release Form Parents	___	___	___	___	Record on
Client	___	___	___	___	back.)
Tape(s) Session 1 ..	___	___	___	___	___
2 ..	___	___	___	___	___
3 ..	___	___	___	___	___
4 ..	___	___	___	___	___
5 ..	___	___	___	___	___
6 ..	___	___	___	___	___
Interview Notes Session 1 ..	___	___	___	___	___
Form #9 2 ..	___	___	___	___	___
plus notes to 3 ..	___	___	___	___	___
supervisor 4 ..	___	___	___	___	___
5 ..	___	___	___	___	___
6 ..	___	___	___	___	___
Copies of Test Answer Sheets	___	___	___	___	___
Copies of Test Interpretation	___	___	___	___	___
Inquiries (letters) to					
_____	___	___	___	___	___
_____	___	___	___	___	___
Reports to					
_____	___	___	___	___	___
_____	___	___	___	___	___
Other Activities or Forms					
_____	___	___	___	___	___
_____	___	___	___	___	___
Termination Form #11	___	___	___	___	___
Case Summary	___	___	___	___	___

*Dr. Joseph W. Hollis is Director of Doctoral Program in Counseling and Guidance and Professor of Psychology-Counseling, Ball State University. Printed by permission.

Form #12, p.1 of 2 pp.

Supervisor's Comments (Please date and sign each one):

Form #12, p.2 of 2 pp.

CHECK SHEET FOR CLIENT FOLDER
Joseph W. Hollis*

One copy in each Case File

Counselor _____ Counselor No. ____

Client _____ M ___ F ___ Age ____ Client No. ____
Marital Status Single ____ Married ____ Separated ____ Divorced ____ Widowed ____
Number of Children Total ____ In home ____

Activity or Form	Completion Date	Submitted Date	Faculty Reviewed Date	Initials	Supervisor's Comments
Intake Form #8	____	____	____	____	(Check here.
Release Form Parents	____	____	____	____	Record on
Client	____	____	____	____	back.)
Tape(s) Session 1	____	____	____	____	____
2	____	____	____	____	____
3	____	____	____	____	____
4	____	____	____	____	____
5	____	____	____	____	____
6	____	____	____	____	____
Interview Notes Session 1	____	____	____	____	____
Form #9 2	____	____	____	____	____
plus notes to 3	____	____	____	____	____
supervisor 4	____	____	____	____	____
5	____	____	____	____	____
6	____	____	____	____	____
Copies of Test Answer Sheets	____	____	____	____	____
Copies of Test Interpretation	____	____	____	____	____

Inquiries (letters) to

_____ ____ ____ ____ ____ ____

_____ ____ ____ ____ ____ ____

Reports to

_____ ____ ____ ____ ____ ____

_____ ____ ____ ____ ____ ____

Other Activities or Forms

_____ ____ ____ ____ ____ ____

_____ ____ ____ ____ ____ ____

Termination Form #11 _____ ____ ____ ____ ____ ____

Case Summary _____ ____ ____ ____ ____ ____

---

*Dr. Joseph W. Hollis is Director of Doctoral Program in Counseling and Guidance and Professor of Psychology-Counseling, Ball State University. Printed by permission.

Form #12, p.1 of 2 pp.

Supervisor's Comments (Please date and sign each one):

Form #12, p.2 of 2 pp.

CHECK SHEET FOR CLIENT FOLDER
Joseph W. Hollis*

One copy in each Case File

Counselor _____ Counselor No. ____

Client _____ M ___ F ___ Age ___ Client No. ____
Marital Status   Single ___ Married ___ Separated ___ Divorced ___ Widowed ___
Number of Children   Total ___ In home ___

Activity or Form	Completion Date	Submitted Date	Faculty Date	Reviewed Initials	Supervisor's Comments
Intake Form #8	___	___	___	___	(Check here. Record on back.)
Release Form Parents	___	___	___	___	
Client	___	___	___	___	
Tape(s) Session 1	___	___	___	___	___
2	___	___	___	___	___
3	___	___	___	___	___
4	___	___	___	___	___
5	___	___	___	___	___
6	___	___	___	___	___
Interview Notes Form #9 plus notes to supervisor Session 1	___	___	___	___	___
2	___	___	___	___	___
3	___	___	___	___	___
4	___	___	___	___	___
5	___	___	___	___	___
6	___	___	___	___	___
Copies of Test Answer Sheets	___	___	___	___	___
Copies of Test Interpretation	___	___	___	___	___
Inquiries (letters) to					
_____	___	___	___	___	___
_____	___	___	___	___	___
Reports to					
_____	___	___	___	___	___
_____	___	___	___	___	___
Other Activities or Forms					
_____	___	___	___	___	___
_____	___	___	___	___	___
Termination Form #11	___	___	___	___	___
Case Summary	___	___	___	___	___

*Dr. Joseph W. Hollis is Director of Doctoral Program in Counseling and Guidance and Professor of Psychology-Counseling, Ball State University. Printed by permission.

Form #12, p.1 of 2 pp.

Supervisor's Comments (Please date and sign each one):

Form #12, p.2 of 2 pp.

CHAPTER VI

TESTS, TEST INTERPRETATIONS AND THE COUNSELOR

The interpretation and use of tests in counseling can present major problems to the practicum counselor. No specific prescription can be presented to alleviate these concerns. Some student counselors have little or no training or understanding in the use of tests and often shy completely away from any use whatsoever. Other counseling students know far less than they may think they do and rapidly find themselves in over their heads.

Tests are not magic! They can help to answer questions you may have about specific clients and tests may help clients to obtain information about themselves.

An interesting phenomenon to remember is that test results only indicate the way an individual responded to given tests items and do not represent actual truth or fact. Therefore, the test results must be interpreted so as to communicate in terms of the client's needs. Clients often see in test results what they want to see or what they fear seeing. This perception is compounded by the common client misconception that the test has in some way magically tapped the "real person" no matter how they answered the test questions.

Most often tests compare an individual with a specific group of individuals. Therefore, the test must be administered in an identical manner to the individual as it was to the comparison groups. Having the skill to administer the test in the prescribed manner often requires the tester to have been trained in the administration of the specific test. Simply reading the directions and administering a test is not acceptable. The student counselor not trained extensively in testing is well advised to make referrals to psychometrists or others with extensive training in the use of psychological tests.

TEST SELECTION AND INTERPRETATION

Rather than a discussion of test selection for the practicum counselor, the appropriate discussion is what information tests can provide. Most important to this discussion is the concept of translating test information requests into specific questions. This questioning does not mean generalized questions such as "What is the youngster's personality like?" but rather questions like "Does he or she have the potential to do college level work?" From the specific questions which are to be answered, the test administrator can make accurate selection of tests. A frustrating experience to the psychometrist is to receive a testing request that indicates a desire only for a client to be tested without regard to questions to be answered by the testing.

Rather than selecting and utilizing tests because it "seems like the thing to do" or because the counselor has expertise with a given test, test selection must be made in regard to the specific question(s) that are to be answered. The counselor making a referral for psychometric work-up and supplying the specific questions to be answered need not be aware of the appropriateness of the tests selected assuming that the referral was to a competent professional person. If the counselor does make the choice to refer his or her client for testing, a request also should be made for the tester to provide an interpretation of the test results, not merely administer the tests.

Tests, then, can be perceived as structured interviews that allow for comparison of an individual to groups of people. Next to learning to translate desired information into specific questions, the most difficult dimension of testing for the counselor is the interpretation of test results to the counselee.

The major concept in test interpretation is not so much what you say as what the client hears you say or how the client interprets what you say. As with counseling, test interpretations require the interpreter to pay attention to the client's feelings and understanding. The client, not the test or the interpretation, is of most importance. The language or system of test interpretation is dictated by the ability of the client to understand. Thus the client's ability, personality, and emotional condition determine the interpretation language.

Since the purpose of the test interpretation is to help the client understand more about self, the primary emphasis needs to be upon the discrepancy between the client's perception and the results as obtained from the tests. Many tests other than personality tests lend themselves to the use of percentiles as an understandable mode of interpretation. A useful technique in this regard is the drawing of a line and dividing it into ten segments; asking the client to mark along the line where he or she thinks they would fall in comparison to other people regarding the specific dimension to be discussed. The interpretation then can be centered upon the discrepancy that exists.

The client needs to understand the actual factor that is being measured. An affirmative response to a counselor question such as "Do you know what I.Q. is?" does not assure client understanding of a complicated factor such as intelligence. The question of "What does that mean to you?" must be actively pursued rather than merely asked of the client. The client must be made aware of the flexibility and limitation of tests!

Many times testing, particularly projective testing, can provide "hunches" about the client. Such "hunches" usually are better pursued in a subsequent counseling session as opposed to a test interpretation session.

A number of aids are available to the counselor in regard to tests and testing. Most prominent of these is <u>The Mental Measurements Yearbook</u> edited by Buros. The book is updated often, contains information on nearly all tests in print in regard to statistical information, critiques, and pertinent research. The responsible practicum counselor should become familiar with <u>The Mental Measurements Yearbook</u> and should study the manual on each test used.

No matter what degree of expertise the counselor has in testing and test interpretation, regardless of decisions to test or refer, it is mandatory that tests not be given for just the sake of testing. Tests are tools, not magic materials, and although potentially helpful to the client and to the counseling process, not an end in themselves.

TEST SELECTION GUIDE

John A. Axelson[*]

Purpose of Measurement	Description
1) General Aptitude	Provides an estimate of an individual's ability to learn by requiring him to perform mental activities that are regarded as evidence of intelligence. Such tests emphasize knowledge of vocabulary and ability to reason. Some tests in this category yield a single total score and others yield separate scores based on both verbal and nonverbal questions.
2) Special Aptitudes	Used in estimating future success of a person in various occupations or further education. In general, characteristics of the person which are believed to be important for success on a job or in further education. Examples of these characteristics are: memory, spatial perception, word fluency, speed, and verbal reasoning. Combinations of these characteristics would be associated with such activities as mechanical, clerical, engineering, mathematics, drafting, dress designing, journalism, business, etc.
3) Achievement	Designed to determine the amount of progress made toward the attainment of a specified goal such as science, mathematics, English, reading, history, etc. Achievement tests are different from aptitude tests in that aptitude refers to the innate ability to achieve while achievement refers to the knowledge and skills that have been acquired. For example, finger dexterity, speed of perception, and spatial visualization are not taught but may be important in some subjects or jobs; skills in mathematics or reading are developed to different levels in the classroom.
4) Interests	Designed to permit a person to record in an organized manner his likes and dislikes, or preferences, in a number of different situations, such as a liking for occupations, choice between activities, or reactions to peculiarities of people. A person's choices then are compared with the choices previously made by successful people in the various occupations, such as physician, production manager, office worker, and sales manager. Or, an inventory may be scored to indicate a larger interest area, such as computational, persuasive, musical, or social service. An interest score is no indicator of the ability of the person, although a person may have a greater chance for success in work which he likes to do.
5) Personality	Designed to measure personal adjustment, to describe a person in terms of his personality traits, or to discover the nature of his problems.

---

[*]Dr. John A. Axelson is Director, Counseling Laboratory, Northern Illinois University. Printed by permission.

TEST USE AND INTERPRETATION

John P. McGowan[*]

A. Develop short, clear, concise methods of <u>describing</u> to the client the purpose of the test he has taken and the meanings of the results--get this out of the way before you begin the interpretation of actual test scores--then, you can concentrate on <u>reactions</u> to the actual test scores rather than to run the risk of being trapped into a technical discussion of the purpose of the test, its construction, etc., during the interpretation period.

B. Make test data meaningful in terms of the <u>client's behavior</u>--make the transfer from the test score to the client's behavior. Ask yourself the following questions: "What does the score mean in terms of client behavior?" and, "How can I express the scores to him/her in such a way that he/she can relate them to his/her past, present, and anticipated future behavior?"

C. Do not become <u>over-identified</u> with the client's test scores. The test scores are his/her, not yours. Present test material in such a way that the client can question it, discuss it, reject it, or accept it, without having to reject or accept you by doing so.

D. Know how you <u>perform yourself</u> on objective tests and try to work out, as best you can, a reasonable acceptance of your own test scores. Generally, this will mean you are able to work with test scores and to interpret them objectively to clients. If you think test scores are either "very good" or "no good," you will be communicating this feeling in many ways to the clients with whom you are working. Avoid projecting your own subjective feelings into the objective tests that you are using.

---

[*]Dr. John P. McGowan is Professor and Provost, University of Missouri. Printed by permission.

TESTS AND TESTING

by

Jane and Edwin Duckworth*

Tests and testing can be of immense concern to the beginning practicum student. Such questions as, "How do I find out about a particular test?", "How do I interpret tests?", and "What are some of the ethical concerns about testing that I need to know?" are common. This article concerns answering these questions specifically, plus giving an annotated bibliography of books we have found especially helpful for students to use in the area of testing.

How to find out information about tests

The way to find information concerning tests depends upon the amount of time you have. If a client is coming in to see you in an hour or two, or even the next day, it would be difficult to do much investigation. However, some things can be done quickly that may help you.

1. Ask your practicum supervisor and/or another faculty member for help. In most psychology and counselor-education departments one or two people have expertise concerning a particular test. The major problem will be discovering who they are and if they are available. If you are doing your practicum work in a field setting (i.e., public school or mental health agency), persons familiar with tests may be available at the practicum site to assist you.

2. Ask a fellow practicum student for help. You may be amazed at the amount of expertise available from your fellow students. They may have been working with tests for years or at the very least be able to identify someone else you may ask for help.

3. Look for the test manual for the particular test you will be interpreting. These manuals are usually on file at the university or college where you are training. People to ask for assistance in finding the manual would be the secretary in the psychology or counselor-education department, the receptionist in the counseling center or the reference librarian in the library. Some libraries maintain a file of tests and manuals. You will find the test manual most useful for information on what the scores for the test mean, with what groups your client is being compared to

---

*Dr. Jane Duckworth is Assistant Professor of Psychology-Counseling, Ball State University. Dr. Edwin Duckworth is a counseling and clinical psychologist in private practice. Original material prepared for this publication.

derive his or her score, and the reliability and validity of the test. Even if you are in a field setting, if a test is used often, in all likelihood the manual will be on file.

4. Look in the Buros Mental Measurements Yearbook. This book is one of the most useful references regarding tests and testing. Besides general information about the test, two or more reviews concerning each test are provided by people with different points of views. In about 30 minutes you can gain a wealth of information about a test from experts in the field. A word of warning, however, the Mental Measurements Yearbook is published in new editions about every six years. The newer book does not always have every test in it since the test may have been reviewed adequately in an earlier edition; therefore, if you do not find the test you want in one edition, it most likely is reviewed in an earlier edition unless the test was published since the last edition of the Yearbook. Keep looking! This Yearbook is so useful that if you are going to be working extensively with tests, it would be worth your while to buy the current Yearbook or have your agency purchase it. A copy is typically found in college and university libraries, counseling centers, counselor-education departments, and psychology departments.

If you will be working with tests continually in your counseling work and have more time to look for information, then other things you can do to become an "expert" are the following:

1. One of the best things you can do is to take some courses in testing. A must is a general survey course usually called Tests and Measurements. You will learn about general testing terms, plus an overview of the different types of tests available. Once you have an overview, you may want to specialize in certain types of tests (i.e., personality, intelligence, or projectives). If you do, then further courses usually are available in these areas. If your particular school does not offer what you need, you may be able to get an extension or correspondence course from another school that would meet your needs.

2. If the particular courses needed are not available, many workshops are given around the country that might be helpful. For example, the Bender-Gestalt and Rorschach have been taught recently in a series of workshops. Some workshops have even been free. The MMPI (Minnesota Multiphasic Personality Inventory) is taught in a workshop

once a year through the University of Minnesota. Other similar workshops are available.

3. Belonging to the local psychometric organization is helpful. The organization may be associated with the state APGA or APA organization. Through these organizations you can discover what others are doing with tests and you can possibly get workshops started.

4. Information about particular tests may be obtained by writing to test publishers. They will usually inundate you with information and will sometimes put you on a mailing list, if they have one, for further information. One caution here is that the publisher usually presents the advantages of a test and generally tends to downplay the weaknesses and limitations.

5. Exhibits by test publishers at conventions are good places to browse. You can acquire much information by examining their materials and talking with the personnel on duty.

6. A professional library of your own may be started. If you cannot afford many books at the start, ask the agency director for which you work if he or she would be willing to make some purchases to keep available in the agency. At the end of this article is a short annotated bibliography of books we have found very useful to own. By asking colleagues and reviewing books they consider valuable, you soon will be able to identify the books you want to obtain for your professional library.

Interpreting the test(s) to a client

Many pitfalls are possible in interpreting. If you follow some of the directions and suggestions given in this section and also ask for help from your practicum supervisor and/or other faculty members, test interpretation can become a very therapeutic skill for you and a very useful adjunct to your counseling.

Before you start interpreting a test you should know it well. If the client should ask you a question about the test to which you don't know the answer, it is better to say you don't know but that you will try to find the answer rather than to try to bluff your way through.

Pre-Interpretation. Other information that would be useful to have before the interpretation would be the answers to such questions as the following:

1. Why was the test given (requested by the client, ordered by an agency or school, etc.?

2. What norms are being used in the interpretation? Phrasing the question in another way, to what group of people is your client being compared—people in general, high school seniors, college graduates, and so forth. The client's test score could change considerably according to the norming group being used. Also, if local norms are available, you will be able to indicate how your client compares to the people with whom the client comes in contact every day. Sometimes the local norms are appreciably higher or lower than the original norms of the test.

3. How old is the test data you are using for interpretation? Occasionally, you are asked to interpret tests that are over a year old. In this case, you may want to be more cautious in your interpretation because the client may have made some drastic changes since the test was given originally. For example, interest inventory results change quite rapidly between the ages of 15 and 25. Personality inventories similarly can be outdated by major changes in a person's life.

4. What does the client want to know about the test? By asking what the client expects to find out from a test, you can find the client's set toward the test and also misconceptions about it. Then, you will be better prepared to answer the client's questions and correct misconceptions.

5. What does the administration, school, teacher, or agency want the client to know about the test? In some settings you are not allowed to divulge certain information. You need an understanding of what your limitations are before you proceed with the interpretation.

Once you have the answers to the previous questions and to others that occur to you, you are better prepared to do the interpretations.

<u>Interpretation</u>. Some points to remember about interpretations which can help you to do a good job.

1. Interpret slowly and use simple language. Remember that the terms you use may not be familiar to the client; therefore, you will need to check with the person to see if he or she understands what you are saying. Phrase your interpretation in his/her language. If the client is a child, use simpler words than you would if the client is in college and has had some psychological background. A question which is helpful to ask yourself is "Would I have understood the interpretation before I became

a counselor?" In other words, are you interpreting the test in layman's language or in psychological jargon. Using examples which the client can easily understand to illustrate your interpretation is helpful.

2. Be kind and gentle in your interpretation. It helps to ask yourself a question, "Would I like to hear what I am saying (about this test)?" If you give positive information first and then the negative aspects of the test, the results are not so hard for the client to take.

3. If possible, use percentile ranks and ranges with the client to indicate where he/she scores on the test. People seem to understand percentages easier than they do other types of scores. However, with some tests you will not be able to use percentages, so read the manual thoroughly and understand exactly what the score you are interpreting means. The more knowledgeable you are about the scores, the easier for you to explain to the client in a way he/she will understand.

4. Your client needs to understand that the test is not infallible. You can foster this feeling by using such words as "probably means," "possibly means," "it looks like," "I wonder if," and "could it mean that (such and such is true)?" If you use generalities rather than words that designate specificity, you are safer and less likely to antagonize the client into rejecting the test altogether. If the client does dispute the test results, try to find out why he/she does. The client may have a very good reason!

5. In relation to the previous point, it is sometimes helpful to ask the client how he/she felt when he/she took the test (if he/she can remember). This information lets you know something about how valid the test is since it gives you an indication of the client's mood and frame of reference when answering it For some tests, this mood and frame of reference can be a vital to know in order to make an accurate interpretation.

6. After you are through interpreting if you have the time, ask the client to give you a brief summary of what he/she learned from the test. This information is your chance to check what has been remembered and to correct any misinterpretations that the client may have. Also, clients tend to remember test results better if they have to indicate what they mean to them.

7. If compatible with agency policy, you may want to give a copy of the test profile or results to the client to keep. If the client has given you an adequate summary of your interpretation of the test, providing a copy of the results may help the client remember the pertinent points. Also, the report can be reviewed later by the client when under less stress. To most clients, the test interpretation you do is an anxiety provoking experience. This anxiety means he/she may not be able to adequately absorb all the information you give at the test interpretation time. Having a copy can help the client do a better job of recalling information given during the test interpretation.

8. If you are counseling with a client as well as interpreting a test, then think of this test interpretation as a structured interview during which you can find out much information about the client. You can find out such items as how he/she handles negative and positive comments and how he/she relates to authority figures (you). This information can be very useful to incorporate into further counseling sessions and also into the test interpretation.

If all these do's and don'ts seem rather overwhelming to you and you are nervous about the whole test interpretation, a very helpful technique to use to reduce this anxiety and improve your interpretation skills is to role-play the test interpretation with a fellow practicum or willing friend. Select a person who does not know the test you are going to interpret. This way the person with whom you are role playing can give you accurate feedback as to whether or not the test and the test results are understood from your interpretation, not from previous knowledge about it. If you tape record the role playing, you can then play it back at your leisure and discover rough points that need smoothing out. You also can tell where you did well and spend some time analyzing those times to see what you are doing right.

The ideal way to begin a test interpretation is to be calm and confident yourself, to be very supportive of the client and to know your test well!

Ethical points to remember

Tests should be treated as confidential material similar to case notes; therefore, test folders should not be left around your office where people can see them. Keep the folders in locked file cabinets when you are not in your office. The following are a few of the more important points on the ethics of testing.

Keep the information in the test folders confidential. Only certain specified personnel should have access to it, depending upon your agency's rules. Do not go beyond the rules. Be very conservative in how you use test information about clients with others, including your fellow counselors. It is especially dangerous to be discussing a case in an office when the door is open so that others such as secretaries or clients can hear you talking.

Find out to what outside agencies and people you must give client test information if they ask for it, such as courts, welfare departments, other schools, parents, government, and make sure the client realizes this fact if it may occur with this case. Obtain release forms from the client or parents if they are necessary.

Your professional ethical responsibility is to learn as much information as possible about the test you are going to be interpreting. You are responsible for many peoples' feelings and futures when you do interpretations even when you don't give the interpretation to the client directly, but rather report to another agency. It is incumbent upon you to keep up with the latest information in your area of testing and to be challenging yourself constantly to be better.

In conclusion then, remember tests are tools to be used to better understand the client Like all tools; tests can be misused by the inept craftsman and do much damage. In the hands of a skilled craftsman however tests can help the client to enjoy a more productive and fulfilling life.

References

Books

Buros, O. *Mental measurements yearbooks*, 3rd, 4th, 5th, 6th, and 7th eds. Highland Park, N. J.: Gryphon Press, 1949, 1953, 1959, 1965, 1975.

Buros, O. *Tests in print-two: an index to tests, tests reviews, and the literature on specific tests.* Highland Park, N. J.: Gryphon Press, 1974.

Campbell, D. *Handbook for the strong vocational interest blank.* Stanford, CA: Stanford University Press, 1971.

Dahlstrom, G., Welsh, L. and Dahlstrom, L. *The MMPI handbook: Vol. 1.* Minneapolis: University of Minnesota Press, 1972.

Duckworth, J. and Duckworth, E. *MMPI interpretation manual for counselors and clinicians.* Muncie, Indiana: Accelerated Development, Inc., 1974.

Freeman, L. *Theory and practice of psychological testing.* New York: Holt, Rinehart, Winston, 1973.

Goldman, L. Using tests in counseling. 2nd ed. New York: Appleton-Century-Crofts, 1971.

Koppitz, E. Bender gestalt test for young children. New York: Grune Stratton, 1963.

Journals

JOURNAL OF CLINICAL AND CONSULTING PSYCHOLOGY. Reports research done on the MMPI and other clinical tests.

JOURNAL OF COUNSELING PSYCHOLOGY. Reports research done with other current tests.

NOTES

CHAPTER VII

INFORMATION PROCESSING

Information processing is an important aspect of all counseling and psychotherapy. The student counselor will be involved not only in the usual information processing that occurs in counseling sessions and within the school or community agency but also in the information processing associated with the practicum course. Records and reports are important in any counseling center and equally so in a course.

One of the first tasks in practicum after identifying the setting where the counseling sessions will be held is to learn the procedures for information processing within the setting. Each school or agency has forms, procedures, and security regulations on information. The practices within that school or agency must be followed.

Another aspect of practicum is that each practicum counselor's tapes, reports, and records as well as actual counseling sessions will be observed and reviewed by others. The concern for the client always must be foremost; however, you as a practicum counselor must recognize the purpose of the practicum is also to assist you in your development. The observations and reviews of your information are for that end. Write your material so that it can be reviewed without harm to the client and with the purpose of obtaining feedback that may be helpful to the client and you.

New federal regulations may make your notes, records, and reports about an individual available to the person. Therefore, recognize that your notes probably are no longer "yours" alone. Therefore, perform under the assumption that the client has the rights to review and also that the client has the rights to a process for removal or revision of items which are inaccurate or potentially damaging. The objectivity statements of what was done or said may remain; however, these are often meaningless or easily misinterpreted unless supported with sufficient information to provide a realistic picture of the timing, setting, and conditions.

Counselors will be affected by a recent federal law which is one of the most controversial on record. The "Family Educational Rights and Privacy Act of 1974" has been designed to protect the rights of students of all ages from unfair evaluations placed confidentially into their files. Students under certain guidelines have access to academic records. This access to records will include comments by counselors, letters of recommendation, and teacher evaluations. If a student feels an injustice has been done, he or she can require a hearing to challenge any information which might be inaccurate or misleading.

In this chapter sections of Public Law 93-380 and the proposed changes are reproduced. A potential counselor or psychotherapist should be aware of the law, informed as to its content and have an understanding of the possible ramifications of the bill in relation to records kept by counselors. A review of the law and any changes in it plus a review of the procedures for the setting where you will do your practicum is recommended before you start counseling.

INFORMATION PROCESSES IN COUNSELING AND PSYCHOTHERAPY

Joseph W. Hollis*

Counseling necessitates not only information exchange between the client and counselor but also information processing internally by each. The more the information can be of significance to the client, the greater the potential for change during the counseling session(s). The kind of information depends upon the client's needs, the extent of development, and the situation.

Counselors gain information not only through what the client says but also how expressed. The change in speed with which spoken, the loudness or softness, and the inflection on words or phrases are important communicators of information. Often the client communicates more through how things are said than through what is said. The same may be true for what and how the counselor speaks.

Body language is another important means of information transmittal. The changes in body positions and when those changes occur are cues for the counselor and the client. When does the client have eye contact with you, the counselor? When do the tears come? In discussion of what topics do the muscles begin to be more tense or less tense? What happens just prior to major shifts in body position? At what times does the client pick, pull, or scrape at objects such as paper, edge of the desk, or hairs on own arm, head, or leg? All of these actions are communicators of information that the counselor can process for facilitating the counseling activities.

Information processing in counseling can enable client and counselor to increase effective counseling in all three domains--affective, cognitive, and psychomotor. The intrinsic information processing within, between and among the three domains is what counseling produces. The client gains a new self concept, "grasps" the feelings at the moment and under different conditions, examines attitudes, clarifies or formulates a value structure, and transfers those psychological "make-ups" into muscular (motor) action or modifications.

The information needed by the client may come during counseling by integrating intrinsically the bits of information that have been internally insulated from one another. Personal-social counseling and psychotherapy often involve assisting the client in re-examining

---

*Dr. Joseph W. Hollis is Director of the Doctoral Program in Counseling and Guidance and Professor of Psychology-Counseling, Ball State University. Original material prepared for this publication.

perceptions, concepts, and feelings and by so doing produce modifications in them. Many counseling and psychotherapeutic techniques are for those purposes.

At times the client's progress will depend upon having additional information from other sources. During practicum, the student counselor may use tests to facilitate the client gaining information about self. At other times, resource materials may be used either during the counseling session or as home work for the client. At still other times the client may consult with other persons, visit certain places, or have try-out experiences to gain the necessary information.

As can be deducted from the preceding statements, information is a tool of counseling and then information processing becomes an integral aspect of all counseling activities. The client and counselor integrate information during the counseling and psychotherapy.

A client may be confused or frustrated because of

- --lack of information and/or the lack of knowing where or how to obtain the information
- --integration of information, e.g., lack of having done the integration or the inability to do so
- --interpretation of information, e.g., failure to interpret, inability or know how to interpret, or misinterpret
- --implication of information, e.g., misunderstanding the implications, ignoring or not having the implications, inability to understand, or the lack of opportunity to gain an understanding of the implications.

Each student counselor or psychotherapist must consider how the client can be assisted through information processing during and between counseling sessions. The information processing must be intrinsic; however, the source of the information may be the counselor, other persons, places (businesses, industries, social settings, community agencies, schools, or various geographical areas), or resource materials. Obtaining information is of itself not sufficient. The integration, interpretation, analyzing implications, and transferring into action are essential in information processing and particularly so during the counseling sessions.

Knowledge alone does not produce change. Counselors and psychotherapists know that well; thus, they use the counseling sessions to enable clients to go beyond the knowledge or knowledge acquisition stage. Knowledge within the counseling sessions can be personalized and intrinsically processed by the client and as such can be the stimulus that initiates a subsequent action.

Facts from the rest of the world's point of view and facts as perceived by the client not only may be different but also may be in conflict. The differences in interpretation or perceptions may be because of difference in value structures that have developed over years as a result of various experiences. Thus, producing a change in the information processing by the client may in itself be a major aspect of the total counseling or psychotherapy. A change in self-concept may result in a change in intrinsic information processing.

Student Counselor's Functions

From a pragmatic point of view the student counselor or student psychotherapist may ask "What can I do to facilitate the information processing during practicum?" To answer straightforward in a minimum number of words will by necessity omit much that could and should be included. However, the following is a list which might be labelled The Least You Can Do Is--

--help client identify what's needed in working with his or her problem or concern

--help client identify resources for gaining pertinent information

--develop realistic approach for obtaining information from the resources that have been identified

--help client integrate related information

--assist client in gathering pertinent information prior to decision making

--identify situations and approaches for exploratory and try-out experiences that the client may utilize

--identify means for obtaining feedback from reality testing resulting from implementation of a tentative decision, exploration, or try-out

--assist client in evaluating and utilizing feedback

--facilitate intrinsic processing for value development, value clarification and attitude modification.

PROTECTION OF THE RIGHTS AND PRIVACY OF PARENTS AND STUDENTS[1]

Sec. 513
(a) Part C of the General Education Provisions Act is further amended by adding at the end thereof the following new section:

"PROTECTION OF THE RIGHTS AND PRIVACY OF PARENTS AND STUDENTS

"Sec. 438
(a)(1) No funds shall be made available under any applicable program to any State or local educational agency, any institution of higher education, any community college, any school, agency offering a preschool program, or any other educational institution which has a policy of denying, or which effectively prevents, the parents of students attending any school of such agency, or attending such institution of higher education, community college, school, preschool, or other educational institution, the right to inspect and review any and all official records, files, and data directly related to their children, including all material that is incorporated into each student's cumulative record folder, and intended for school use or to be available to parties outside the school or school system, and specifically including, but not necessarily limited to, identifying data, academic work completed, level of achievement (grades, standardized achievement test scores), attendance data, scores on standardized intelligence, aptitude, and psychological tests, interest inventory results, health data, family background information, teacher or counselor ratings and observations, and verified reports of serious or recurrent behavior patterns. Where such records or data include information on more than one student, the parents of any student shall be entitled to receive, or be informed of, that part of such record or data as pertains to their child. Each recipient shall establish appropriate procedures for the granting of a request by parents for access to their child's school records within a reasonable period of time, but in no case more than forty-five days after the request has been made.

"(2) Parents shall have an opportunity for a hearing to challenge the content of their child's school records, to insure that the records are not inaccurate, misleading, or otherwise in violation of the privacy or other rights of students, and to provide an opportunity for the correction or deletion of any such inaccurate, misleading, or otherwise inappropriate data contained therein.

"(b)(1) No funds shall be made available under any applicable program to any State or local educational agency, any institution of higher education, any community college, any school, agency offering a preschool program, or any other educational institution which has a policy of permitting the release of personally identifiable records or files (or personal information contained therein) of students without the written consent of their parents to any individual, agency, or organization, other than to the following--

"(A) other school officials, including teachers within the educational institution or local educational agency who have legitimate educational interests;

"(B) officials of other schools or school systems in which the student intends to enroll, upon condition that the student's parents be notified of the transfer, receive a copy of the record if desired, and have an opportunity for a hearing to challenge the content of the record;

"(C) authorized representatives of (i) the Comptroller General of the United States, (ii) the Secretary, (iii) an administrative head of an education agency (as defined in section 409 of this Act), or (iv) State educational authorities, under the conditions set forth in paragraph (3) of this subection; and

---

[1] Education Amendments of 1974, Statutes at Large, LXXXVIII, sec. 513-516, 571-575 (1974). (The sections of the Education Amendments of 1974, Public Law 93-380, 93rd Congress, H.R. 69, August 21, 1974, that apply most appropriately to counselors are known as Family Educational Rights and Privacy Act of 1974 /frequently referred to as Buckley Amendment/.)

"(D) in connection with a student's application for, or receipt of, financial aid.

"(2) No funds shall be made available under any applicable program to any State or local educational agency, any institution of higher education, any community college, any school, agency offering a preschool program, or any other educational institution which has a policy or practice of furnishing, in any form, any personally identifiable information contained in personal school records, to any persons other than those listed in subsection (b)(1) unless—

"(A) there is written consent from the student's parents specifying records to be released, the reasons for such release, and to whom, and with a copy of the records to be released to the student's parents and the student if desired by the parents, or

"(B) such information is furnished in compliance with judicial order, or pursuant to any lawfully issued subpoena, upon condition that parents and the students are notified of all such orders or subpoenas in advance of the compliance therewith by the educational institution or agency.

"(3) Nothing contained in this section shall preclude authorized representatives of (a) the Comptroller General of the United States, (B) the Secretary, (C) an administrative head of an education agency or (D) State educational authorities from having access to student or other records which may be necessary in connection with the audit and evaluation of Federally-supported education program, or in connection with the enforcement of the Federal legal requirements which relate to such programs: <u>Provided</u>, That, except when collection of personally identifiable data is specifically authorized by Federal law, any data collected by such officials with respect to individual students shall not include information (including social security numbers) which would permit the personal identification of such students or their parents after the data so obtained has been collected.

"(4) (A) With respect to subsections (c)(1) and (c)(2) and (c)(3), all persons, agencies, or organizations desiring access to the records of a student shall be required to sign a written form which shall be kept permanently with the file of the student, but only for inspection by the parents or student, indicating specifically the legitimate educational or other interest that each person, agency, or organization has in seeking this information. Such form shall be available to parents and to the school official responsible for record maintenance as a means of auditing the operation of the system.

"(B) With respect to this subsection, personal information shall only be transferred to a third party on the condition that such party will not permit any other party to have access to such information without the written consent of the parents of the student.

"(c) The Secretary shall adopt appropriate regulations to protect the rights of privacy of students and their families in connection with any surveys or data-gathering activities conducted, assisted, or authorized by the Secretary or an administrative head of an education agency. Regulations established under this subsection shall include provisions controlling the use, dissemination, and protection of such data. No survey or data-gathering activities shall be conducted by the Secretary, or an administrative head of an education agency under an applicable program, unless such activities are authorized by law.

"(d) For the purposes of this section, whenever a student has attained eighteen years of age, or is attending an institution of postsecondary education the permission or consent required of and the rights accorded to the parents of the student shall thereafter only be required of and accorded to the student.

"(e) No funds shall be made available under any applicable program unless the recipient of such funds informs the parents of students, or the students, if they are eighteen years of age or older, or are attending an institution of postsecondary education, of the rights accorded them in this section.

"(f) The Secretary, or an administrative head of an education agency, shall take appropriate actions to enforce provisions of this section and to deal with violations of this section, according to the provisions of this Act, except that action to terminate assistance may be taken only if the Secretary finds there has been a failure to comply with the provisions of this section, and he has determined that compliance canot be secured by voluntary means.

"(g) The Secretary shall establish or designate an office and review board within the Department of Health, Education, and Welfare for the purpose of investigating, processing, reviewing, and adjudicating violations of the provisions of this section and complaints which may be filed concerning alleged violations of this section, according to the procedures contained in sections 434 and 437 of this Act.".

/Sec. 513/
(b)(1)(i) The provisions of this section shall become effective ninety days after the date of enactment of section 438 of the General Education Provisions Act.

   (2)(i) This section may be cited as the "Family Educational Rights and Privacy Act of 1974".

PROTECTION OF PUPIL RIGHTS

Sec. 514
(a) Part C of the General Education Provisions Act is further amended by adding after section 438 the following new section:

"PROTECTION OF PUPIL RIGHTS

"Sec. 439. All instructional material, including teacher's manuals, films, tapes, or other supplementary instructional material which will be used in connection with any research or experimentation program or project shall be available for inspection by the parents or guardians of the children engaged in such program or project. For the purpose of this section 'research or experimentation program or project' means any program or project in any applicable program designed to explore or develop new or unproven teaching methods or techniques."

(b) The amendment made by subsection (a) shall be effective upon enactment of this Act.

LIMITATION ON WITHHOLDING OF FEDERAL FUNDS

Sec. 515
(a) Part C of the General Education Provisions Act is further amended by adding after section 439 the following new section:

"LIMITATION ON WITHHOLDING OF FEDERAL FUNDS

"Sec. 440. Except as provided in section 438(b)(1)(D) of this Act, the refusal of a State or local educational agency or institution of higher education, community college, school, agency offering a preschool program, or other educational institution to provide personally identifiable data on students or their families, as a part of any applicable program, to any Federal office, agency, department, or other third party, on the grounds that it constitutes a violation of the right to privacy and confidentiality of students or their parents, shall not constitute sufficient grounds for the suspension or termination of Federal assistance. Such a refusal shall also not constitute sufficient grounds for a denial of, a refusal to consider, or a delay in the consideration of, funding for such a recipient in succeeding fiscal years. In the case of any dispute arising under this section, reasonable notice and opportunity for a hearing shall be afforded the applicant.".

(b) The amendment made by subsection (a) shall be effective upon enactment of this Act.

APPOINTMENT OF MEMBERS OF AND FUNCTIONING OF ADVISORY COUNCILS

Sec. 516

(a) Section 443 of the General Education Provisions Act is amended by inserting "(a)" after "Sec. 433." and by adding at the end thereof the following: "(b) Where the President fails to appoint a member to fill a vacancy in the membership of a Presidential advisory council within sixty days after it occurs (or after the effective date of the statute creating such council), then the Secretary shall immediately appoint a member to fill such vacancy.".

(b) The amendment made by subsection (a) shall be effective upon enactment of this Act.

MAJOR AMENDMENTS TO THE FAMILY EDUCATIONAL RIGHTS

AND PRIVACY ACT OF 1974

The following items are proposed either as additions or modifications from the original Family Educational Rights and Privacy Act of 1974. This listing is not meant to serve as a substitute for a thorough reading of both the law and the proposed rules.

1. Educational records are re-defined--Sec. 438 (a)(4)(A).

2. Four areas are exempt from the definition of educational records--Sec. 438 (a)(4)(B).

3. A category of "directory information" is established--Sec. 438(a)(5)(A) and (B).

4. The term "student" is defined--Sec 438 (a)(6).

5. The release of information without informed written consent is delineated--Sec. 438 (b)(1)(A) through (I).

6. Requirements of educational institution for maintaining a record of individuals, agencies, or organizations which have requested or obtained access to a student's education record--Sec. 438 (b)(4)(A).

7. The rights are extended to any student who is attending or has attended an educational institution--99.3 proposed rules.

8. Educational institutions must provide, at least annually, notice to parents and eligible students of the rights afforded them by this law. Eight categories are identified--99.5 proposed rules.

A reading of the proposed rules is absolutely necessary for a total understanding of the requirements set forth in the law. To facilitate your reading and understanding of the proposed rules three explanatory notes are in order. First, comment sections are used in lieu of lengthy preamble for ease of reading and to highlight the substance of the proposed rules. Second, where statutory language is repeated in the proposed rules, it is so indicated by use of brackets. Third, the proposed rules reproduced are the ones most applicable to counseling. The final decisions on proposed rules had not been made at the time the Practicum Manual went to press.

PROPOSED RULES[1]
PL 93-568

Sec. 438

(a)(1)(A) No funds shall be made available under any applicable program to any educational agency or institution which has a policy of denying or which effectively prevents, the parents of students who are or have been in attendance at a school of such agency or at such institution, as the case may be, the right to inspect and review the education records of their children. If any material or document in the education record of a student includes information on more than one student, the parents of one of such students shall have the right to inspect and review only such part of such material or document as related to such student or to be informed of the specific information contained in such part of such material. Each educational agency or institution shall establish appropriate procedures for the granting of a request by parents for access to the education records of their children within a reasonable period of time, but in no case more than forty-five days after the request has been made.

(B) The first sentence of subparagraph (a) shall not operate to make available to students in institutions of postsecondary education the following materials:

(i) financial records of the parents of the student or any information contained therein;

(ii) confidential letters and statements of recommendation, which were placed in the education records prior to January 1, 1975, if such letters or statements are not used for purposes other than those for which they were specifically intended;

(iii) if the student has signed a waiver of the student's right of access under this subsection in accordance with subparagraph (c), confidential recommendations--

(I) respecting admission to any educational agency or institution,

(II) respecting an application for employment, and

(III) respecting the receipt of an honor or honorary recognition.

(C) A student or a person applying for admission may waive his right of access to confidential statements described in clause (iii) of subparagraph (B), except that such wavier shall apply to recommendations only if (i) the student is, upon request, notified of the names of all persons making confidential recommendations and (ii) such recommendations are used solely for the purpose for which they were specifically intended. Such waivers may not be recurred /sic/ as a condition for admission to, receipt of financial aid from, or receipt of any other services or benefits from such agency or institution.

(2) No funds shall be made available under any applicable program to any educational agency or institution unless the parents of students who are or have been in attendance at a school of such agency or at such institution are provided an opportunity for a hearing by such agency or institution, in accordance with regulations of the Secretary, to challenge the content of such student's education records, in order to insure that the records are not inaccurate, misleading, or otherwise in violation of the privacy or other rights of student, and to provide an opportunity for the correction or deletion of any such inaccurate, misleading, or otherwise inappropriate data contained therein and to insert into such records a written explanation of the parents respecting the content of such records.

---

[1] U.S. "Proposed Rules, PL 93-568," *Federal Register*, XL, No. 3, January 6, 1975, 1208-1209.

(3) For the purposes of this section the term "educational agency or institution" means any public or private agency or institution which is the recipient of funds under any applicable program.

(4)(A) For the purposes of this section, the term "education records" means, except as may be provided otherwise in subparagraph (B), those records, files, documents, and other materials which--

(i) contain information directly related to a student; and

(ii) are maintained by an educational agency or institution, or by a person acting for such agency or institution.

(B) The term "education records" does not include--

(i) records of institutional, supervisory, and administrative personnel and educational personnel ancillary thereto which are in the sole possession of the maker thereof and which are not accessible or revealed to any other person except a substitute;

(ii) if the personnel of a law enforcement unit do not have access to education records under subsection (b)(1), the records and documents of such law enforcement unit which (I) are kept apart from records described in subparagraph (A), (II) are maintained solely for law enforcement purposes and (III) are not made available to persons other than law enforcement officials of the same jurisdiction;

(iii) in the case of persons who are employed by an educational agency or institution but who are not in attendance at such agency or institution, records made and maintained in the normal course of business which relate exclusively to such person in that person's capacity as an employee and are not available for use for any other purpose; or

(iv) records on a student who is 18 years of age or older, or is attending an institution of postsecondary education, which are created or maintained by a physician, psychiatrist, psychologist, or other recognized professional or para-professional acting in his professional or para-professional capacity, or assisting in that capacity, and which are created, maintained, or used only in connection with the provision of treatment to the student, and are not available to anyone other than persons providing such treatment; provided, however, that such records can be personally reviewed by a physician or other appropriate professional of the student's choice.

(5)(A) For the purpose of this section the term "directory information" relating to a student includes the following: the student's name, address, telephone listing, date and place of birth, major field of study, participation in officially recognized activities and sports, weight and heights of members of athletic teams, dates of attendance, degrees and awards received, and the most recent previous educational agency or institution attended by the student.

(B) Any educational agency or institution making public directory information shall give public notice of the categories of information which it has designated as such information with respect to each student attending the institution or agency and shall allow a reasonable period of time after such notice has been given for a parent to inform the institution or agency that any or all of the information designated should not be released without the parent's prior consent.

(6) For the purposes of this section, the term "student" includes any person with respect to whom an educational agency or institution maintains education records or personally identifiable information, but does not include a person who has not been in attendance at such agency or institution.

(b)(1) No funds shall be made available under any applicable program to any educational agency or institution which has a policy or practice of permitting the release of education records (or personally identifiable information contained therein other than directory information, as defined in paragraph (5) of subsection (a)) of students without the written consent of their parents to any individual, agency, or organization, other than to the following--

    (A) other school officials, including teachers within the educational institution or local educational agency who have been determined by such agency or institution to have legitimate educational interests;

    (B) officials of other schools or school systems in which the student seeks or, intends to enroll, upon condition that the student's parents be notified of the transfer, receive a copy of the record if desired, and have an opportunity for a hearing to challenge the content of the record;

    (C) authorized representatives of (i) the Comptroller General of the United States, (ii) the Secretary, (iii) an administrative head of an education agency (as defined in section 408(c) of this Act), or (iv) State educational authorities, under the conditions set forth in paragraph (3) of this subsection; and

    (D) in connection with a student's applications for, or receipt of, financial aid;

    (E) State and local officials or authorities to which such information is specifically required to be reported or disclosed pursuant to State statute adopted prior to November 19, 1974;

    (F) organizations conducting studies for, or on behalf of, educational agencies or institutions for the purpose of developing, validating, or administering predictive tests, administering student aid programs, and improving institution, if such studies are conducted in such a manner as will not permit the personal identification of students and their parents by persons other than representatives of such organizations and such information will be destroyed when no longer needed for the purpose for which it is conducted;

    (G) accrediting organizations in order to carry out their accrediting functions;

    (H) parents of a dependent study of such parents, as defined in section 152 of the Internal Revenue Code of 1954; and

    (I) subject to regulations of the Secretary in connection with an emergency, appropriate persons if the knowledge of such information is necessary to protect the health or safety of the student or other persons.

(2) No funds shall be made available under any applicable program to any education agency or institution which has a policy or practice of releassing, or providing access to, any persoanlly identifiable information in education records other than directory information, or as is permitted under paragraph (1) of this subsection unless--

    (A) there is written consent from the student's parents specifying records to be released, the reasons for such release, and to whom, and with a copy of the records to be released to the student's parents and the student if desired by the parents, or

    (B) such information is furnished in compliance with judicial order, or pursuant to any lawfully issued subpoena, upon condition that parents and the students are notified of all such orders or subpoenas in advance of the compliance therewith by the educational institution or agency.

(3) Nothing contained in this section shall preclude authorized representatives of (A) the Comptroller General of the United States, (B) the Secretary, (C) an administrative head of an education agency or (D) State educational authorities from having access to student or other records which may be necessary in connection with the audit and

evaluation of Federally supported education programs, or in connection with the enforcement of the Federal legal requirements which relate to such programs: <u>Provided</u>, That except when collection of personally identifiable information is specifically authorized by Federal law, any data collected by such officials shall be protected in a manner which will not permit the personal identification of students and their parents by other than those officials, and such personally identifiable data shall be destroyed when no longer needed for such audit, evaluation, and enforcement of Federal legal requirements.

(4) (A) Each educational agency or institution shall maintain a record, kept with the education records of each student, which will indicate all individuals (other than those specified in paragraph (1)(A) of this subsection), agencies or organizations which have requested or obtained access to a student's education records maintained by such educational agency or institution, and which will indicate specifically the legitimate interest that each such person, agency, or organization has in obtaining this information. Such a record of access shall be available only to parents, to the school official and his assistants who are responsible for the custody of such records, and to persons or organizations authorized in, and under the conditions of, clauses (A) and (C) of paragraph (1) as a means of auditing the operation of the system.

(B) With respect to this subsection, personal information shall only be transferred to a third party on the condition that such party will not permit any other party to have access to such information without the written consent of the parents of the student.

(c) The Secretary shall adopt appropriate regulations to protect the rights of privacy of students and their families in connection with any surveys or data-gathering activities conducted, assisted, or authorized by the Secretary or an administrative head of an education agency. Regulations established under this subsection shall include provisions controlling the use, dissemination, and protection of such data. No survey or data-gathering activities shall be conducted by the Secretary, or an administrative head of an education agency under an applicable program, unless such activities are authorized by law.

(d) For the purposes of this section, whenever a student has attained eighteen years of age, or is attending an institution of postsecondary education the permission or consent required of and the rights accorded to the parents of the student shall thereafter only be required of and accorded to the student.

(e) No funds shall be made available under any applicable program to any educational agency or institutions unless such agency or institution informs the parents of students, or the students, if they are eighteen years of age or older, or are attending an institution of postsecondary education of the rights accorded them by this section.

(f) The Secretary, or an administrative head of an education agency, shall take appropriate actions to enforce provisions of this section and to deal with violations of this section, according to the provisions of this Act, except that action to terminate assistance may be taken only if the Secretary finds there has been a failure to comply with the provisions of this section, and he has determined that compliance cannot be secured by voluntary means.

(g) The Secretary shall establish or designate an office and review board within the Department of Health, Education, and Welfare for the purpose of investigating, processing, reviewing, and adjudicating violations of the provisions of this section and complaints which may be filed concerning alleged violations of this section. Except for the conduct of hearings, none of the functions of the Secretary under this section shall be carried out in any of the regional office of such Department.

CHAPTER VIII

EVALUATION OF PRACTICUM STUDENT AND SUPERVISOR

Included in this chapter is an article entitled "Possible Alternatives for Evaluating Counseling Students," as well as several forms to be used in the evaluation of practicum counselors and supervisors.

Assigning of grades to student counselors has been a millstone around instructors' necks. Those of us who teach practicum find that determining the effectiveness of our practicum course and/or the effectiveness of those students enrolled in practicum is often difficult to measure. "Learning to counsel" is often such a subjective assignment that evaluating the work of a practicum counselor needs not only to encompass the counseling process but also to include the practicum counselor's philosophy and behavior outside of the counseling cubicle.

In order to assess the effectiveness of a practicum counselor, an evaluation might be made by his or her

(a) peers

(b) practicum instructor

(c) field supervisor

(d) self and

(e) counselees.

Sample assessment instruments for different evaluators are provided in this chapter. The instruments can be used to gain information helpful in planning activities for improving counseling skills of those students evaluated. The evaluation forms that are presented may not be considered useful in _all_ practicum settings and may not be related to a student or professor's indices of therapeutic effectiveness. As an example, possibly a counselee might express much satisfaction with his or her counselor because the counselee found the counseling experience a pleasant personal relationship experience even though it did not solve the problem which motivated the counselee to seek counseling in the first place.

POSSIBLE ALTERNATIVES FOR EVALUATING
COUNSELING PRACTICUM STUDENTS

Kenneth Dimick and Frank Krause*

Our hope in writing this paper is to stimulate counselor educators, practicing counselors, and students training to become counselors to think about, discuss, and experiment with new and better ways of making counseling practicum courses more meaningful, relevant, and useful. However, we do recognize that such experimentation must at the same time meet the necessity of adequately fulfilling the professional and institutional obligations and responsibilities for evaluation of the prospective counselor.

Our experience has taught us that the training and inevitable evaluation of counseling practicum students presents unique problems. We certainly agree with the fact that many problems which do exist in a counseling practicum are really extensions or intensifications of problems inherent in our educational structure. Grades do seem to get in the way of effective learning!

The completion of practicum, however, in actuality usually gives license to the student to earn a living counseling. The grade of "A" in a social psychology or personality course, for example, really does not give the student permit to go out into the world and "social psych" or "personality" people. But each time a counselor educators gives a passing grade to a practicum student the counselor educator is saying in essence "I certify this person to be helpful and non-detrimental to the counselees he comes in contact with."

Another problem that is intensified in practicum instruction is the expected end result --a certain level of excellence--but nobody, student or counselor educator, really knows what that level is.

Finally this is all expected to be done in a specified length of time. This does not take into consideration that we as individuals learn and grow at different rates. This and the other problems we mentioned contribute to the dilemma we as counselor educators experience.

The Counselor Educators Dilemma

We as practicum supervisors have come to believe that the most effective way to promote a student's growth (e.g. effective counseling by the student) is the promotion of a warm, friendly, non-threatening atmosphere. We have also come to realize that this is at best difficult when also contracting to fulfill the role of possible executioner. We feel the practicum instructor could be a more effective agent of change were he not responsible for evaluation. By the same token we feel he could be a more effective evaluator were he not responsible for facilitating growth.

Yet we as counselor educators contract to fulfill these antithetical responsibilities. The result, although tolerable for a number of years, has inhibited optimal learning and optimal evaluation.

This is much the same dilemma the school counselor faces when agreeeing to be both counselor and disciplinarian within a school. Both duties need to be performed, yet when the same person tries to do both jobs either one or the other and, unfortunately, usually both roles become less effective than they might be.

The Practicum Student's Dilemma

Our contention is that threat is seen by our students as being detrimental to their maximum learning. With all the practicum student has at stake in being evaluated by his practicum instructor it is not difficult to really see why a student does not wish to display his weaknesses or inadequacies.

---

*Reprinted by permission from ILLINOIS GUIDANCE AND PERSONNEL JOURNAL, No. 2 (Spring, 1971), pp. 15-17.

Instructors make comments such as "bring me your worst tapes, those are the ones I can help you with the most." This may very well be true but does the student really want the instructor to hear his "worst tapes" when he is aware that this person will decide his professional fate?

Perhaps we expect too much from our practicum students. The counselor educator would like for his students to be open. But what i the instructor doesn't like what he hears. "Did you hear about the student who flunked practicum because he told his instructor . . .?" Such an environment promotes "closedness" not "openness."

The counselor educator is clearly engaged in playing roles. The student is often in a quandary as to which role his professor is playing at a given instant.

Do you say the same things in front of a jury that you may have confidentially discussed with your lawyer outside of court? It seems that you do so only if you are extremely secure within yourself and do not worry about the people who have been convicted that were not guilty.

What Then?

If there were an easy solution to these dilemmas it would no doubt have been in practice for some time.

We do not propose that there is an easy solution. Neither do we wish to leave the idea, "here is the problem you figure out what to do with it." Instead we propose experimentation with alternative ways for evaluating practicum students.

We are presenting a few alternatives which we believe have merit at least as ideas for experimentation. These ideas may prove impractical or may present problems even greater than the problems they are designed to circumvent.

The idea is then, not to figure out which of the following alternatives might "get the job done," but rather to encourage ideas and experimentation in practicum evaluation.

Specific Alternatives

1) Present a continuum of practicum and practicum related experiences (pre-practicum, practicum, advanced practicum, internship) and set up specific criteria in terms of counseling exompetencies which must be demonstrated by the student before he moves from one experience to the next (e.g. must be able to develop a relationship with another person before leaving pre-practicum for practicum). Do away with these experiences as classes thus allowing some students to spend six days in pre-practicum while other students might spend six months there. This in essence becomes a pass (as opposed to pass-fail) system. Degree or certification levels would have levels within the continuum of experience that would be required for completion (e.g. practicum completed for M.A., advanced practicum completed for Ed.S., internship completed for Ph.D.). All students would begin their training in the pre-practicum segment of the continuum.

2) Since we have such little evidence of what skills and techniques on the part of the counselor contribute to effective counseling, another alternative might be that of making the grades of practicum students entirely dependent upon the outcome or growth of their clients. This would emphasize that counseling is for the growth of clients rather than an exercise for the counselor to demonstrate his skills. This alternative would deal with the real meaning of counseling and thus the primary reason for practicum. There have been a number of methods employed in various research designs to measure client change and/or growth. Pre- and post-tests by all clients counseled by practicum students with such paper and pencil tests as the POI, Tennessee Self-Concept Scale, MMPI, etc. Measures such as client self-report, or reports from others associated with the client might also be possible ways of determining client growth.

3) Assign a practicum instructor for all but the last two weeks of the class time. This instructor's role would be that of teaching students to become better counselors. Both the students and the instructor would be aware that this instructor would have nothing whatsoever to do with the grade evaluations of the students. In the last two weeks another instructor would replace the first instructor with the responsibility of evaluating the individual student. This

alternative could be modified by having a team of evaluators measure the effectiveness of each student. The practicality of such a plan might be enhanced if two practicum classes were being taught simultaneously, by two different instructors. The two instructors could then merely switch classes for the evaluation phase of the class.

4) Utilize student or peer group evaluation. One method of doing this would be to take twenty-five students in practicum, splitting them up into five groups of five to critique and evaluate each other. Each week the groups would need to choose the one best and one worst counselor. The top person from each group would then go to the next highest group while the least effective in each group goes to the next lowest group. By the end of the term the students would have ranked or at least grouped their peers from best to worst.

5) Make practicum a pass-fail class without time limits. Some students could pass in one week and some students might never pass. But students would only get credit for the class when they passed it.

We have presented this paper with the hope that those professionals in the field of counseling might examine ways in which training, most specifically training in practicum, might most effectively help to prepare counselors. We sincerely hope that some of the alternatives or combinations of these alternatives may lead toward the development of more effective methods of training counselors.

References

Altucher, N., "Constructive Use of the Supervisory Relationship," Journal of Counseling Psychology, 1967, 14:165-170.

Carkhuff, R. R. and Truax, C. B., "Training in Counseling and Psychotherapy: An Evaluation of an Integrated Didactic and Experiential Approach," Journal of Consulting Psychology, 1965, 29:333-336.

Fraleigh, Patrick W. and Buchheimer, Arnold, "The Use of Peer Groups in Practicum Supervision," Counselor Education and Supervision, Summer, 1969, 8:4, 284-288.

Kirk, Barbara A., "Internship in Counseling Psychology: Goals and Issues," Journal of Counseling Psychology, 1970, 17:1, 88-90.

Rioch, Margaret J., Elkes, C., Flint, A. A., et al., "Pilot Project in Training Mental Health Counselors," U.S. Department of Health, Education, and Welfare; Public Health Service Publication, Washington, D.C.: No. 1254, 1965.

COOPERATING PRACTICUM SITE SUPERVISOR'S EVALUATION OF STUDENT COUNSELOR*

DIRECTIONS: This evaluation form is to be completed by the practicum site person who is supervising the student counselor at the practicum site. When the evaluation form has been completed, please forward it to the practicum supervisor in the college or university.

Name of Student Counselor _____
Name of School or Other Community Agency
    Where Practicum Was Done _____
School Grade Levels or Kinds of Clients
    With Whom Student Counselor Worked _____
Name of Rater _____ Position of Rater _____
Period Covered by This Rating _____

Directions: Circle the number which best describes the area.

0. Not observed
1. Unsatisfactory
2. Adequate
3. Does well
4. Outstanding

AREAS

1. The Practicum Counselor's Personal Characteristics

    A sensitive person 4 3 2 1 0
    Personal appearance 4 3 2 1 0
    Degree of acceptance of others' values 4 3 2 1 0
    Awareness of own strengths and weaknesses 4 3 2 1 0
    Openness to growth and learning 4 3 2 1 0
    Conducts self in a professional manner 4 3 2 1 0

    Comments:

2. The Practicum Counselor's Communication and Coordination Skills

    Ability to communicate with others 4 3 2 1 0
    Works cooperatively with others 4 3 2 1 0
    Able to bring about changes in the school setting 4 3 2 1 0
    Able to communicate with parents and teachers while
      still maintaining confidence with own clients 4 3 2 1 0
    Ability to convey information orally and in written form 4 3 2 1 0

    Comments:

---

*Printed by permission from Dr. Thomas J. Caulfield, Chairman, Counselor Education, Canisius College.

Form #13, p.1 of 4 pp.

                                                        0. Not observed
                                                      1. Unsatisfactory
                                                    2. Adequate
                                                  3. Does well
                AREAS   4. Outstanding

3. The Practicum Counselor's Skill in Counseling

   Ability to provide a theoretical rationale for
     use of own counseling procedures 4 3 2 1 0
   Awareness of ethical standards and confidentiality 4 3 2 1 0
   Awareness of own personal and professional limitations . 4 3 2 1 0
   Ability to apply knowledge, research and theory from
     other disciplines to the counselee's situation 4 3 2 1 0
   Awareness of the youth culture and its implications in
     areas of sex, drugs, and moral concerns 4 3 2 1 0
   Responds at the counselee's level 4 3 2 1 0
     If not, circle whether   below or above
   Assumes leadership 4 3 2 1 0
     If not, circle whether too much or too little
   Perceptive in handling the counselee's cues 4 3 2 1 0
   Acceptance of the counselee 4 3 2 1 0
   Conveys a pleasant mood or relaxed atmosphere in the interview . 4 3 2 1 0
     If not, circle whether too much or not enough
   Seems sincere in working with the counselee 4 3 2 1 0
     If not, circle whether too much or too little
   Understands the situation the counselee is trying to present ... 4 3 2 1 0
   Gains the confidence of the counselee 4 3 2 1 0
   Is a good listener 4 3 2 1 0
   Facilitative in specifying the problem in concrete terms 4 3 2 1 0
   Emphatically able to bring client to the affective
     level of awareness 4 3 2 1 0
   Real and genuine in the relationship 4 3 2 1 0
   Able to facilitate the counselee's resolution of concerns 4 3 2 1 0
   Effectiveness of this counselor as evaluated by clients 4 3 2 1 0
   Ability as a counselor, overall evaluation 4 3 2 1 0

   Comments:

4. The Practicum Counselor's Skills in the Information Services Area

   Aware of vocational development theories 4 3 2 1 0
   Familiar with current practices in the informational service area 4 3 2 1 0
   Able to use current sources of information 4 3 2 1 0
   Able to assist teachers and administrators integrate various
     aspects and kinds of information into the curriculum . 4 3 2 1 0
   Able to help students interpret and accumulate information
     in light of personal needs 4 3 2 1 0
   Able to help staff, parents, and others interpret and accumulate
     information in light of personal needs 4 3 2 1 0

   Comments:

                                                      Form #13, p.2 of 4 pp.

AREAS

0. Not observed
1. Unsatisfactory
2. Adequate
3. Does well
4. Outstanding

5. The Practicum Counselor's Assessment and Appraisal Skills

Able to help counselees integrate and assimilate test
  and non-test data 4 3 2 1 0
Able to help others involved with the counselee to
  assimilate test and non-test data 4 3 2 1 0
Able to help other pupil personnel services team members
  by providing case study materials 4 3 2 1 0
Able to administer tests 4 3 2 1 0
Able to interpret tests 4 3 2 1 0
Able to conduct follow-up studies related to placement
  and can use the results with counselees 4 3 2 1 0

Comments:

6. The Practicum Counselor's Placement Skills

Knowledgeable of available placement referral sources 4 3 2 1 0
Able to make reasonable and effective referrals 4 3 2 1 0
Able to offer students and others appropriate referral sources 4 3 2 1 0
Knowledgeable of referral sources available in the following areas:
  a. training 4 3 2 1 0
  b. special education needs 4 3 2 1 0
  c. employment services 4 3 2 1 0
  d. psychological services 4 3 2 1 0

Comments:

7. The Practicum Counselor's Potentialities

Possesses potential for becoming an effective counselor 4 3 2 1 0
Possesses potential for supervisory work in the area of
  guidance and counseling 4 3 2 1 0
"Over-all" evaluation of this counselor's effectiveness 4 3 2 1 0

Comments:

Form #13, p.3 of 4 pp.

SUMMARY NOTES:

Student Counselor's strong points:

Student Counselor's needs for improvement:

Would you employ this counselor to work for you? Yes____   No____   Uncertain____

Has this evaluation been discussed with the practicum counselor? Yes____   No____

General comments:

Based on the preceding information I recommend a grade of _____ for the student counselor.

Rater's Signature_____   Date_____

Evaluation held_____   Attended by_____

Form #13, p.4 or 4 pp.

COUNSELEE RATING SHEET*

SUGGESTED USE: Practicum counselors may use this rating sheet to elicit information from their counselees. The sheet is given to a counselee by the practicum counselor in order to encourage the counselee to express real feelings about the counseling process.

Counselee Name_____   Date_____

DIRECTIONS FOR THE COUNSELEE: Please complete the sentences on the front and back of this sheet. Express <u>your real feelings</u> about the interview that you have just had. Please try to complete each statement in a few words.

1. Before the interview began I thought

2. During the interview

3. I feel that my counselor

4. If I have another interview

*Printed by permission from Dr. William E. Hopke, Head, Guidance and Personnel Services, North Carolina State University at Raleigh.

Form #14, p.1 of 2 pp.

5. My vocational plans are

6. I believe that my ability

7. I think that my interests

8. My school record

9. The real thing that I

10. This interview was

Form #14, p.2 of 2 pp.

COUNSELEE RATING SHEET*

SUGGESTED USE: Practicum counselors may use this rating sheet to elicit information from their counselees. The sheet is given to a counselee by the practicum counselor in order to encourage the counselee to express real feelings about the counseling process.

Counselee Name_____ Date_____

DIRECTIONS FOR THE COUNSELEE: Please complete the sentences on the front and back of this sheet. Express your real feelings about the interview that you have just had. Please try to complete each statement in a few words.

1. Before the interview began I thought

2. During the interview

3. I feel that my counselor

4. If I have another interview

---

*Printed by permission from Dr. William E. Hopke, Head, Guidance and Personnel Services, North Carolina State University at Raleigh.

Form #14, p.1 of 2 pp.

5. My vocational plans are

6. I believe that my ability

7. I think that my interests

8. My school record

9. The real thing that I

10. This interview was

Form #14, p.2 of 2 pp.

COUNSELEE RATING SHEET*

SUGGESTED USE: Practicum counselors may use this rating sheet to elicit information from their counselees. The sheet is given to a counselee by the practicum counselor in order to encourage the counselee to express real feelings about the counseling process.

Counselee Name_____   Date_____

DIRECTIONS FOR THE COUNSELEE: Please complete the sentences on the front and back of this sheet. Express <u>your real feelings</u> about the interview that you have just had. Please try to complete each statement in a few words.

1. Before the interview began I thought

2. During the interview

3. I feel that my counselor

4. If I have another interview

_____

*Printed by permission from Dr. William E. Hopke, Head, Guidance and Personnel Services, North Carolina State University at Raleigh.

Form #14, p.1 of 2 pp.

5. My vocational plans are

6. I believe that my ability

7. I think that my interests

8. My school record

9. The real thing that I

10. This interview was

Form #14, p.2 of 2 pp.

COUNSELEE RATING SHEET*

SUGGESTED USE: Practicum counselors may use this rating sheet to elicit information from their counselees. The sheet is given to a counselee by the practicum counselor in order to encourage the counselee to express real feelings about the counseling process.

Counselee Name_____   Date_____

DIRECTIONS FOR THE COUNSELEE: Please complete the sentences on the front and back of this sheet. Express <u>your real feelings</u> about the interview that you have just had. Please try to complete each statement in a few words.

1. Before the interview began I thought

2. During the interview

3. I feel that my counselor

4. If I have another interview

---

*Printed by permission from Dr. William E. Hopke, Head, Guidance and Personnel Services, North Carolina State University at Raleigh.

Form #14, p.1 of 2 pp.

5. My vocational plans are

6. I believe that my ability

7. I think that my interests

8. My school record

9. The real thing that I

10. This interview was

Form #14, p.2 of 2 pp.

SELF-RATING BY THE STUDENT COUNSELOR

SUGGESTED USE: The practicum counselor may use this sheet as a self-evaluation form after a therapy session.

Date   Counselee Name_____   Practicum Counselor Name_____

DIRECTIONS: The student counselor following a therapy session is to answer each question. The questions serve as a self-rating initiator and may enable the student counselor to determine means for improvement in his or her counseling.

Preparation for the Interview   Yes   ?   No

1. Was I physically in good condition and mentally alert? . . . . ___ ___ ___

2. Did I schedule sufficient time for the interview? . . . . ___ ___ ___

3. Was there provision for privacy and reasonable freedom from interruption? ___ ___ ___

4. Did I have the physical space where we met arranged so as to suggest welcome and an atmosphere conducive to counseling? . . . . ___ ___ ___

5. Did I have a background of available data about the client that would help me to understand him or her better in the interview but would not bias me? . . . . ___ ___ ___

6. Did I have information about the educational and vocational opportunities and other facts that the client might need? . . . . ___ ___ ___

7. Had I previously established a reputation for seeing the client's point of view, being genuinely helpful, and not disclosing confidences? . . . . . ___ ___ ___

Comments:

Beginning the Interview

1. Was I sensitive to the client and did I use an appropriate approach? . . . ___ ___ ___

2. Was I able to create a psychological atmosphere in which the client was stimulated to take the responsibility of thinking through the situation? ___ ___ ___

3. Was I successful in maintaining free communication between us? . . . . . . ___ ___ ___

Comments:

Form #15, p.1 of 2 pp.

Development of the Interview   Yes   ?   No

1. Did the client feel free to express negative feelings?. . . . . ___ ___ ___

2. Did the client have the opportunity to release tension? . . . . ___ ___ ___

3. Was my attitude one of reflecting objectivity while expressing caring?. . ___ ___ ___

4. Was I sincere and did I show genuine respect for the client?. . . . . . . ___ ___ ___

5. Was my own attitude, so far as I know, free from bias?. . . . . ___ ___ ___

6. Did I follow the leads suggested by the client? . . . . ___ ___ ___

7. Did I help the client to clarify and expand positive feelings?. . . . . . ___ ___ ___

8. Did the client establish a more forward looking, positive, hopeful
    attitude during the interview or series of interviews?. . . . . ___ ___ ___

9. Was I able to give the information needed when the client was
    ready to use it?. . . . . ___ ___ ___

10. Was information provided in a manner which caused the client to
    move forward realistically in his or her thinking?. . . . . ___ ___ ___

Comments:

Planning for Next Session   Yes   ?   No

1. Was I able to identify areas with which to follow through for
    next session? . . . . ___ ___ ___

2. Was I able to help client identify things to do between this
    interview and the next one? . . . . ___ ___ ___

3. Was I able to help client gain a clear view of what might be
    done in the next session? . . . . ___ ___ ___

4. Did I establish with the client a definite meeting time and
    place for the next session? . . . . ___ ___ ___

5. Have I identified techniques that might be considered for the
    next session? . . . . ___ ___ ___

6. Have I identified the materials and/or preparation I will
    need for the next session?. . . . . ___ ___ ___

Comments:

Form #15, p.2 of 2 pp.

SELF-RATING BY THE STUDENT COUNSELOR

SUGGESTED USE: The practicum counselor may use this sheet as a self-evaluation form after a therapy session.

Date _____ Counselee Name _____ Practicum Counselor Name _____

DIRECTIONS: The student counselor following a therapy session is to answer each question. The questions serve as a self-rating initiator and may enable the student counselor to determine means for improvement in his or her counseling.

Preparation for the Interview   Yes   ?   No

1. Was I physically in good condition and mentally alert? . . . . ___ ___ ___
2. Did I schedule sufficient time for the interview?. . . . . ___ ___ ___
3. Was there provision for privacy and reasonable freedom from interruption?   ___ ___ ___
4. Did I have the physical space where we met arranged so as to suggest welcome and an atmosphere conducive to counseling? . . . . ___ ___ ___
5. Did I have a background of available data about the client that would help me to understand him or her better in the interview but would not bias me? . . . . ___ ___ ___
6. Did I have information about the educational and vocational opportunities and other facts that the client might need?. . . . . ___ ___ ___
7. Had I previously established a reputation for seeing the client's point of view, being genuinely helpful, and not disclosing confidences?. . . . . ___ ___ ___

Comments:

Beginning the Interview

1. Was I sensitive to the client and did I use an appropriate approach? . . . ___ ___ ___
2. Was I able to create a psychological atmosphere in which the client was stimulated to take the responsibility of thinking through the situation?   ___ ___ ___
3. Was I successful in maintaining free communication between us? . . . . . . ___ ___ ___

Comments:

Form #15, p.1 of 2 pp.

Development of the Interview   Yes   ?   No

1. Did the client feel free to express negative feelings?. . . . .   ___ ___ ___

2. Did the client have the opportunity to release tension? . . . .   ___ ___ ___

3. Was my attitude one of reflecting objectivity while expressing caring?. .   ___ ___ ___

4. Was I sincere and did I show genuine respect for the client?. . . . . . .   ___ ___ ___

5. Was my own attitude, so far as I know, free from bias?. . . . .   ___ ___ ___

6. Did I follow the leads suggested by the client? . . . .   ___ ___ ___

7. Did I help the client to clarify and expand positive feelings?. . . . . .   ___ ___ ___

8. Did the client establish a more forward looking, positive, hopeful
   attitude during the interview or series of interviews?. . . . .   ___ ___ ___

9. Was I able to give the information needed when the client was
   ready to use it?. . . . .   ___ ___ ___

10. Was information provided in a manner which caused the client to
    move forward realistically in his or her thinking?. . . . .   ___ ___ ___

Comments:

Planning for Next Session   Yes   ?   No

1. Was I able to identify areas with which to follow through for
   next session? . . . .   ___ ___ ___

2. Was I able to help client identify things to do between this
   interview and the next one? . . . .   ___ ___ ___

3. Was I able to help client gain a clear view of what might be
   done in the next session? . . . .   ___ ___ ___

4. Did I establish with the client a definite meeting time and
   place for the next session? . . . .   ___ ___ ___

5. Have I identified techniques that might be considered for the
   next session? . . . .   ___ ___ ___

6. Have I identified the materials and/or preparation I will
   need for the next session?. . . . .   ___ ___ ___

Comments:

Form #15, p.2 of 2 pp.

SELF-RATING BY THE STUDENT COUNSELOR

SUGGESTED USE: The practicum counselor may use this sheet as a self-evaluation form after a therapy session.

Date _____ Counselee Name _____ Practicum Counselor Name _____

DIRECTIONS: The student counselor following a therapy session is to answer each question. The questions serve as a self-rating initiator and may enable the student counselor to determine means for improvement in his or her counseling.

Preparation for the Interview   Yes   ?   No

1. Was I physically in good condition and mentally alert? . . . . ___ ___ ___

2. Did I schedule sufficient time for the interview? . . . . ___ ___ ___

3. Was there provision for privacy and reasonable freedom from interruption? ___ ___ ___

4. Did I have the physical space where we met arranged so as to suggest welcome and an atmosphere conducive to counseling? . . . . ___ ___ ___

5. Did I have a background of available data about the client that would help me to understand him or her better in the interview but would not bias me? . . . . ___ ___ ___

6. Did I have information about the educational and vocational opportunities and other facts that the client might need? . . . . ___ ___ ___

7. Had I previously established a reputation for seeing the client's point of view, being genuinely helpful, and not disclosing confidences? . . . . . ___ ___ ___

Comments:

Beginning the Interview

1. Was I sensitive to the client and did I use an appropriate approach? . . . ___ ___ ___

2. Was I able to create a psychological atmosphere in which the client was stimulated to take the responsibility of thinking through the situation? ___ ___ ___

3. Was I successful in maintaining free communication between us? . . . . . . ___ ___ ___

Comments:

Form #15, p.1 of 2 pp.

Development of the Interview   Yes   ?   No

1. Did the client feel free to express negative feelings?. . . . .   ___ ___ ___

2. Did the client have the opportunity to release tension? . . . .   ___ ___ ___

3. Was my attitude one of reflecting objectivity while expressing caring?. .   ___ ___ ___

4. Was I sincere and did I show genuine respect for the client?. . . . . . .   ___ ___ ___

5. Was my own attitude, so far as I know, free from bias?. . . . .   ___ ___ ___

6. Did I follow the leads suggested by the client? . . . .   ___ ___ ___

7. Did I help the client to clarify and expand positive feelings?. . . . . .   ___ ___ ___

8. Did the client establish a more forward looking, positive, hopeful
    attitude during the interview or series of interviews?. . . . .   ___ ___ ___

9. Was I able to give the information needed when the client was
    ready to use it?. . . . .   ___ ___ ___

10. Was information provided in a manner which caused the client to
    move forward realistically in his or her thinking?. . . . .   ___ ___ ___

Comments:

Planning for Next Session   Yes   ?   No

1. Was I able to identify areas with which to follow through for
    next session?. . . . .   ___ ___ ___

2. Was I able to help client identify things to do between this
    interview and the next one? . . . .   ___ ___ ___

3. Was I able to help client gain a clear view of what might be
    done in the next session?. . . . .   ___ ___ ___

4. Did I establish with the client a definite meeting time and
    place for the next session?. . . . .   ___ ___ ___

5. Have I identified techniques that might be considered for the
    next session?. . . . .   ___ ___ ___

6. Have I identified the materials and/or preparation I will
    need for the next session?. . . . .   ___ ___ ___

Comments:

Form #15, p.2 of 2 pp.

SELF-RATING BY THE STUDENT COUNSELOR

SUGGESTED USE: The practicum counselor may use this sheet as a self-evaluation form after a therapy session.

Date _____ Counselee Name _____ Practicum Counselor Name _____

DIRECTIONS: The student counselor following a therapy session is to answer each question. The questions serve as a self-rating initiator and may enable the student counselor to determine means for improvement in his or her counseling.

Preparation for the Interview   Yes   ?   No

1. Was I physically in good condition and mentally alert? . . . .   ___ ___ ___

2. Did I schedule sufficient time for the interview? . . . .   ___ ___ ___

3. Was there provision for privacy and reasonable freedom from interruption?   ___ ___ ___

4. Did I have the physical space where we met arranged so as to suggest welcome and an atmosphere conducive to counseling? . . . .   ___ ___ ___

5. Did I have a background of available data about the client that would help me to understand him or her better in the interview but would not bias me? . . . .   ___ ___ ___

6. Did I have information about the educational and vocational opportunities and other facts that the client might need? . . . .   ___ ___ ___

7. Had I previously established a reputation for seeing the client's point of view, being genuinely helpful, and not disclosing confidences? . . . .   ___ ___ ___

Comments:

Beginning the Interview

1. Was I sensitive to the client and did I use an appropriate approach? . . .   ___ ___ ___

2. Was I able to create a psychological atmosphere in which the client was stimulated to take the responsibility of thinking through the situation?   ___ ___ ___

3. Was I successful in maintaining free communication between us? . . . . . .   ___ ___ ___

Comments:

Form #15, p.1 of 2 pp.

Development of the Interview   Yes   ?   No

1. Did the client feel free to express negative feelings?. . . . .   ___ ___ ___

2. Did the client have the opportunity to release tension? . . . .   ___ ___ ___

3. Was my attitude one of reflecting objectivity while expressing caring?. .   ___ ___ ___

4. Was I sincere and did I show genuine respect for the client?. . . . . . .   ___ ___ ___

5. Was my own attitude, so far as I know, free from bias?. . . . .   ___ ___ ___

6. Did I follow the leads suggested by the client? . . . .   ___ ___ ___

7. Did I help the client to clarify and expand positive feelings?. . . . . .   ___ ___ ___

8. Did the client establish a more forward looking, positive, hopeful
    attitude during the interview or series of interviews?. . . . .   ___ ___ ___

9. Was I able to give the information needed when the client was
    ready to use it?. . . . .   ___ ___ ___

10. Was information provided in a manner which caused the client to
    move forward realistically in his or her thinking?. . . . .   ___ ___ ___

Comments:

Planning for Next Session   Yes   ?   No

1. Was I able to identify areas with which to follow through for
    next session? . . . .   ___ ___ ___

2. Was I able to help client identify things to do between this
    interview and the next one? . . . .   ___ ___ ___

3. Was I able to help client gain a clear view of what might be
    done in the next session? . . . .   ___ ___ ___

4. Did I establish with the client a definite meeting time and
    place for the next session? . . . .   ___ ___ ___

5. Have I identified techniques that might be considered for the
    next session? . . . .   ___ ___ ___

6. Have I identified the materials and/or preparation I will
    need for the next session?. . . . .   ___ ___ ___

Comments:

Form #15, p.2 of 2 pp.

SUPERVISOR'S EVALUATION AND REPORT REGARDING STUDENT COUNSELOR

Name of Student Counselor _____

DIRECTIONS: The supervisor's evaluation of a practicum student's competences is indicated by completing the form. The extent to which the student counselor possesses each competence is identified by circling a mark on the scale accompanying each dimension or characteristic. The supervisor circles a number on the continuum from 1, which is "Poor," to 7, which is "Good," or indicates that the dimension is "Not Applicable" by circling the asterisk. The evaluation is to be completed periodically in order to provide the practicum student with feedback on performance and as a basic for identifying areas for additional emphases.

Student Counselor's Relationship with Supervisor

	Poor		Average			Good		NA
	1	2	3	4	5	6	7	*

1. <u>Involvement</u>--Has the student counselor demonstrated involvement and seriousness of being a counselor? . . . . . 1 2 3 4 5 6 7 *

2. <u>Growth</u>--
   a. Is supervision used to further the student counselor's development? . . . . 1 2 3 4 5 6 7 *
   b. Is the counseling experience used to further the student counselor's development? . . . . 1 2 3 4 5 6 7 *
   c. Has the student counselor shown personal growth? . . . . 1 2 3 4 5 6 7 *

3. <u>Rapport</u>--How easy has it been to communicate with the student counselor? . . . . 1 2 3 4 5 6 7 *

4. <u>Awareness of Limitations</u>--
   a. Ability to share competencies and skills with peers and supervisors . . . . 1 2 3 4 5 6 7 *
   b. Humility to share deficiencies with peers and supervisors . . . . 1 2 3 4 5 6 7 *

Counseling Relationship

1. Ease of beginning an interview . . . . 1 2 3 4 5 6 7 *
2. Demonstrate sensitivity to counselee feelings . . . . 1 2 3 4 5 6 7 *
3. Permit counselee expression . . . . 1 2 3 4 5 6 7 *
4. Facilitate counselee expression . . . . 1 2 3 4 5 6 7 *
5. Focus on content or problem . . . . 1 2 3 4 5 6 7 *
6. Focus on person . . . . 1 2 3 4 5 6 7 *
7. Initiate a working relationship . . . . 1 2 3 4 5 6 7 *
8. Communicate acceptance . . . . 1 2 3 4 5 6 7 *
9. Communicate understanding . . . . 1 2 3 4 5 6 7 *

Organization and Preparation

1. Organize case material . . . . 1 2 3 4 5 6 7 *
2. Recognize implications of case material . . . . 1 2 3 4 5 6 7 *
3. Recognize discrepancies and meaning of inconsistent information . . . . 1 2 3 4 5 6 7 *
4. Consider various approaches and the   . . . 1 2 3 4 5 6 7 *
5. Aware of counselee readiness . . . . 1 2 3 4 5 6 7 *
6. Define goals tentatively . . . . 1 2 3 4 5 6 7 *
7. Utilize appropriate structure . . . . 1 2 3 4 5 6 7 *
8. Distinguish between immediate and long term goals . . . . . 1 2 3 4 5 6 7 *

Form #16, p.1 of 2 pp.

```
                                                      Poor      Average     Good  NA
                                                      1    2    3    4    5    6    7    *
```

Implementation

1. Accurate use of tests technically 1   2   3   4   5   6   7   *
2. Dealing with affect
    a. Recognizing positive affect 1   2   3   4   5   6   7   *
    b. Handling positive affect 1   2   3   4   5   6   7   *
    c. Recognizing negative affect 1   2   3   4   5   6   7   *
    d. Handling negative affect 1   2   3   4   5   6   7   *
3. Present unpleasant information 1   2   3   4   5   6   7   *
4. Recognize impact of student counselor behavior and
   activities 1   2   3   4   5   6   7   *
5. Recognize the importance of timing on imparting
   information 1   2   3   4   5   6   7   *
6. Perceive the nature and significance of the process
   accurately 1   2   3   4   5   6   7   *
7. Focus on specific behaviors 1   2   3   4   5   6   7   *
8. Integration of data 1   2   3   4   5   6   7   *
9. Agree upon goals mutually 1   2   3   4   5   6   7   *
10. Termination of a case 1   2   3   4   5   6   7   *

Prognosis

What is this student counselor's promise as a counselor? _____

_____
_____
_____
_____
_____

_____   _____
      (Date)   (Signature of Supervisor)

My signature indicates that I have read the report(s) presented above and have had an opportunity to discuss the material with my supervisor.

_____   _____
      (Date)   (Signature of Student Counselor)

Form #16, p.2 of 2 pp.

SUPERVISOR'S EVALUATION AND REPORT REGARDING STUDENT COUNSELOR

Name of Student Counselor _____

DIRECTIONS: The supervisor's evaluation of a practicum student's competences is indicated by completing the form. The extent to which the student counselor possesses each competence is identified by circling a mark on the scale accompanying each dimension or characteristic. The supervisor circles a number on the continuum from 1, which is "Poor," to 7, which is "Good," or indicates that the dimension is "Not Applicable" by circling the asterisk. The evaluation is to be completed periodically in order to provide the practicum student with feedback on performance and as a basic for identifying areas for additional emphases.

Student Counselor's Relationship with Supervisor

```
                                               Poor    Average    Good   NA
                                               1   2   3   4   5   6   7  *
```

1. *Involvement*—Has the student counselor demonstrated involvement and seriousness of being a counselor? ..... 1 2 3 4 5 6 7 *

2. *Growth*—
   a. Is supervision used to further the student counselor's development? .... 1 2 3 4 5 6 7 *
   b. Is the counseling experience used to further the student counselor's development? .... 1 2 3 4 5 6 7 *
   c. Has the student counselor shown personal growth? .... 1 2 3 4 5 6 7 *

3. *Rapport*—How easy has it been to communicate with the student counselor? .... 1 2 3 4 5 6 7 *

4. *Awareness of Limitations*—
   a. Ability to share competencies and skills with peers and supervisors .... 1 2 3 4 5 6 7 *
   b. Humility to share deficiencies with peers and supervisors .. .. 1 2 3 4 5 6 7 *

Counseling Relationship

1. Ease of beginning an interview .... 1 2 3 4 5 6 7 *
2. Demonstrate sensitivity to counselee feelings .... 1 2 3 4 5 6 7 *
3. Permit counselee expression .... 1 2 3 4 5 6 7 *
4. Facilitate counselee expression .... 1 2 3 4 5 6 7 *
5. Focus on content or problem .... 1 2 3 4 5 6 7 *
6. Focus on person .... 1 2 3 4 5 6 7 *
7. Initiate a working relationship .... 1 2 3 4 5 6 7 *
8. Communicate acceptance .... 1 2 3 4 5 6 7 *
9. Communicate understanding .... 1 2 3 4 5 6 7 *

Organization and Preparation

1. Organize case material .... 1 2 3 4 5 6 7 *
2. Recognize implications of case material .... 1 2 3 4 5 6 7 *
3. Recognize discrepancies and meaning of inconsistent information .... 1 2 3 4 5 6 7 *
4. Consider various approaches and the .... 1 2 3 4 5 6 7 *
5. Aware of counselee readiness .... 1 2 3 4 5 6 7 *
6. Define goals tentatively .... 1 2 3 4 5 6 7 *
7. Utilize appropriate structure .... 1 2 3 4 5 6 7 *
8. Distinguish between immediate and long term goals ..... 1 2 3 4 5 6 7 *

Form #16, p.1 of 2 pp.

```
                                                      Poor    Average    Good  NA
                                                      1   2   3   4   5   6   7   *
```

Implementation

```
1.  Accurate use of tests technically . . . . . . . . . . .1   2   3   4   5   6   7   *
2.  Dealing with affect
    a. Recognizing positive affect . . . . . . . . . . . . .1   2   3   4   5   6   7   *
    b. Handling positive affect  . . . . . . . . . . . . . .1   2   3   4   5   6   7   *
    c. Recognizing negative affect . . . . . . . . . . . . .1   2   3   4   5   6   7   *
    d. Handling negative affect  . . . . . . . . . . . . . .1   2   3   4   5   6   7   *
3.  Present unpleasant information . . . . . . . . . . . . .1   2   3   4   5   6   7   *
4.  Recognize impact of student counselor behavior and
    activities . . . . . . . . . . . . . . . . . . . . . . .1   2   3   4   5   6   7   *
5.  Recognize the importance of timing on imparting
    information  . . . . . . . . . . . . . . . . . . . . . .1   2   3   4   5   6   7   *
6.  Perceive the nature and significance of the process
    accurately . . . . . . . . . . . . . . . . . . . . . . .1   2   3   4   5   6   7   *
7.  Focus on specific behaviors  . . . . . . . . . . . . . .1   2   3   4   5   6   7   *
8.  Integration of data  . . . . . . . . . . . . . . . . . .1   2   3   4   5   6   7   *
9.  Agree upon goals mutually  . . . . . . . . . . . . . . .1   2   3   4   5   6   7   *
10. Termination of a case  . . . . . . . . . . . . . . . . .1   2   3   4   5   6   7   *
```

Prognosis

What is this student counselor's promise as a counselor? _____

_____

_____

_____

_____

_____

_____   _____
       (Date)   (Signature of Supervisor)

My signature indicates that I have read the report(s) presented above and have had an opportunity to discuss the material with my supervisor.

_____   _____
       (Date)   (Signature of Student Counselor)

Form #16, p.2 of 2 pp.

COUNSELING PRACTICUM TAPES

WEEKLY EVALUATION RECORD

Practicum Student Name _____

DIRECTIONS: Supervisors or peers who are critiqueing practicum student's tapes are urged to use this subjective evaluation form once a week. This record has the advantage of allowing both critiquer and practicum student to understand the weekly progress made.

REMARKS (Based on all tapes critiqued during the week):

CHECK ONE:
___ Practicum Supervisor
___ Field Supervisor
___ Peer

Date_____   CRITIQUER SIGNATURE_____
- -
REMARKS (Based on all tapes critiqued during the week):

CHECK ONE:
___ Practicum Supervisor
___ Field Supervisor
___ Peer

Date_____   CRITIQUER SIGNATURE_____
- -
REMARKS (Based on all tapes critiqued during the week):

CHECK ONE:
___ Practicum Supervisor
___ Field Supervisor
___ Peer

Date_____   CRITIQUER SIGNATURE_____

Form #17, p.1 of 2 pp.

REMARKS (Based on all tapes critiqued during the week):

CHECK ONE:
___ Practicum Supervisor
___ Field Supervisor
___ Peer

Date_____ CRITIQUER SIGNATURE_____

REMARKS (Based on all tapes critiqued during the week):

CHECK ONE:
___ Practicum Supervisor
___ Field Supervisor
___ Peer

Date_____ CRITIQUER SIGNATURE_____

REMARKS (Based on all tapes critiqued during the week):

CHECK ONE:
___ Practicum Supervisor
___ Field Supervisor
___ Peer

Date_____ CRITIQUER SIGNATURE_____

REMARKS (Based on all tapes critiqued during the week):

CHECK ONE:
___ Practicum Supervisor
___ Field Supervisor
___ Peer

Date_____ CRITIQUER SIGNATURE_____

Form #17, p.2 of 2 pp.

COUNSELING PRACTICUM TAPES

WEEKLY EVALUATION RECORD

Practicum Student Name_____

DIRECTIONS: Supervisors or peers who are critiqueing practicum student's tapes are urged to use this subjective evaluation form once a week. This record has the advantage of allowing both critiquer and practicum student to understand the weekly progress made.

REMARKS (Based on all tapes critiqued during the week):

CHECK ONE:
___ Practicum Supervisor
___ Field Supervisor
___ Peer

Date_____ CRITIQUER SIGNATURE_____
- -
REMARKS (Based on all tapes critiqued during the week):

CHECK ONE:
___ Practicum Supervisor
___ Field Supervisor
___ Peer

Date_____ CRITIQUER SIGNATURE_____
- -
REMARKS (Based on all tapes critiqued during the week):

CHECK ONE:
___ Practicum Supervisor
___ Field Supervisor
___ Peer

Date_____ CRITIQUER SIGNATURE_____

Form #17, p.1 of 2 pp.

REMARKS (Based on all tapes critiqued during the week):

CHECK ONE:
___ Practicum Supervisor
___ Field Supervisor
___ Peer

Date_____ CRITIQUER SIGNATURE_____

REMARKS (Based on all tapes critiqued during the week):

CHECK ONE:
___ Practicum Supervisor
___ Field Supervisor
___ Peer

Date_____ CRITIQUER SIGNATURE_____

REMARKS (Based on all tapes critiqued during the week):

CHECK ONE:
___ Practicum Supervisor
___ Field Supervisor
___ Peer

Date_____ CRITIQUER SIGNATURE_____

REMARKS (Based on all tapes critiqued during the week):

CHECK ONE:
___ Practicum Supervisor
___ Field Supervisor
___ Peer

Date_____ CRITIQUER SIGNATURE_____

Form #17, p.2 of 2 pp.

COUNSELING PRACTICUM
INTERVIEW RATING FORM

Gordon Poling*

Client Name or   Practicum
  Identification _____   Counselor Name _____

CHECK ONE:
____ Audio Tape   Signature of Supervisor
____ Video Tape   or Observer _____
____ Observation
____ Other (Specify)   Date of Interview _____

DIRECTIONS: Practicum supervisor or peer of the practicum student is to mark a rating for each item and as much as possible is to provide remarks that will help the practicum counselor in his or her development.

SPECIFIC CRITERIA	RATING (best to least)	REMARKS
1. OPENING: Was opening unstructured, friendly, and pleasant? Any role definition needed? Any introduction necessary?	5 4 3 2 1	
2. RAPPORT: Did practicum counselor establish good rapport with counselee? Was the stage set for a productive interview?	5 4 3 2 1	
3. INTERVIEW RESPONSIBILITY: If not assumed by the counselee, did practicum counselor assume appropriate level of responsibility for interview conduct? Practicum counselor or counselee initiative?	5 4 3 2 1	
4. INTERACTION: Were the counselee and practicum counselor really communicating in a meaningful manner?	5 4 3 2 1	
5. ACCEPTANCE/PERMISSIVENESS: Was the practicum counselor accepting and permissive of counselee emotion, feelings and expressed thoughts?	5 4 3 2 1	
6. REFLECTIONS OF FEELINGS: Did practicum counselor reflect and react to feelings or did interview remain on an intellectual level?	5 4 3 2 1	

*Dr. Gordon Poling is Professor, School of Education, University of South Dakota. Printed by permission.

Form #18, p.1 of 2 pp.

SPECIFIC CRITERIA	RATING (best to least)	REMARKS

7. **PRACTICUM COUNSELOR RESPONSES:** Were practicum counselor responses appropriate in view of what the counselee was expressing or were responses concerned with trivia and minutia? Meaningful questions?   5 4 3 2 1

8. **VALUE MANAGEMENTS:** How did the practicum counselor cope with values? Were attempts made to impose counselor values during the interview?   5 4 3 2 1

9. **COUNSELING RELATIONSHIP:** Were practicum counselor-counselee relationships conducive to productive counseling? Was a counseling relationship established?   5 4 3 2 1

10. **CLOSING:** Was closing practicum counselor or counselee initiated? Was it abrupt brusque? Any follow-up or further interview scheduling accomplished?   5 4 3 2 1

11. **GENERAL TECHNIQUES:** How well did the practicum counselor conduct the mechanics of the interview?   5 4 3 2 1

    A. Duration of interview: Was the interview too long or too short? Should interview have been terminated sooner or later?
    B. Vocabulary level: Was practicum counselor vocabulary appropriate for the counselee?
    C. Mannerisms: Did the practicum counselor display any mannerism which might have adversely affected the interview or portions thereof?
    D. Verbosity: Did the practicum counselor dominate the interview, interrupt, override, or become too wordy?
    E. Silences: Were silences broken to meet practicum counselor needs or were they dealt with in an effectual manner?

COMMENTS FOR PRACTICUM COUNSELOR ASSISTANCE: Additional comments that might assist the practicum counselor in areas not covered by the preceding suggestions.

Form #18, p.2 of 2 pp.

COUNSELING PRACTICUM
INTERVIEW RATING FORM

Gordon Poling*

Client Name or
  Identification _____

Practicum
  Counselor Name _____

CHECK ONE:
____ Audio Tape
____ Video Tape
____ Observation
____ Other (Specify)

Signature of Supervisor
  or Observer _____

Date of Interview _____

DIRECTIONS: Practicum supervisor or peer of the practicum student is to mark a rating for each item and as much as possible is to provide remarks that will help the practicum counselor in his or her development.

SPECIFIC CRITERIA	RATING (best to least)	REMARKS
1. OPENING: Was opening unstructured, friendly, and pleasant? Any role definition needed? Any introduction necessary?	5 4 3 2 1	
2. RAPPORT: Did practicum counselor establish good rapport with counselee? Was the stage set for a productive interview?	5 4 3 2 1	
3. INTERVIEW RESPONSIBILITY: If not assumed by the counselee, did practicum counselor assume appropriate level of responsibility for interview conduct? Practicum counselor or counselee initiative?	5 4 3 2 1	
4. INTERACTION: Were the counselee and practicum counselor really communicating in a meaningful manner?	5 4 3 2 1	
5. ACCEPTANCE/PERMISSIVENESS: Was the practicum counselor accepting and permissive of counselee emotion, feelings and expressed thoughts?	5 4 3 2 1	
6. REFLECTIONS OF FEELINGS: Did practicum counselor reflect and react to feelings or did interview remain on an intellectual level?	5 4 3 2 1	

*Dr. Gordon Poling is Professor, School of Education, University of South Dakota. Printed by permission.

Form #18, p.1 of 2 pp.

SPECIFIC CRITERIA	RATING (best to least)	REMARKS
7. PRACTICUM COUNSELOR RESPONSES: Were practicum counselor responses appropriate in view of what the counselee was expressing or were responses concerned with trivia and minutia? Meaningful questions?	5 4 3 2 1	
8. VALUE MANAGEMENTS: How did the practicum counselor cope with values? Were attempts made to impose counselor values during the interview?	5 4 3 2 1	
9. COUNSELING RELATIONSHIP: Were practicum counselor-counselee relationships conducive to productive counseling? Was a counseling relationship established?	5 4 3 2 1	
10. CLOSING: Was closing practicum counselor or counselee initiated? Was it abrupt brusque? Any follow-up or further interview scheduling accomplished?	5 4 3 2 1	
11. GENERAL TECHNIQUES: How well did the practicum counselor conduct the mechanics of the interview?	5 4 3 2 1	

    A. Duration of interview: Was the interview too long or too short? Should interview have been terminated sooner or later?
    B. Vocabulary level: Was practicum counselor vocabulary appropriate for the counselee?
    C. Mannerisms: Did the practicum counselor display any mannerism which might have adversely affected the interview or portions thereof?
    D. Verbosity: Did the practicum counselor dominate the interview, interrupt, override, or become too wordy?
    E. Silences: Were silences broken to meet practicum counselor needs or were they dealt with in an effectual manner?

COMMENTS FOR PRACTICUM COUNSELOR ASSISTANCE: Additional comments that might assist the practicum counselor in areas not covered by the preceding suggestions.

Form #18, p.2 of 2 pp.

COUNSELING PRACTICUM
INTERVIEW RATING FORM

Gordon Poling*

Client Name or
   Identification _____

Practicum
   Counselor Name _____

CHECK ONE:
_____ Audio Tape
_____ Video Tape
_____ Observation
_____ Other (Specify)

Signature of Supervisor
   or Observer _____

Date of Interview _____

DIRECTIONS: Practicum supervisor or peer of the practicum student is to mark a rating for each item and as much as possible is to provide remarks that will help the practicum counselor in his or her development.

SPECIFIC CRITERIA	RATING (best to least)	REMARKS
1. OPENING: Was opening unstructured, friendly, and pleasant? Any role definition needed? Any introduction necessary?	5 4 3 2 1	
2. RAPPORT: Did practicum counselor establish good rapport with counselee? Was the stage set for a productive interview?	5 4 3 2 1	
3. INTERVIEW RESPONSIBILITY: If not assumed by the counselee, did practicum counselor assume appropriate level of responsibility for interview conduct? Practicum counselor or counselee initiative?	5 4 3 2 1	
4. INTERACTION: Were the counselee and practicum counselor really communicating in a meaningful manner?	5 4 3 2 1	
5. ACCEPTANCE/PERMISSIVENESS: Was the practicum counselor accepting and permissive of counselee emotion, feelings and expressed thoughts?	5 4 3 2 1	
6. REFLECTIONS OF FEELINGS: Did practicum counselor reflect and react to feelings or did interview remain on an intellectual level?	5 4 3 2 1	

*Dr. Gordon Poling is Professor, School of Education, University of South Dakota. Printed by permission.

Form #18, p.1 of 2 pp.

SPECIFIC CRITERIA	RATING (best to least)	REMARKS
7. PRACTICUM COUNSELOR RESPONSES: Were practicum counselor responses appropriate in view of what the counselee was expressing or were responses concerned with trivia and minutia? Meaningful questions?	5 4 3 2 1	
8. VALUE MANAGEMENTS: How did the practicum counselor cope with values? Were attempts made to impose counselor values during the interview?	5 4 3 2 1	
9. COUNSELING RELATIONSHIP: Were practicum counselor-counselee relationships conducive to productive counseling? Was a counseling relationship established?	5 4 3 2 1	
10. CLOSING: Was closing practicum counselor or counselee initiated? Was it abrupt brusque? Any follow-up or further interview scheduling accomplished?	5 4 3 2 1	

11. GENERAL TECHNIQUES: How well did the practicum counselor conduct the mechanics of the interview?
 	
   A. Duration of interview: Was the interview too long or too short? Should interview have been terminated sooner or later?
   B. Vocabulary level: Was practicum counselor vocabulary appropriate for the counselee?
   C. Mannerisms: Did the practicum counselor display any mannerism which might have adversely affected the interview or portions thereof?
   D. Verbosity: Did the practicum counselor dominate the interview, interrupt, override, or become too wordy?
   E. Silences: Were silences broken to meet practicum counselor needs or were they dealt with in an effectual manner?
	5 4 3 2 1	

COMMENTS FOR PRACTICUM COUNSELOR ASSISTANCE: Additional comments that might assist the practicum counselor in areas not covered by the preceding suggestions.

COUNSELING PRACTICUM
INTERVIEW RATING FORM

Gordon Poling*

Client Name or
Identification _____

Practicum
Counselor Name _____

CHECK ONE:
____ Audio Tape
____ Video Tape
____ Observation
____ Other (Specify)

Signature of Supervisor
or Observer _____

Date of Interview _____

DIRECTIONS: Practicum supervisor or peer of the practicum student is to mark a rating for each item and as much as possible is to provide remarks that will help the practicum counselor in his or her development.

SPECIFIC CRITERIA	RATING (best to least)	REMARKS
1. OPENING: Was opening unstructured, friendly, and pleasant? Any role definition needed? Any introduction necessary?	5 4 3 2 1	
2. RAPPORT: Did practicum counselor establish good rapport with counselee? Was the stage set for a productive interview?	5 4 3 2 1	
3. INTERVIEW RESPONSIBILITY: If not assumed by the counselee, did practicum counselor assume appropriate level of responsibility for interview conduct? Practicum counselor or counselee initiative?	5 4 3 2 1	
4. INTERACTION: Were the counselee and practicum counselor really communicating in a meaningful manner?	5 4 3 2 1	
5. ACCEPTANCE/PERMISSIVENESS: Was the practicum counselor accepting and permissive of counselee emotion, feelings and expressed thoughts?	5 4 3 2 1	
6. REFLECTIONS OF FEELINGS: Did practicum counselor reflect and react to feelings or did interview remain on an intellectual level?	5 4 3 2 1	

*Dr. Gordon Poling is Professor, School of Education, University of South Dakota. Printed by permission.

Form #18, p.1 of 2 pp.

SPECIFIC CRITERIA	RATING (best to least)	REMARKS
7. PRACTICUM COUNSELOR RESPONSES: Were practicum counselor responses appropriate in view of what the counselee was expressing or were responses concerned with trivia and minutia? Meaningful questions?	5 4 3 2 1	
8. VALUE MANAGEMENTS: How did the practicum counselor cope with values? Were attempts made to impose counselor values during the interview?	5 4 3 2 1	
9. COUNSELING RELATIONSHIP: Were practicum counselor-counselee relationships conducive to productive counseling? Was a counseling relationship established?	5 4 3 2 1	
10. CLOSING: Was closing practicum counselor or counselee initiated? Was it abrupt brusque? Any follow-up or further interview scheduling accomplished?	5 4 3 2 1	
11. GENERAL TECHNIQUES: How well did the practicum counselor conduct the mechanics of the interview? A. Duration of interview: Was the interview too long or too short? Should interview have been terminated sooner or later? B. Vocabulary level: Was practicum counselor vocabulary appropriate for the counselee? C. Mannerisms: Did the practicum counselor display any mannerism which might have adversely affected the interview or portions thereof? D. Verbosity: Did the practicum counselor dominate the interview, interrupt, override, or become too wordy? E. Silences: Were silences broken to meet practicum counselor needs or were they dealt with in an effectual manner?	5 4 3 2 1	

COMMENTS FOR PRACTICUM COUNSELOR ASSISTANCE: Additional comments that might assist the practicum counselor in areas not covered by the preceding suggestions.

Form #18, p.2 of 2 pp.

COUNSELING PRACTICUM
INTERVIEW RATING FORM

Gordon Poling*

Client Name or
Identification _____   Practicum
                                   Counselor Name _____

CHECK ONE:
____ Audio Tape   Signature of Supervisor
____ Video Tape   or Observer _____
____ Observation
____ Other (Specify)   Date of Interview _____

DIRECTIONS: Practicum supervisor or peer of the practicum student is to mark a rating for each item and as much as possible is to provide remarks that will help the practicum counselor in his or her development.

SPECIFIC CRITERIA	RATING (best to least)	REMARKS
1. OPENING: Was opening unstructured, friendly, and pleasant? Any role definition needed? Any introduction necessary?	5 4 3 2 1	
2. RAPPORT: Did practicum counselor establish good rapport with counselee? Was the stage set for a productive interview?	5 4 3 2 1	
3. INTERVIEW RESPONSIBILITY: If not assumed by the counselee, did practicum counselor assume appropriate level of responsibility for interview conduct? Practicum counselor or counselee initiative?	5 4 3 2 1	
4. INTERACTION: Were the counselee and practicum counselor really communicating in a meaningful manner?	5 4 3 2 1	
5. ACCEPTANCE/PERMISSIVENESS: Was the practicum counselor accepting and permissive of counselee emotion, feelings and expressed thoughts?	5 4 3 2 1	
6. REFLECTIONS OF FEELINGS: Did practicum counselor reflect and react to feelings or did interview remain on an intellectual level?	5 4 3 2 1	

*Dr. Gordon Poling is Professor, School of Education, University of South Dakota. Printed by permission.

Form #18, p.1 of 2 pp.

SPECIFIC CRITERIA	RATING (best to least)	REMARKS
7. PRACTICUM COUNSELOR RESPONSES: Were practicum counselor responses appropriate in view of what the counselee was expressing or were responses concerned with trivia and minutia? Meaningful questions?	5 4 3 2 1	
8. VALUE MANAGEMENTS: How did the practicum counselor cope with values? Were attempts made to impose counselor values during the interview?	5 4 3 2 1	
9. COUNSELING RELATIONSHIP: Were practicum counselor-counselee relationships conducive to productive counseling? Was a counseling relationship established?	5 4 3 2 1	
10. CLOSING: Was closing practicum counselor or counselee initiated? Was it abrupt brusque? Any follow-up or further interview scheduling accomplished?	5 4 3 2 1	
11. GENERAL TECHNIQUES: How well did the practicum counselor conduct the mechanics of the interview?	5 4 3 2 1	

    A. Duration of interview: Was the interview too long or too short? Should interview have been terminated sooner or later?
    B. Vocabulary level: Was practicum counselor vocabulary appropriate for the counselee?
    C. Mannerisms: Did the practicum counselor display any mannerism which might have adversely affected the interview or portions thereof?
    D. Verbosity: Did the practicum counselor dominate the interview, interrupt, override, or become too wordy?
    E. Silences: Were silences broken to meet practicum counselor needs or were they dealt with in an effectual manner?

COMMENTS FOR PRACTICUM COUNSELOR ASSISTANCE: Additional comments that might assist the practicum counselor in areas not covered by the preceding suggestions.

Form #18, p.2 of 2 pp.

SUPERVISOR EVALUATION OF PRACTICUM COUNSELOR*

SUGGESTED USE: This form is to be used to check competencies in counseling practicum. The form may be completed after each supervised counseling session or may cover several supervisions over a period of time. The form is appropriate for individual or group counseling.

ALTERNATE USE: The student counselor may ask a peer to observe a counseling session and mark the evaluation.

Name of Practicum Counselor _____

Name of Client _____

Date of Supervision _____ or Period Covered by the Evaluation _____

DIRECTIONS: The supervisor following each counseling session which has been supervised or after several supervisions covering a period of time is to circle a number which best evaluates the practicum counselor on each competence at that point in time.

		Poor	Adequate	Good
	General Supervision Comments			
1.	Demonstrates a personal commitment in developing professional competencies.	1 2	3 4	5 6
2.	Invests time and energy in becoming a counselor.	1 2	3 4	5 6
3.	Accepts and uses constructive criticism to enhance self-development and counseling skills.	1 2	3 4	5 6
4.	Engages in open, comfortable and clear communication with peers and supervisors.	1 2	3 4	5 6
5.	Recognizes own competencies and skills and shares these with peers and supervisors.	1 2	3 4	5 6
6.	Recognizes own deficiencies and actively works to overcome them with peers and supervisors.	1 2	3 4	5 6
7.	Completes case reports and record punctually and conscientiously.	1 2	3 4	5 6

---

*Printed by permission from Dr. Harold Hackney, Assistant Professor, Purdue University. This form was designed by two graduate students based upon material drawn from COUNSELING STRATEGIES AND OBJECTIVES by H. Hackney and S. Nye, Prentice-Hall, 1973.

Form #19, p.1 of 4 pp.

		Poor	Adequate	Good

The Counseling Process

		Poor	Adequate	Good
8.	Researches the referral prior to the first interview.	1 2	3 4	5 6
9.	Keeps appointments on time.	1 2	3 4	5 6
10.	Begins the interview smoothly.	1 2	3 4	5 6
11.	Explains the nature and objectives of counseling when appropriate.	1 2	3 4	5 6
12.	Is relaxed and comfortable in the interview.	1 2	3 4	5 6
13.	Communicates interest in and acceptance of the client.	1 2	3 4	5 6
14.	Facilitates client expression of concerns and feelings.	1 2	3 4	5 6
15.	Focuses on the content of the client's problems.	1 2	3 4	5 6
16.	Recognizes and resists manipulation by the client.	1 2	3 4	5 6
17.	Recognizes and deals with positive effect of the client.	1 2	3 4	5 6
18.	Recognizes and deals with negative effect of the client.	1 2	3 4	5 6
19.	Is spontaneous in the interview.	1 2	3 4	5 6
20.	Uses silence effectively in the interview.	1 2	3 4	5 6
21.	Is aware of own feelings in the counseling session.	1 2	3 4	5 6
22.	Communicates own feelings to the client when appropriate.	1 2	3 4	5 6
23.	Recognizes and skillfully interprets the client's covert messages.	1 2	3 4	5 6
24.	Facilitates realistic goal-setting with the client.	1 2	3 4	5 6
25.	Encourages appropriate action-step planning with the client.	1 2	3 4	5 6
26.	Employs judgment in the timing and use of different techniques and strategies	1 2	3 4	5 6
27.	Initiates periodic evaluation of goals, action-steps and process during counseling.	1 2	3 4	5 6

Form #19, p.2 of 4 pp.

		Poor	Adequate	Good
28.	Explains, administers and interprets tests correctly.	1 2	3 4	5 6
29.	Terminates the interview smoothly.	1 2	3 4	5 6

The Conceptualization Process

		Poor	Adequate	Good
30.	Focuses on specific behaviors and their consequences, implications, and contingencies.	1 2	3 4	5 6
31.	Recognizes and pursues discrepancies and meaning of inconsistent information.	1 2	3 4	5 6
32.	Uses relevant case data in planning both immediate and long-range goals.	1 2	3 4	5 6
33.	Uses relevant case data in considering various strategies and their implication.	1 2	3 4	5 6
34.	Bases decisions on a theoretically sound and consistent rationale of human behavior.	1 2	3 4	5 6
35.	Is perceptive in evaluating the effects of own counseling techniques.	1 2	3 4	5 6
36.	Demonstrates ethical behavior in the counseling activity and case management.	1 2	3 4	5 6

Form #19, p.3 of 4 pp.

Additional Comments and/or Suggestions

_____
_____
_____
_____
_____
_____
_____
_____
_____
_____
_____
_____
_____
_____

_____   _____
  Date   Practicum Supervisor

My signature indicates that I have read the above report and have discussed the content with my supervisor. It does not necessarily indicate that I agree with the report in part or in whole.

_____   _____
  Date   Signature of Practicum Student

Form #19, p.4 of 4 pp.

SUPERVISOR EVALUATION OF PRACTICUM COUNSELOR*

SUGGESTED USE: This form is to be used to check competencies in counseling practicum. The form may be completed after each supervised counseling session or may cover several supervisions over a period of time. The form is appropriate for individual or group counseling.

ALTERNATE USE: The student counselor may ask a peer to observe a counseling session and mark the evaluation.

Name of Practicum Counselor _____

Name of Client _____

Date of Supervision _____ or Period Covered by the Evaluation _____

DIRECTIONS: The supervisor following each counseling session which has been supervised or after several supervisions covering a period of time is to circle a number which best evaluates the practicum counselor on each competence at that point in time.

	Poor	Adequate	Good
General Supervision Comments			
1. Demonstrates a personal commitment in developing professional competencies.	1 2	3 4	5 6
2. Invests time and energy in becoming a counselor.	1 2	3 4	5 6
3. Accepts and uses constructive criticism to enhance self-development and counseling skills.	1 2	3 4	5 6
4. Engages in open, comfortable and clear communication with peers and supervisors.	1 2	3 4	5 6
5. Recognizes own competencies and skills and shares these with peers and supervisors.	1 2	3 4	5 6
6. Recognizes own deficiencies and actively works to overcome them with peers and supervisors.	1 2	3 4	5 6
7. Completes case reports and record punctually and conscientiously.	1 2	3 4	5 6

---

*Printed by permission from Dr. Harold Hackney, Assistant Professor, Purdue University. This form was designed by two graduate students based upon material drawn from COUNSELING STRATEGIES AND OBJECTIVES by H. Hackney and S. Nye, Prentice-Hall, 1973.

		Poor	Adequate	Good
	## The Counseling Process			
8.	Researches the referral prior to the first interview.	1 2	3 4	5 6
9.	Keeps appointments on time.	1 2	3 4	5 6
10.	Begins the interview smoothly.	1 2	3 4	5 6
11.	Explains the nature and objectives of counseling when appropriate.	1 2	3 4	5 6
12.	Is relaxed and comfortable in the interview.	1 2	3 4	5 6
13.	Communicates interest in and acceptance of the client.	1 2	3 4	5 6
14.	Facilitates client expression of concerns and feelings.	1 2	3 4	5 6
15.	Focuses on the content of the client's problems.	1 2	3 4	5 6
16.	Recognizes and resists manipulation by the client.	1 2	3 4	5 6
17.	Recognizes and deals with positive effect of the client.	1 2	3 4	5 6
18.	Recognizes and deals with negative effect of the client.	1 2	3 4	5 6
19.	Is spontaneous in the interview.	1 2	3 4	5 6
20.	Uses silence effectively in the interview.	1 2	3 4	5 6
21.	Is aware of own feelings in the counseling session.	1 2	3 4	5 6
22.	Communicates own feelings to the client when appropriate.	1 2	3 4	5 6
23.	Recognizes and skillfully interprets the client's covert messages.	1 2	3 4	5 6
24.	Facilitates realistic goal-setting with the client.	1 2	3 4	5 6
25.	Encourages appropriate action-step planning with the client.	1 2	3 4	5 6
26.	Employs judgment in the timing and use of different techniques and strategies	1 2	3 4	5 6
27.	Initiates periodic evaluation of goals, action-steps and process during counseling.	1 2	3 4	5 6

Form #19, p.2 of 4 pp.

		Poor	Adequate	Good
28.	Explains, administers and interprets tests correctly.	1 2	3 4	5 6
29.	Terminates the interview smoothly.	1 2	3 4	5 6

The Conceptualization Process

		Poor	Adequate	Good
30.	Focuses on specific behaviors and their consequences, implications, and contingencies.	1 2	3 4	5 6
31.	Recognizes and pursues discrepancies and meaning of inconsistent information.	1 2	3 4	5 6
32.	Uses relevant case data in planning both immediate and long-range goals.	1 2	3 4	5 6
33.	Uses relevant case data in considering various strategies and their implication.	1 2	3 4	5 6
34.	Bases decisions on a theoretically sound and consistent rationale of human behavior.	1 2	3 4	5 6
35.	Is perceptive in evaluating the effects of own counseling techniques.	1 2	3 4	5 6
36.	Demonstrates ethical behavior in the counseling activity and case management.	1 2	3 4	5 6

Form #19, p.3 of 4 pp.

Additional Comments and/or Suggestions

_____
_____
_____
_____
_____
_____
_____
_____
_____
_____
_____
_____
_____
_____

_____   _____
Date   Practicum Supervisor

My signature indicates that I have read the above report and have discussed the content with my supervisor. It does not necessarily indicate that I agree with the report in part or in whole.

_____   _____
Date   Signature of Practicum Student

Form #19, p.4 of 4 pp.

STUDENT COUNSELOR EVALUATION OF SUPERVISOR*

SUGGESTED USE: The practicum supervisor could obtain feedback on the supervision by asking student counselors to complete this form. The evaluation could be done at mid-term and/or final. The purposes are twofold: (1) to provide feedback for improving supervision and (2) to encourage communication between the supervisor and the student counselor.

Name of Practicum Supervisor_____

Period covered_____ to _____

DIRECTIONS: The student counselor when asked to do so is to make an evaluation of the supervision received. Circle the number which best represents how you, the student counselor, feel about the supervision received. After the form is completed, the supervisor may suggest a meeting to discuss the supervision desired.

		Poor	Adequate	Good
1.	Gives time and energy in observing, tape processing and case conferences.	1 2	3 4	5 6
2.	Accepts and respects me as a person.	1 2	3 4	5 6
3.	Recognizes and encourages further development of my strengths and capabilities.	1 2	3 4	5 6
4.	Gives me useful feedback when I do something well.	1 2	3 4	5 6
5.	Provides me the freedom to develop flexible and effective counseling styles.	1 2	3 4	5 6
6.	Encourages and listens to my ideas and suggestions for developing my counseling skills.	1 2	3 4	5 6
7.	Provides suggestions for developing my counseling skills.	1 2	3 4	5 6
8.	Helps me to understand the implications and dynamics of the counseling approaches I use.	1 2	3 4	5 6
9.	Encourages me to use new and different techniques when appropriate.	1 2	3 4	5 6
10.	Is spontaneous and flexible in the supervisory sessions.	1 2	3 4	5 6

*Printed by permission from Dr. Harold Hackney, Assistant Professor, Purdue University. This form was designed by two graduate students based upon material drawn from COUNSELING STRATEGIES AND OBJECTIVES by H. Hackney and S. Nye, Prentice-Hall, 1973.

Form #20, p.1 of 3 pp.

		Poor	Adequate	Good
11.	Helps me to define and achieve specific concrete goals for myself during the practicum experience.	1 2	3 4	5 6
12.	Gives me useful feedback when I do something wrong.	1 2	3 4	5 6
13.	Allows me to discuss problems I encounter in my practicum setting.	1 2	3 4	5 6
14.	Pays amount of attention to both me and my clients.	1 2	3 4	5 6
15.	Focuses on both verbal and nonverbal behavior in me and in my clients.	1 2	3 4	5 6
16.	Helps me define and maintain ethical behavior in counseling and case management.	1 2	3 4	5 6
17.	Encourages me to engage in professional behavior.	1 2	3 4	5 6
18.	Maintains confidentiality in material discussed in supervisory sessions.	1 2	3 4	5 6
19.	Deals with both content and effect when supervising.	1 2	3 4	5 6
20.	Focuses on the implications, consequences and contingencies of specific behaviors in counseling and supervision.	1 2	3 4	5 6
21.	Helps me organize relevant case data in planning goals and strategies with my client.	1 2	3 4	5 6
22.	Helps me to formulate a theoretically sound rationale of human behavior.	1 2	3 4	5 6
23.	Offers resource information when I request or need it.	1 2	3 4	5 6
24.	Helps me develop increased skill in critiquing and gaining insight from my counseling tapes.	1 2	3 4	5 6
25.	Allows and encourages me to evaluate myself.	1 2	3 4	5 6
26.	Explains his/her criteria for evaluation clearly and in behavioral terms.	1 2	3 4	5 6
27.	Applies his/her criteria fairly in evaluating my counseling performance.	1 2	3 4	5 6

Form #20, p.2 of 3 pp.

Additional Comments and/or Suggestions
_____
_____
_____
_____
_____
_____
_____
_____

_____   _____
      Date   Practicum Student

My signature indicates that I have read the above report and have discussed the content with my supervisee. It does not necessarily indicate that I agree with the report in part or in whole.

_____   _____
      Date   Signature of Supervisor

Form #20, p.3 of 3 pp.

BIBLIOGRAPHY

Often we are asked by our students for a list of related reading that might add to their understanding of themselves and/or the counseling process. As many of you know, compiling a bibliography on the subject of counseling is quite easy. However, we have endeavored to present a very concise, pertinent and current list of really useful sources. Hopefully, the practicum student and/or instructor will find this list facilitative for the additional enrichment they might be seeking.

THE COUNSELOR AS A PERSON

Bardwick, J.; Douvan, E.; and Gutmann, D. FEMININE PERSONALITY AND CONFLICT. Belmont, Calif.: Brooks/Cole, 1970.

Beers, C. A MIND THAT FOUND ITSELF. Rev. ed. New York: Doubleday, 1948.

Bessell, H., and Palomares, U. METHODS IN HUMAN DEVELOPMENT. San Diego, Calif.: Human Development Training Institute, 1970.

Carkhuff, R. R. THE ART OF HELPING. Amherst, Mass.: Human Resource Development Press, 1972.

Carkhuff, R. R. THE DEVELOPMENT OF HUMAN RESOURCES: EDUCATION, PSYCHOLOGY AND SOCIAL CHANGE. New York: Holt, Rinehart and Winston, 1971.

Collins, A. H. THE LONELY AND AFRAID. New York: Odyssey Press, 1969.

Dinkmeyer, D. DEVELOPING UNDERSTANDING OF SELF AND OTHERS (DUSO, D-1). Circle Pines, Minn.: American Guidance Service, 1970.

Fitts, W. E. THE EXPERIENCE OF PSYCHOTHERAPY. New York: VanNostrand Reinhold, 1965.

Frankl, V. E. MAN'S SEARCH FOR MEANING. Rev. ed. Boston: Beacon Press, 1963.

Jourard, S. M. THE TRANSPARENT SELF. 2d ed. New York: VanNostrand Reinhold, 1971.

Laing, R. D. THE DIVIDED SELF. New York: Pantheon Books, 1969.

Loevinger, J. THE MEANING AND MEASUREMENT OF EGO DEVELOPMENT. San Francisco: Jossey-Bass, 1970.

Mace, D., and Mace, V. WE CAN HAVE BETTER MARRIAGES IF WE REALLY WANT THEM. Nashville, Tennessee: Abingdon Press, 1974.

Maslow, A. THE FARTHER REACHES OF HUMAN NATURE. New York: Viking Press, 1971.

May, R., ed. EXISTENCE. New York: Basic Books, 1958.

Perls, F. S. IN AND OUT OF THE GARBAGE PAIL. Lafayette, California: Real People Press, 1969.

Rogers, C. FREEDOM TO LEARN. Columbus, Ohio: Charles E. Merrill, 1969.

Rogers, C. R., and Stevens, B. PERSON TO PERSON. Lafayette, California: Real People Press, 1967.

Skinner, B. F. BEYOND FREEDOM AND DIGNITY. New York: Knopf, 1971.

Toffler, A. FUTURE SHOCK. New York: Bantam Books, 1970.

Viscott, D. THE MAKING OF A PSYCHIATRIST. New York: Arbor House, 1972.

Williams, K. THE SCHOOL COUNSELOR. London: Methuen, 1973.

THE COUNSELING PROCESS

Allen, T., and Whiteley, J. W. DIMENSIONS OF EFFECTIVE COUNSELING. Columbus, Ohio: Charles E. Merrill, 1968.

Appley, D. G., and Winder, A. E. T-GROUPS AND THERAPY IN A CHANGING SOCIETY. San Francisco: Jossey-Bass, Inc., 1973.

Arbuckle, D. S. COUNSELING: PHILOSOPHY, THEORY AND PRACTICE. 2d ed. Boston: Allyn and Bacon, 1970.

Assagioli, R. THE ACT OF WILL. New York: Viking Press, 1973.

Axline, V. PLAY THERAPY. Rev. ed. New York: Ballantine, 1969.

Barclay, J. R. FOUNDATIONS OF COUNSELING STRATEGIES. New York: Wiley, 1971.

Bart, P. "Depression in Middle-Aged Women." WOMEN IN SEXIST SOCIETY: STUDIES IN POWER AND POWERLESSNESS. Edited by V. Gornick and B. Moran. New York: Basic Books, 1971.

Becuar, R. SKILLS FOR EFFECTIVE COMMUNICATION: A GUIDE FOR BUILDING RELATIONSHIPS. New York: Wiley, 1974.

Belcher, D. W. COMPENSATION ADMINISTRATION. Englewood Cliffs, New Jersey: Prentice-Hall, Inc., 1974.

Belkin, G. PRACTICAL COUNSELING IN THE SCHOOLS. Dubuque, Iowa: Wm. C. Brown Company Publishers, 1975.

Belliveau, F., and Richter, L. UNDERSTANDING HUMAN SEXUAL INADEQUACY. New York: Bantam Books, 1970.

Benjamin, A., ed. THE HELPING INTERVIEW. Boston: Houghton Mifflin, 1969.

Berger, M., ed. VIDEOTAPE TECHNIQUES IN PSYCHIATRIC TRAINING AND TREATMENT. New York: Brunner/Mazel, 1970.

Bergin, A., and Garfield, S., eds. HANDBOOK OF PSYCHOTHERAPY AND BEHAVIOR CHANGE. New York: Wiley, 1971.

Berzon, B., and Solomon, L. N., eds. NEW PERSPECTIVES IN ENCOUNTER GROUPS. San Francisco, Calif.: Jossey-Bass, 1972.

Blatner, H. A. ACTING-IN. New York: Springer Publishing Company, 1973.

Blocher, D. H. DEVELOPMENTAL COUNSELING. New York: Ronald Press, 1974.

Bordin, E. S. PSYCHOLOGICAL COUNSELING. 2d ed. New York: Appleton-Century-Crofts, 1968.

Brammer, L. M., and Shostrom, E. L. THERAPEUTIC PSYCHOLOGY. Englewood Cliffs, New Jersey: Prentice-Hall, 1968.

Brodsky, S. L. PSYCHOLOGISTS IN THE CRIMINAL JUSTICE SYSTEM. Washington, D. C.: American Association of Correctional Psychologists, 1972.

Campbell, D. P. THE RESULTS OF COUNSELING. Philadelphia: Saunders, 1965.

Carkhuff, R. R., and Berenson, B. G. BEYOND COUNSELING AND PSYCHOTHERAPY. New York: Rinehart and Winston, 1967.

Chesler, P. WOMEN AND MADNESS. New York: Doubleday, 1972.

Comfort, A. THE JOY OF SEX: A CORDON BLEU GUIDE TO LOVEMAKING. New York: Crown, 1972.

Cook, B., and Stone, B. COUNSELING WOMEN. SPECIAL TOPICS IN COUNSELING. GUIDANCE MONOGRAPH SERIES, Series VII. Edited by Shelley C. Stone and Bruce Sertzer. Boston: Houghton Mifflin Company, 1973.

Cottle, W. C., and Downie, N. M. PREPARATION FOR COUNSELING. 2d ed. Englewood Cliffs, New Jersey: Prentice-Hall, 1970.

Cronbach, L. J., and Drenth, P. J. D. MENTAL TESTS AND CULTURAL ADAPTATION. The Hague, The Netherlands: Mouton Publishers, 1972.

Danish, S., and Haver, A. HELPING SKILLS. New York: Behavioral Publications, 1973.

Dimick, K. M., and Huff, V. E. CHILD COUNSELING. Dubuque, Iowa: W. C. Brown, 1970.

Dinkmeyer, D. C., and Dreikurs, R. ENCOURAGING CHILDREN TO LEARN. New York: Prentice-Hall, 1963.

Dinkmeyer, D. C. GUIDANCE AND COUNSELING IN THE ELEMENTARY SCHOOL. New York: Holt, Rinehart and Winston, 1967.

Dreyfus, E. A. YOUTH: SEARCH FOR MEANING. Columbus, Ohio: Charles E. Merrill, 1972.

Farber, J. THE STUDENT AS NIGGER. New York: Pocket Books, 1969.

Garrett, A. INTERVIEWING: ITS PRINCIPLES AND METHODS. New York: Family Service Association, 1972.

Ginott, H. G. BETWEEN PARENT AND CHILD. New York: MacMillan, 1965.

Gluckstern, N., and Ivey, A. BASIC ATTENDING SKILLS: AN INTRODUCTION TO MICROCOUNSELING AND HELPING. Amherst, Mass.: Microtraining Associates, 1974.

Gordon, T. PARENT EFFECTIVENESS TRAINING. New York: Wyden, 1970.

Gum, M. F. THE ELEMENTARY SCHOOL GUIDANCE COUNSELOR: A DEVELOPMENTAL MODEL. St. Paul, Minn.: Minnesota Department of Education, 1969.

Hansen, J. C. GUIDANCE SERVICES IN ELEMENTARY SCHOOLS. Washington, D. C.: A.P.G.A., 1971.

Hardy, R. E., and Cull, J. G. THERAPEUTIC NEEDS OF THE FAMILY. Springfield, Illinois: Charles C. Thomas, Publisher, 1974.

Haworth, M., ed. CHILD PSYCHOTHERAPY. New York: Basic Books, 1964.

Hendrickson, D. E., and Krause, F. H. COUNSELING AND PSYCHOTHERAPY: TRAINING AND SUPERVISION. Columbus, Ohio: Charles E. Merrill, 1972.

Ivey, A. MICROCOUNSELING: INNOVATIONS IN INTERVIEWING TRAINING. Springfield, Ill.: C. C. Thomas, 1971.

Katz, R. L. EMPATHY: ITS NATURE AND USES. New York: Free Press of Glencoe, 1963.

Kaufman, S. DIARY OF A MAD HOUSEWIFE. New York: Bantam Books, 1968.

Kohlberg, L., and Turiel, E. MORALIZATION: THE COGNITIVE DEVELOPMENTAL APPROACH. New York: Holt, Rinehart and Winston, 1974.

Krantzler, M. CREATIVE DIVORCE: A NEW OPPORTUNITY FOR PERSONAL GROWTH. New York: M. Evans and Co., Inc., 1974.

Krause, F. H., and Hendrickson, D. E. COUNSELING TECHNIQUES WITH YOUTH. Columbus, Ohio: Charles E. Merrill, 1972.

Kroth, J. A. COUNSELING PSYCHOLOGY AND GUIDANCE. Springfield, Illinois: C. C. Thomas, Publisher, 1973.

Krumboltz, J. D., ed. REVOLUTION IN COUNSELING: IMPLICATIONS OF BEHAVIORAL SCIENCE. Boston: Houghton Mifflin, 1966.

Levin, P. A., ed. CONTEMPORARY PROBLEMS OF DRUG ABUSE. Acton, Massachusetts: Publishing Sciences Group Inc., 1974.

Litwack, L.; Getson, R.; and Saltzman, G., eds. RESEARCH IN COUNSELING. Itasca, Illinois: F. E. Peacock, 1968.

Matthews, E. E., et al. COUNSELING GIRLS AND WOMEN OVER THE LIFESPAN. Washington, D. C.: A.P.G.A., 1972.

McIntire, R. W. FOR LOVE OF CHILDREN. Del Mar: CRM Books, 1970.

Meltzoff, J., and Kornreich, M. RESEARCH IN PSYCHOTHERAPY. New York: Atherton Press, 1970.

Osipow, S. H., and Walsh, W. B. STRATEGIES IN COUNSELING FOR BEHAVIOR CHANGE. New York: Appleton-Century-Crofts, 1970.

Patterson, C. H., ed. THE COUNSELOR IN THE SCHOOL: SELECTED READINGS. New York: McGraw-Hill, 1967.

Reuben, D. HOW TO GET MORE OUT OF SEX THAN YOU EVER THOUGHT YOU COULD. New York: David McKay, 1974.

Sattler, J. M. ASSESSMENT OF CHILDREN'S INTELLIGENCE. Philadelphia: W. B. Saunders, 1974.

Super, D. E. COMPUTER-ASSISTED COUNSELING. New York: Teachers College Press, 1970.

Thoresen, C. E., and Mahoney, M. BEHAVIORAL SELF-CONTROL. New York: Holt, Rinehart and Winston, 1974.

Thorne, F. C. PSYCHOLOGICAL CASE HANDLING. Brandon, Vermont: Clinical Psychology Publishing Company, 1968. 2 vols.

Tolbert, E. L. INTRODUCTION TO COUNSELING. 2d ed. New York: McGraw-Hill, 1972.

Truax, C. B., and Carkhuff, R. R. TOWARD EFFECTIVE COUNSELING AND PSYCHOTHERAPY: TRAINING AND PRACTICE. Chicago: Aldine, 1967.

Tyler, L. E. THE WORK OF THE COUNSELOR. 3d ed. New York: Appleton-Century-Crofts, 1969.

Ware, C., and Gold, B. K. THE LOS ANGELES CITY COLLEGE PEER COUNSELING PROGRAM. Washington, D. C.: American Association of Junior Colleges, 1971.

Williamson, E. G. COUNSELING ADOLESCENTS. New York: McGraw-Hill, 1950.

Woody, R. H., and Woody, J. D. SEXUAL, MARITAL, AND FAMILIAL RELATIONS: THERAPEUTIC INTERVENTIONS FOR PROFESSIONAL HELPING. Springfield, Illinois: Charles C. Thomas, 1973.

PHILOSOPHICAL AND THEORETICAL BASE OF COUNSELING

Adler, A. UNDERSTANDING HUMAN NATURE. New York: Humanities Press, 1962 reprint 1928 ed.

Arbuckle, D. S. COUNSELING: PHILOSOPHY, THEORY AND PRACTICE. 2d ed. Boston: Allyn and Bacon, 1970.

Arbuckle, D. S., ed. COUNSELING AND PSYCHOTHERAPY: AN OVERVIEW. New York: McGraw-Hill, 1967.

Ard, B. N., ed. COUNSELING AND PSYCHOTHERAPY, CLASSICS ON THEORIES AND ISSUES. Palo Alto, California: Science and Behavior Books, 1966.

Bandura, A. PRINCIPLES OF BEHAVIOR MODIFICATION. New York: Holt, Rinehart and Winston, 1969.

Barclay, J. R. COUNSELING AND PHILOSOPHY: A THEORETICAL EXPOSITION. Boston: Houghton Mifflin, 1968.

Barry, R., and Wolf, B. MOTIVES, VALUES AND REALITIES: A FRAMEWORK FOR COUNSELING. New York: Teachers College Press, Columbia University, 1965.

Beck, C. E. PHILOSOPHICAL FOUNDATIONS OF GUIDANCE. Englewood Cliffs, New Jersey: Prentice-Hall, 1963.

Blocher, D. H. DEVELOPMENTAL COUNSELING. New York: Ronald Press, 1966.

Blum, G. S. PSYCHOANALYTIC THEORIES OF PERSONALITY. New York: McGraw-Hill, 1953.

Bordin, E. S. PSYCHOLOGICAL COUNSELING. 2d ed. New York: Appleton-Century-Crofts, 1968.

Brammer, L. M., and Shostrom, E. L. THERAPEUTIC PSYCHOLOGY: FUNDAMENTALS OF COUNSELING AND PSYCHOTHERAPY. 2d ed. Englewood Cliffs, New Jersey: Prentice-Hall, 1968.

Bühler, C., and llen, M. INTRODUCTION TO HUMANISTIC PSYCHOLOGY. Monterey, California: Brooks-Cole, 1972.

Burton, A., et al. SCHIZOPHRENIA AS A LIFE STYLE. New York: Springer Publishing Company, 1974.

Combs, A. W., ed. PERCEIVING, BEHAVING, BECOMING. Assoc. for Supvn. and Curriculum Development, NEA, 1962 Yearbook.

Corsini, R. J. CURRENT PSYCHOTHERAPIES. Itasca, Illinois: F. E. Peacock Publishers, Inc., 1973.

Curran, C. A. COUNSELING AND PSYCHOTHERAPY: THE PURSUIT OF VALUES. New York: Sheed, 1968.

Dollard, J., and Miller, N. E. PERSONALITY AND PSYCHOTHERAPY. New York: McGraw-Hill, 1950.

Dreikurs, R., and Soltz, V. CHILDREN: THE CHALLENGE. New York: Hawthorn Books, 1964.

Dreikurs, R. PSYCHOLOGY IN THE CLASSROOM. Rev. ed. New York: Harper and Row, 1968.

Dugan, W. E., ed. COUNSELING POINTS OF VIEW. Minneapolis: University of Minnesota Press, 1959.

Ellis, A. HUMANISTIC PSYCHOTHERAPY: THE RATIONAL-EMOTIVE APPROACH. New York: The Julian Press, Inc., 1973.

Ellis, A. REASON AND EMOTION IN PSYCHOTHERAPY. New York: Lyle Stuart, 1962.

Erikson, E. H. YOUTH AND CRISIS. New York: W. W. Norton, 1968.

Ford, D. H., and Urban, H. B. SYSTEMS OF PSYCHOTHERAPY: A COMPARATIVE STUDY. New York: Wiley, 1963.

Fraiberg, S. THE MAGIC YEARS. New York: Scribner, 1968.

Freud, A. THE EGO AND THE MECHANISMS OF DEFENSE. Rev. ed. New York: International Universities Press, 1967.

Freud, S. A GENERAL INTRODUCTION TO PSYCHOANALYSIS. Rev. trans. New York: Simon and Schuster, 1969.

Freud, S. OUTLINE OF PSYCHOANALYSIS. Rev. ed. New York: Norton, 1970.

Freud, S. BASIC WRITINGS OF SIGMUND FREUD. New York: Modern Library, 1938.

Fullmer, D. W., and Bernard, H. COUNSELING: CONTENT AND PROCESS. Chicago: Science Research Associates, 1964.

Gazda, G. M., ed. BASIC APPROACHES TO GROUP PSYCHOTHERAPY AND GROUP COUNSELING. Springfield, Illinois: Charles Thomas, 1970.

Glanz, E. C. FOUNDATIONS AND PRINCIPLES OF GUIDANCE. Boston: Allyn and Bacon, 1964.

Glasser, W. REALITY THERAPY: A NEW APPROACH TO PSYCHIATRY. New York: Harper and Row, 1965.

Glueck, W. F. PERSONNEL: A DIAGNOSTIC APPROACH. Dallas: Business Publications, Inc., 1974.

Hahn, M. E. PSYCHOEVALUATION: ADAPTATION-DISTRIBUTION-ADJUSTMENT. New York: McGraw-Hill, 1963.

Hall, C. S., and Lindzey, G. THEORIES OF PERSONALITY. 2d ed. New York: Wiley, 1970.

Hansen, D. A., ed. EXPLORATIONS IN SOCIOLOGY AND COUNSELING. Boston: Houghton Mifflin, 1969.

Harms, E., and Schreiber, P., eds. HANDBOOK OF COUNSELING TECHNIQUES. New York: Pergamon Press, 1963.

Harper, R. A. PSYCHOANALYSIS AND PSYCHOTHERAPY: 36 SYSTEMS. Englewood Cliffs, New Jersey: Prentice-Hall, 1959.

Harris, T. A. I'M OK. YOU'RE OK. New York: Harper and Row, 1969.

Hart, J. T., and Tomlinson, T. M. NEW DIRECTIONS IN CLIENT-CENTERED THERAPY. Boston: Houghton Mifflin, 1970.

Horney, K. THE NEUROTIC PERSONALITY OF OUR TIME. New York: Norton, 1937.

Johnson, D. E., and Vestermark, M. J. BARRIERS AND HAZARDS IN COUNSELING. Boston: Houghton Mifflin, 1970.

Jones, A. J. PRINCIPLES OF GUIDANCE. 6th ed. New York: McGraw-Hill, 1970.

Jourard, S. M., and Overlade, D. C. DISCLOSING MAN TO HIMSELF. Princeton, New Jersey: VanNostrand Reinhold, 1968.

Kell, B. L., and Burow, J. M. DEVELOPMENTAL COUNSELING AND THERAPY. Boston: Houghton Mifflin, 1970.

Kemp, C. G. INTANGIBLES IN COUNSELING. Boston: Houghton Mifflin, 1967.

Krumboltz, J. D., and Thoreson, C. E., eds. BEHAVIORAL COUNSELING CASES AND TECHNIQUES. New York: Holt, Rinehart and Winston, 1969.

Krumboltz, J. D., ed. REVOLUTION IN COUNSELING: IMPLICATIONS OF BEHAVIORAL SCIENCE. Boston: Houghton Mifflin, 1966.

Lewis, E. C. THE PSYCHOLOGY OF COUNSELING. New York: Holt, Rinehart and Winston, 1970.

Litwack, L., Getson, R., and Saltzman, G., eds. RESEARCH IN COUNSELING. Itasca, Illinois: F. E. Peacock, 1968.

London, P., and Rosenhan, D. THE MODES AND MORALS OF PSYCHOTHERAPY. New York: Holt, Rinehart and Winston, 1970.

Loughary, J. W., ed. COUNSELING, A GROWING PROFESSION. Washington: American Personnel Guidance Association, 1966.

Lowe, C. M. VALUE ORIENTATIONS IN COUNSELING AND PSYCHOTHERAPY. San Francisco: Chandler, 1969.

Maslow, A. H. THE PSYCHOLOGY OF SCIENCE: A RECONNAISSANCE. New York: Harper and Row, 1966.

Maslow, A. H. TOWARD A PSYCHOLOGY OF BEING. Princeton, New Jersey: VanNostrand Reinhold, 1968.

McCary, J. L., ed. PSYCHOLOGY OF PERSONALITY. New York: Grove Press, 1959.

McGowan, J. F., and Schmidt, L. D., eds. COUNSELING: READINGS IN THEORY AND PRACTICE. New York: Holt, Rinehart and Winston, 1962.

Mikulas, W. L. BEHAVIOR MODIFICATION: AN OVERVIEW. New York: Harper and Row, 1972.

Moser, L. E., and Moser, R. S. COUNSELING AND GUIDANCE: AN EXPLORATION. Englewood Cliffs, New Jersey: Prentice-Hall, 1963.

Munroe, R. L. SCHOOLS OF PSYCHOANALYTIC THOUGHT. New York: Holt, Rinehart and Winston, 1955.

Patterson, C. H. THEORIES OF COUNSELING AND PSYCHOTHERAPY. New York: Harper and Row, 1973.

Pepinsky, H. B., and Pepinsky, P. N. COUNSELING THEORY AND PRACTICE. New York: Ronald Press, 1954.

Perls, F., et al. GESTALT THERAPY: EXCITEMENT AND GROWTH IN THE HUMAN PERSONALITY. New York: Julian Messner, 1969.

Perls, F. GESTALT THERAPY VERBATIM. Lafayette, Calif.: Real People Press, 1969.

Raths, L. E.; Harmin, M.; and Simon, S. B. VALUES AND TEACHING. Columbus, Ohio: Charles E. Merrill Books, 1966.

Redl, F., and Wineman, D. WHEN WE DEAL WITH CHILDREN. New York: Free Press, 1966.

Rogers, C. R. CLIENT CENTERED THERAPY. Boston: Houghton-Mifflin, 1951

Rogers, C. R. ON BECOMING A PERSON. Boston: Houghton-Mifflin, 1961.

Satir, V. M. CONJOINT FAMILY THERAPY. Rev. ed. Palo Alto, California: Science and Behavior Books, 1967.

Schutz, W. C. JOY: EXPANDING HUMAN AWARENESS. New York: Grove Press, 1967.

Shertzer, B. E., and Stone, S. C. FUNDAMENTALS OF COUNSELING. 2d ed. Boston: Houghton Mifflin, 1974.

Skinner, B. F. WALDEN II. New York: Macmillan, 1948.

Stefflre, B., and Matheny, K. THE FUNCTION OF COUNSELING THEORY. Boston: Houghton-Mifflin, 1968.

Tolbert, E. L. INTRODUCTION TO COUNSELING. 2d ed. New York: McGraw-Hill, 1972.

Van Kaam, A. EXISTENTIAL FOUNDATIONS OF PSYCHOLOGY. New York: Duquesne University Press, 1966.

Warnath, C. F., and Stewart, L. H. THE COUNSELOR AND SOCIETY: A CULTURAL APPROACH. Boston: Houghton Mifflin, 1965.

Whiteley, J. M. RESEARCH IN COUNSELING. Columbus, Ohio: Charles E. Merrill, 1967.

Williamson, E. G. HOW TO COUNSEL STUDENTS. New York: McGraw-Hill, 1939.

Williamson, E. G. VOCATIONAL COUNSELING: SOME HISTORICAL, PHILOSOPHICAL AND THEORETICAL PERSPECTIVES. New York: McGraw Hill, 1965.

Wolff, S. CHILDREN UNDER STRESS. London: Penguin Press, 1969.

Wrenn, C. G. THE COUNSELOR IN A CHANGING WORLD. Washington: A.P.G.A., 1962.

OCCUPATIONAL AND EDUCATIONAL INFORMATION

American College Testing Program. HANDBOOK FOR THE ASSESSMENT OF CAREER DEVELOPMENT. Iowa City: Author, 1974.

Bailey, L., and Stadt, D. CAREER EDUCATION: NEW APPROACHES TO HUMAN DEVELOPMENT. Bloomington, Illinois: McKnight, 1973.

Borow, H. CAREER GUIDANCE FOR A NEW AGE. Boston: Houghton-Mifflin, 1973.

CAREER EDUCATION RESOURCE GUIDE. Norristown, New Jersey: Career Programs, General Learning Corporation, 1972.

Chick, J. M. INNOVATIONS IN THE USE OF CAREER INFORMATION. New York: Houghton-Mifflin, 1970.

Crites, J. O. VOCATIONAL PSYCHOLOGY. New York: McGraw Hill, 1969.

Evans, R.; Hoyt, K.; and Mangum, G. CAREER EDUCATION IN THE MIDDLE/JUNIOR HIGH SCHOOL. Salt Lake City: Olympus Publishing Company, 1973.

Ginzberg, E. CAREER GUIDANCE: WHO NEEDS IT, WHO PROVIDES IT, WHO CAN IMPROVE IT? New York: McGraw Hill, 1971.

Holland, J. THE PSYCHOLOGY OF VOCATIONAL CHOICE: A THEORY OF PERSONALITY TYPES AND MODEL ENVIRONMENTS. Waltham, Mass.: Blaisdell, 1966.

Hollis, J. W., and Hollis, L. PERSONALIZING INFORMATION PROCESSES: EDUCATIONAL, OCCUPATIONAL, AND PERSONAL-SOCIAL. New York: Macmillan, 1969.

Hoppock, R. OCCUPATIONAL INFORMATION: WHERE TO GET IT AND HOW TO USE IT. New York: McGraw Hill, 1967.

Hoyt, K.; Evans, R.; Mackin, E.; and Mangum, G. CAREER EDUCATION: WHAT IT IS AND HOW TO DO IT. Salt Lake City: Olympus, 1974.

Isaacson, L. CAREER INFORMATION IN COUNSELING AND TEACHING. Boston: Allyn and Bacon, 1972.

MANPOWER REPORT OF THE PRESIDENT. Washington, D.C.: Superintendent of Documents, U.S. Government Printing Office, 1974.

Marshall, R. RURAL WORKERS IN RURAL LABOR MARKETS. Salt Lake City: Olympus Publishing Company, 1974.

Osipow, S. THEORIES OF CAREER DEVELOPMENT. New York: Appleton-Century-Crofts, 1968.

Peters, J., and Hansen, J. VOCATIONAL GUIDANCE AND CAREER DEVELOPMENT. New York: MacMillan, 1971.

Roe, A. THE PSYCHOLOGY OF OCCUPATIONS. New York: John Wiley and Sons, Inc., 1956.

Rosow, J. M. THE WORKER AND THE JOB: COPING WITH CHANGE. Englewood Cliffs, New Jersey: Prentice-Hall, Inc., 1974.

Saint, A. LEARNING AT WORK: HUMAN RESOURCES AND ORGANIZATIONAL DEVELOPMENT. Chicago: Nelson-Hall Company, 1974.

Super, D. THE PSYCHOLOGY OF CAREERS: AN INTRODUCTION TO VOCATIONAL DEVELOPMENT. New York: Harper and Row, 1957.

Tiedeman, D., and O'Hara, R. P. CAREER DEVELOPMENT: CHOICE AND ADJUSTMENT. New York: College Entrance Examination Board, 1963.

U.S. Dept. of H.E.W. CAREER EDUCATION: A HANDBOOK FOR IMPLEMENTATION. Washington, D.C.: Superintendent of Documents, U.S. Government Printing Office, 1972.

Whitley, M., and Resnikoff, A. PERSPECTIVES ON VOCATIONAL DEVELOPMENT. Washington, D.C.: A.P.G.A., 1972.

Williamson, E. G. VOCATIONAL COUNSELING: SOME HISTORICAL, PHILOSOPHICAL AND THEORETICAL PERSPECTIVES. New York: McGraw Hill, 1965.

Zaccaria, J. THEORIES OF OCCUPATIONAL CHOICE AND VOCATIONAL DEVELOPMENT. Boston: Houghton Mifflin, 1970.

INDEX

A

Agency
   administration of, 24
   policy, 229
   professional practices, 23
Agreement, practicum
   counselor forms, 31, 34
   practicum supervisor and
      practicum counselor
      forms, 31
Altucher, N., 250
American Personnel and
   Guidance Association,
   4, 23, 226
   Ethics, 31, 34, 143, 152-158
American Psychological
   Association, 23, 226
   Ethics, Code of, 31, 34, 143,
      144-151
Axelson, J. A., 222

B

Brown, J. L., 5, 8, 13
Buchheimer, A., 250
Buckley Amendment, 238-241
Buros, O., 221, 225, 230

C

Campbell, D., 230
Canisius College, 14
Carkhuff, R. R., 250
Case reports, 139
   length and depth of, 138
   materials for, 139
   notes regarding, 138
   organization of, 138
   sample of, 139-140
   style of, 138
   summary, 139
   to the client and/or
      his family, 138
   to the school, 139
Case study
   guidelines, 137
Check sheet
   client folder form 197,
      199-218
Child-centered
   competency identification,
      8, 9, 11
Class meetings, 27
Class requirements
   practicum, 5
Client
   folder for, 28, 197-218
Client Expectancy
   Inventory, 162

Clients
   involvement with, 26
   responsibility to, 160-161
   selection of, 159-160
Cluster approach
   competency identification,
      8, 9, 10
Competence
   professional, 25
Competencies, 6-13
   organizing and
      classifying, 11
   some definitions, 6-7
   see also counselor
      competencies
Competency-based counselor
   education, 7
Competency-based instructional
   approaches, 2
Competency cluster approach,
   9, 10
Competency identification
   by analyzing, 8
   by observing, 8
   by poaching, 8
   by polling, 8
Confidential information
   release form, 165
Contractual model instructional approaches, 3
Cook, F. S., 6, 13
Cottrell, C. J., 6, 13
Counselee Rating Sheet
   Form, 255-262
Counselee Release Form,
   Example, 164
Counselee, respect for, 56
Counseling
   approaches 2
   art form, 1
   atmosphere for 54, 55
   instruments for effective-
      ness of, 162
   processes, 53
   role and function, 29
   sessions, number of, 27
   techniques, 53
Counseling practicum interview
   rating form, 279-288
Counseling practicum tapes
   weekly evaluation record
      form, 275-278
Counselor competencies
   assessment focus, 11
   behavior skill, 11, 12
   focus for evaluation, 11
   identifying, 7-11
   judgment, 11, 12
   knowledge, 11
Counselor Educator Dilemma, 248

Course requirements
   suggested, 27
Criteria
   for practicum sites, 23-24

D

Dahlstrom, G., 230
Dahlstrom, L., 230
Department of Health,
   Education and Welfare, 13
Dimick, K. M., 4, 5, 54, 248
Dodl, N., 6, 13
Donn, P. A., 166, 167, 168
Duckworth, E., 224, 230
Duckworth, J., 224, 230

E

Education Amendment of 1974,
   238-241
Elkes, C., 250
Ethics
   American Personnel and
      Guidance Association,
      31, 34, 143, 152-158
   American Psychological
      Association, 31, 34,
      143, 144-151
   counseling and psycho-
      therapy, 143
   testing, 229-230
Evaluation
   alternatives, 248-250
   by counselees, 247
   by field supervisor, 247
   by peers, 247
   by practicum instructor,
      247
   by practicum site super-
      visor, 251-254
   by practicum supervisor,
      247-299, 271-274
   by self, 247
   of practicum counselor,
      17-20, 247-299, 289-296
   of prospective practicum
      site, 23-24
   of student counselor, 15,
      16, 251-254, 271-274
   of supervisor, 297-299
   tapes, 275-278
Evaluation form
   activities by weeks, 17-20

F

Family Education Rights and
   Privacy Act of 1974, 234,
   238-241, 242

Flint, A. A., 250
Folder, client
    purposes, 197
Forms
    agreement by practicum counselor, 34
    agreement, practicum supervisor and practicum counselor, 35
    check sheet for client folder, 197, 199-218
    counselee rating sheet, 255-262
    counselee release form, example, 164
    counseling practicum interview rating, 279-288
    counseling practicum tapes weekly evaluation record, 275-278
    evaluation of practicum counselor, 17-20
    evaluation of supervisor, 297-299
    initial intake, 67-86
    interview notes, 87-136
    parent release form, example, 164
    personal data sheet, 31, 33
    practicum counselors placement and schedule, 36
    practicum site supervisor's evaluation, 251-254
    referral, 169-176
    release of confidential information, 165
    schedule, weekly, 38, 39
    student counselor self-rating, 263-270
    summary of time utilization to meet course requirements, 37
    supervisor evaluation of practicum counselor, 289-296
    supervisor's evaluation and report regarding student counselor, 271-274
    termination report, 177-196
Fraleigh, P. W., 250
Freeman, L., 230
Froehle, T. C., 3, 6, 12, 14, 16, 251

G

Goldman, L., 231
Grading, 5
Group guidance sessions, 15, 16
Guidance department meetings, 15, 16
Guidelines
    case study, 137
    for monitoring weekly behavioral objectives, 14, 15

H

Hackney, H., 297
Hendrickson, D E., 53
Hollis, J. W., 58, 162, 167, 168, 197, 199, 235
Hopke, W. E., 255
Houston, W. R., 6, 8, 9, 12
Huff, V. E., 54

I

Illinois Guidance and Personnel Journal, 248
Individual client needs assessment approach competency identification, 10, 11
Information processing, 233-246
Innovations
    practicum, 4-5
    practicum settings, 21
    practicum supervisors, 21
In-service sessions conducting, 15
Instructional approaches, 1, 3
    collage of, 2
    competency based, 2
    contractual model, 3
    interpersonal process model, 2
    MBO model, 3
    simulation model, 3
    supervised field experience model, 3
    traditional, 21
Interpersonal process model instructional approaches, 2
Interview
    initial intake forms, 53, 63, 67-86
    notes, 65
    notes, form for, 66, 87-136
    notes, function of, 65
    notes, recording of, 66
    notes, structure of, 66
    rating form, 279-288
Inventory of fulfillment of client expectancy, 162

J

Jackson, B., 6, 12

Journal of Clinical and Consulting Psychology, 231
Journal of Counseling Psychology, 231

K

Kirk, B. A., 250
Koppitz, E., 231
Krause, F. H., 4, 5, 53, 248
Kurpius, D. J., 11

L

Laboratory
    structure of, 4
Letter
    to practicum site supervisor, 14
Listening, 54, 55, 63

M

MBO model instructional approaches, 3
Management By Objectives see MBO
McGowan, J. P., 63, 223
Measurement purpose of, 222
Meek, L. R., 4, 5
Mental Measurements Yearbook, 221, 225, 230
Minnesota Multiphasic Personality Inventory, 225

N

NASW
    National Association of Social Workers, 23
National Association of Social Workers NASW, 23
Needs assessment competency identification, 8, 10
Newhauser, C., 6, 13
Nye, S., 297

O

Objectives
    behavioral, 14, 15
Okey, J. R., 7, 8, 12
Orientation
    of new students, 15, 16

P

Parent release form, example 164

Parents
    Letter to, 163
Parker, A. W., 4, 5
Paul, G. L., 12, 13
Personal data sheet
    forms, 31, 33
Poling, G., 279
Practicum
    basic class requirements, 5
    desired content, 2
    general suggestions, 63
    initiating, 25
    innovations, 4-5
    suggestions for, 63
Practicum: a growth
    experience, 1
Practicum counselor
    activities by weeks, 17-20
    evaluation, 247-299
    evaluation by site
        supervisor, 251-254
    functions, 239
Practicum counselor's placement and schedule forms, 31, 36
Practicum experience
    record, 14
Practicum settings
    innovations, 21
Practicum site supervisor
    evaluation, 251-254
Practicum sites, 24
Practicum student
    dilemma, 249-250
Practicum students, 4-5
    see also practicum counselor
Practicum supervisors, 21-22
    evaluation, 247-299
    innovations, 21
Prepracticum students, 4-5
Professional associations, 23
Professional practices
    agency, 23
    school, 23
Program transformation approach to competency identification, 9, 10
Program translation
    competency identification, 8, 9
Psychometric work-up
    referral for, 168
Public Law 93-380,
    65, 138, 234, 238-241

R

Record
    practicum experience, 14
Referral forms, 169-176
Referrals, 15, 16
    letter, 140-141

Referrals (Cont.)
    making, 166
    mechanics of, 167
    psychometric work-up, 168
    to physician, 167
Responsibilities
    for practicum counselor, 159-219
    to clients, 159-219
Richey, R., 6, 13
Rioch, M. J., 250
Ruble, R. A., 138
Rumfelt, D., 163

S

Schedule, weekly
    example of, 32, 38
    form, 39-52
School
    administration of, 24
    professional practices, 23
Simulation model instructional approaches, 3
Student counselor, 1
    self rating, 263-270
    see also practicum
        counselor
Student counselor evaluation of supervisor form, 297-299
Students
    orientation, 15, 16
Students, practicum
    evaluation alternatives, 248-250
Supervised field experience model instructional approaches, 3
Supervision, 1
    individual sessions, 27
    of prepracticum by
        practicum students, 4-5
Supervisor evaluation of practicum counselor form 289-296
Supervisors
    of practicum, 21-22
Supervisor's evaluation and report regarding student counselor form, 271-274
Systems needs assessment approach, 9-10

T

Tapes
    critiques, 27
Task analysis competency identification, 8, 10
Techniques
    clarifying, 53

Techniques (Cont.)
    confronting, 53
    counseling, 53, 58, 59-62
    expressing feelings, 53
    interpreting, 53
    list of, 60-62
    philosophical positions, 58
    psychotherapy, 55, 59-62
    role playing, 53
    understand feelings, 56
Termination report
    forms, 177-196
Testing
    ethics, 229-230
Tests
    achievement, 222
    general aptitude, 222
    information about, 224-227
    interests, 222
    interpretation, 63, 219-221, 223, 226, 227-229
    personality, 222
    pre-interpretation, 226-227
    selection, 219-221
    selection guide, 222
    special aptitudes, 222
    testing, 224-232
    use, 63, 223
Theoretical approach
    to competency identification, 9, 10
Theoretical position
    competency identification, 8, 9, 10
Theories, 60
Thro, E. G., 162
Time utilization to meet course requirements forms, summary of, 31, 37
Truax, C B., 250

W

Welsh, L., 230

ABOUT THE AUTHORS

KENNETH M. DIMICK is an associate professor of Psychology-Counseling in the Department of Counseling Psychology and Guidance Services at Ball State University He received his B.S. and M.Ed. from Oregon State University and his doctorate from the University of Arizona.

Dr Dimick has worked as an elementary school teacher and junior high school counselor. Before taking his present position, he was an assistant professor of counseling at the University of Arizona.

He is co-author of the textbook, Child Counseling, and is also the author of numerous journal articles. His major interests are counselor supervision, group therapy, family counseling and correctional counseling.

FRANK H. KRAUSE received his doctorate from Indiana University and currently is associate professor of Psychology-Counseling in the Department of Counseling Psychology and Guidance Services at Ball State University. He and his wife, Shelley, have spent two of his years with Ball State University living in England, Germany and Spain, where Dr. Krause taught graduate students enrolled in Ball State University's European program. As of July, 1975, Dr. Krause will become Associate Director for Advanced Graduate Program in Counseling for Europe.

Dr. Krause serves as a consultant to the Indiana Soldiers and Sailors Children's Home and Delaware County Sheriff's Department and Jail. He has conducted numerous workshops and in-service training sessions for industry, public schools and community agencies. He has written for professional journals and has co-authored several books in the area of counseling psychology, counseling techniques, and the supervision of counseling and psychotherapy. Most recently he co-edited a book entitled, Counseling and Psychotherapy: Training and Supervision.